AUVERGNE
& THE MASSIF CENTRAL

THE HELM FRENCH REGIONAL GUIDES

***Series Editor:* Arthur Eperon**

The Dordogne and Lot
Arthur and Barbara Eperon

Languedoc and Roussillon
Andrew Sanger

The Loire Valley
Arthur and Barbara Eperon

Provence and the Côte d'Azur
Roger Macdonald

AUVERGNE
& THE MASSIF CENTRAL

Rex Grizell

Photographs by Joe Cornish

CHRISTOPHER HELM
London

Photographs by Joe Cornish
Line illustrations by David Saunders
Maps by Oxford Cartographers

Christopher Helm (Publishers) Ltd,
Imperial House, 21-25 North Street,
Bromley, Kent BR1 1SD

ISBN 0-7470-1220-2

A CIP catalogue record for this book
is available from the British Library

Title page illustration:-
The fine 12th century Chevet of the church of
St. Urcize.

Typeset by Leaper and Gard, Bristol
Printed and bound in Italy

Contents

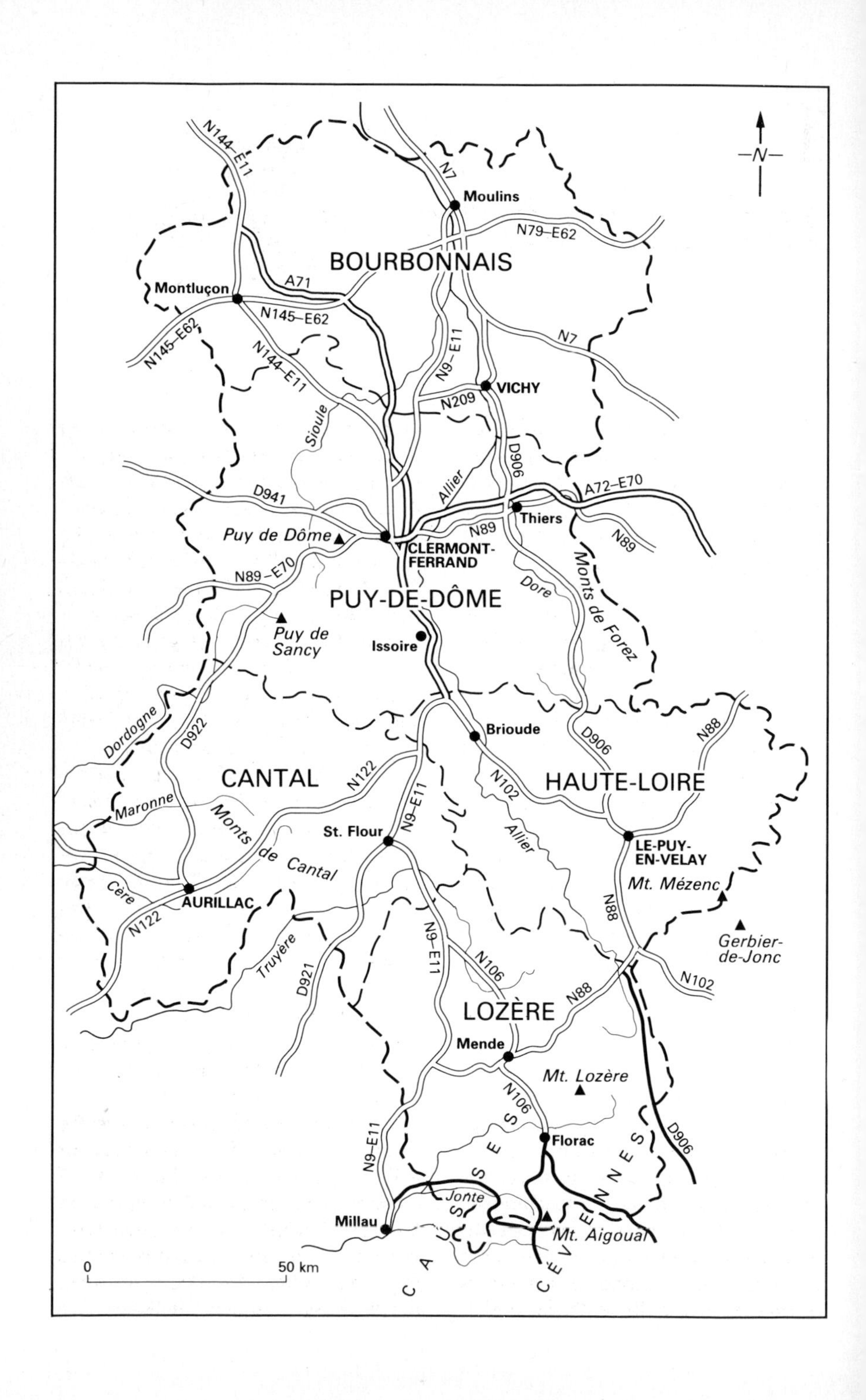
N
BOURBONNAIS
Moulins
N7
N79–E62
N144–E11
Montluçon
A71
N145–E62
N9–E11
VICHY
N209
Sioule
D906
Allier
A72–E70
D941
Thiers
N89
Puy de Dôme
CLERMONT-FERRAND
N89–E70
PUY-DE-DÔME
Dore
Monts de Forez
Puy de Sancy
Issoire
Dordogne
D922
Brioude
D906
N88
CANTAL
N122
HAUTE-LOIRE
N102
Maronne
Monts de Cantal
St. Flour
Allier
LE-PUY-EN-VELAY
Mt. Mézenc
Cère
AURILLAC
Gerbier-de-Jonc
Truyère
D921
N106
LOZÈRE
Mende
Mt. Lozère
Florac
D906
Jonte
Millau
Mt. Aigoual
CAUSSES
CÉVENNES
0
50 km

1
Introduction

Auvergne is an island surrounded by land, physically and in many other respects a country within a country. The land is different, the people are different, the history is different, the weather is different.

It is a wild region formed by a succession of volcanic upheavals, by the timeless wars of rock upon rock, lava against granite. The fires that turned the skies of France red for thousands of years were still burning when the remorseless glaciers of the Ice Ages ground slowly over all, leaving behind new lakes, new contours. Then came countless centuries of erosion by wind and water, of fierce rivers biting down through layer after layer of rock to form the many gorges that break and slash the landscape. The result is a battered region to which age has at last given majestic serenity, its old volcanic peaks ribboned with cloud, its lava slopes now often tree-covered and laced with crystal waterfalls, its green valleys watered by cool streams coming down from the heights and by hot springs surging from the depths of the earth.

In the uplands the plateaux resemble the surface of an undead moon, strewn with the rocks of ages weathered into fantastic shapes which in the distance look like castles or cathedrals or ruined villages. Beneath these plateaux are some of the world's most extensive cave systems, with secrets yet unexplored. Throughout the mountains there are crater lakes and glacial lakes whose still waters mirror the beauty around them. In recent years Man himself has changed the landscape further by creating new lakes behind the barrages of great hydroelectric schemes, diverting rivers, drowning roads and villages. In all a landscape of remarkable complexity, of strange and particular beauty.

This, then, is what the modern visitor finds as a background to a range of country holidays — *vacances vertes* — as they are called in France — unequalled in Europe. The tourist can sit back and do little but enjoy the therapy of the peace, the fresh air, the splendour of Nature. But Auvergne is also a paradise for those who enjoy exercise in the open air; anything from a country stroll to a full day's ramble on mountains and through forest, from white-water canoeing to hang-gliding.

Ramblers and hill-walkers have the chance of going their own way or following some of the hundreds of kilometres of signposted footpaths in the Parc Régional des Volcans d'Auvergne. There are numerous centres for horse-riding and pony-trekking. Horse-drawn caravan holidays are available. There are facilities for rock-climbing, for canoeing or rafting on fast-flowing rivers through spectacular gorges, for sailing and windsurfing on calm lakes. The Puy-de-Dôme is the European headquarters for hang-gliding. There are guided tours of the most impressive grottoes, as well as opportunities for pot-holing and cave exploring. The fishing is superb with coarse fish of all kinds in countless lakes, and trout and some salmon in the rivers.

And for the real motorist, the person who enjoys driving, who likes the excitement of taking the car away from the main roads into unfamiliar territory, finding his own particular beauty spots, peaceful villages and country inns, Auvergne offers limitless variety and opportunity. If not a village inn, your base can be a first-class hotel, even a château, or an organised camp site, or just a tent in the wilds.

Paradoxically, Auvergne is also a haven for the less active, for those whose health is not quite what it might be. There are many spas and thermal springs whose curative properties have been known and used since Roman times. There are few disorders of the human body which one or other of the spas does not treat.

There is plenty of interest, too, for those who like some intellectual content in their travel. The region has some of the finest Norman (Romanesque) churches in Europe (the French for this period is *Roman,* while the French for Roman is *Romain*). There is a lot to interest engineers in the many vast and complex hydro-electric schemes, and in the Garabit viaduct, and others, built by Eiffel. Artists and photographers are never going to run out of subjects here. There is endless variety for the geologist and, perhaps unexpectedly, there is much material for scholars seriously interested in superstition, magic or Satanism.

If, in pre-history, Auvergne was a battleground of fire and ice, of rock and water, it has been the setting, since the first men arrived thousands of years ago, for an unceasing struggle between Man and Nature, for a fight to survive in a land which, though beautiful, has never been rich and has often given the farmer desperately little in return for his labour. It was a conflict in isolation. There can be few regions of the world where it is so obvious to the layman how the land itself, its climate, its topography, the nature of the soil, forged over thousands of years the character of the people who lived there. In Auvergne it produced a race of tough, resourceful, self-reliant men and women, in whom awe of the forces of Nature was bred in the bone, and who in their isolation often looked in complete faith to God for support, and who sought refuge also in superstition and belief in the powers of evil, to explain away or combat ill-fortune and disaster. One way or another they struggled on, living in the heart of France but so cut off that it was not until the 16th century that they learned to speak French.

In France as a whole the Auvergnats are considered to be hard, cagey, difficult to know, and in a country where the usual attitude to money makes the traditional idea of the Scot seem like that of a lunatic spendthrift, they are considered mean. If the Auvergnat is difficult to get the better of in a deal and makes every centime count, it is because for generations they have had to. Auvergne has a lot in common with the highlands of Scotland, a mountainous and beautiful countryside of lakes and sparkling rivers but where the soil is often poor and unrewarding. Both areas have produced a physically tough, canny, reserved people.

Like the Scots, the Arvernes, ancestors of the Auvergnats of today, were Celtic tribes redoubtable in battle. They were very fond of gold and silver jewellery and went into battle wearing all their finery. This little affectation in no way reduced their ferocity. When wounded they would tear open the wounds further with their fingernails and continue the fight with blood-curdling shouts. In more modern times the fortitude of the local peasant farmers in the face of death became legendary. When they felt unwell they would continue to work until they could no longer stand, and only then take to their beds. If they recovered they would work again, for weeks, perhaps for months or years, until the last days came. Then, rather than call the doctor, they would try their own traditional remedies and, if these failed, bowed, uncomplaining, to the will of God.

The famous French author, Chateaubriand, once wrote: 'When, as a child in the moors of my native Brittany, I heard people speaking of the Auvergne and the little Auvergnats it seemed to me that Auvergne was a country far, far away where one saw strange things, and where one dared not go without making one's way under the protection of the Holy Mother.'

Over the centuries many legends have become established in Auvergne illustrating the belief of the people in magic and Satanic powers. Bastards were often accused of being in league with the Devil, who changed them into wolves at the full moon and obliged them to run on all fours through seven parishes a night, afraid of nothing but bullets which had been blessed. One wicked nobleman, Pons de Chapteuil, was said to have become a wolf who savagely attacked adults and ate children, and became a man again only after one of his feet was cut off by a forester he had attacked.

Another revealing story concerns Blaise Pascal, one of France's greatest philosophers and mathematicians, who was an Auvergnat. In his childhood he fell ill and languished for a year without the doctors being able to find the cause of his illness. According to his niece, Marguerite Périer, it was eventually discovered that a spell had been cast upon him by a poor woman whom Pascal's father had refused to help in a law suit. When Monsieur Pascal questioned the woman she admitted that the child was cursed with death and that the only way to cure him was to move the curse to another person. Monsieur Pascal refused to do any such thing. The sorceress then said an animal would do. A cat was obtained and sacrificed and the child regained his health at once.

The peasants went in fear of the Evil Eye, which could make people sterile, take away a mother's milk, or make the cows go dry. As a protection they would keep the skin of a poisonous animal, a snake or a toad, or a live spider, in a pocket. To protect cows they took a tuft of hair from the cow's tail and put it in a hole in the wall of the byre.

They also believed strongly in the medicinal value of charms and amulets. A favourite charm was a piece of serpentine with a hole in the middle to take a cord. Worn around the neck these were believed to cure migraine, protect from lightning, restore milk to nursing mothers, and abate fevers. Similar charms of red cornelian were supposed to stop bleeding, others cured eye troubles or insomnia.

Many plants were thought to have medicinal and protective powers, often correctly as science has since established. Wild plants from the mountain sides were considered more effective than the same ones grown in a herb garden. The maidenhair fern, they said, kept away werewolves, and angelica warded off evil spells.

The salamander was considered the most terrible animal in Auvergne. It was said to harm cows by blowing poisonous air at them. On the other hand it was said to breathe only once a day, presumably just before blowing at the cows. Toads and owls were other creatures much feared. But if the fears were legion, so were the cures. A paste made from chopped snails cured corns. A spider's web stopped bleeding. A poultice of crow's brains treated chilblains. Eel's blood mixed with wine cured drunkenness.

I have put all this in the past tense but even today, when diagnoses are made by scanner, operations carried out by laser, when hearts and lungs can be replaced, there remain many Auvergnats who put their faith in healers to cure them of everything from warts to cancer. The local papers always carry at least half a page of advertisements from mediums, clairvoyants and healers claiming to cure almost everything, remove spells, restore virility, and to turn away harmful vibrations. When I casually mentioned rheumatic twinges to an Auvergnat farmer, he told me seriously that if I always carried a horse chestnut in my pocket, I would have no more trouble. But it had to be from a tree with red flowers.

For all their strangeness the people and the region have made their mark on France. Auvergne is not only beautiful in itself, with a beauty that includes almost nothing soft and idyllic, but is a source of much of the beauty of the gentler France that surrounds it. What is more characteristic of the French landscape than its countless lovely rivers, winding through fertile valleys, reflecting the poplars, and with grassy banks where Frenchmen in their thousands, though each seems to have about a kilometre of river to himself, prove that whatever others may say about their excitability, when it comes to fishing they are men of unshakeable calm and patience. A great many of these lovely rivers are born in the mountains and plateaux of Auvergne, among them the Loire, the Dordogne, the Lot, the Tarn, the Allier. Like the rivers in many mountain areas some of those in Auvergne are reputed to be gold-bearing. In former times prospectors used, like the ancient Greeks, to immerse the fleece of a freshly killed (because more greasy) sheep into the river and later washed out the gold particles caught in it.

In fact, Auvergne is an imprecise term which, in different periods of history, has been used to refer to bigger or smaller regions. At present the official administrative region includes the four départements of Allier, Puy-de-Dôme, Cantal and Haute-Loire. In this book Auvergne has been used in a loose sense to include key points of beauty and interest in and around the Massif Central which may not all be, strictly speaking, in the Auvergne of today. I have included, for example, the Gorges du Tarn, in the département of Lozère, and the Cévennes mountains.

Until the 18th century Auvergne was as populated as other rural parts of France and the people lived in relative contentment in their isolation. But while other regions gradually benefited from improved communications, and so greater facility for selling their produce, and then from new techniques which brought capacity for increased production, Auvergne received none of these advantages, because of the difficulty of its terrain. The foothills of the Massif Central and the mountains themselves which had for so long been a protection now formed a barrier to progress. What had been a defensive wall now shut off Auvergne and its inhabitants from the changing France outside. Gradually the region lapsed into economic stagnation with a resultant falling off in population.

The boom which France experienced after the war under de Gaulle found Auvergne still left aside, neglected by successive governments, while the main stream of European development flowed in other channels. Today, with five per cent of the national territory, the region has less than two and a half per cent of the population, and half of that is in one town.

It was not until Prime Minister Pompidou (later President), himself an Auvergnat, promoted the improvement of major roads in the area, notably the N9 from Clermont-Ferrand to the Mediterranean coast, that things began to change more quickly. An increase in tourism had already given a gentle stimulus to the economy and then in 1982 the new Decentralisation Law further encouraged progress by giving Auvergne more responsibility in deciding its own affairs, together with government aid. New industries were founded, new sources of energy established.

There is no doubt that the region has changed in the past twenty-five years and is still changing. Villages and towns which I visited in the 1950s and 1960s and found looking as if they were still in the Middle Ages, with streets of mud churned up by cattle, decrepit houses and an occasional café-bar of Spartan simplicity, now have neatly cobbled roads, paved squares, flower-decked houses, cafés with coloured umbrellas and comfortable hotels. Even the cows seem cleaner.

There has been a steady growth in tourism, with more amenities for leisure and sporting holidays of all kinds, particularly, in the past few years, for winter sports. At the same time many new enterprises have been created connected with cattle raising, agriculture or forestry.

Auvergne now has confidence in its future. One French writer (it must be admitted, an Auvergnat) says, 'Courage, tenacity, the spirit of enterprise, force of character, these are Auvergnat virtues recognised everywhere, and they will help the region take its place in the modern French landscape.'

All true. However, one quality which the Auvergnat tends to lack is refinement or, if you like, good taste. While the healthier local economy has brought some modernisation, it has often been with no sense of what is appropriate. There have been changes which will surprise some visitors. I know a hotel where a chromium and plastic bar backed by tinted mirrors was installed at the foot of a splendid medieval oak staircase wide enough and shallow enough to ride two horses up side by side, and with an antique cupboard on the landing which would have housed d'Artagnan and the Three Musketeers with room to play a hand of cards.

But only the surface has been scratched. It remains a wonderful, individual region, unlike any other. The main communication routes still bypass the Massif Central. They are nearer the mountains but at their foot. The hinterland remains difficult, sectionised country, full of surprises. The visitor has only to strike out across country and drive for an hour or two on the climbing, tortuous roads, one minute above the clouds, then in the depths of a spectacular gorge, to appreciate what every other visitor to the Massif Central has realised since the first pages of history. This is a region in which Nature dominates all, a landscape of mountains and gorges, rivers and lakes, forests and pastures, valleys and plateaux, all interwoven in the incredible complexity which makes Auvergne a world apart.

The Volcanoes

This is not the place for a geological treatise but no account of Auvergne should omit a brief explanation of its volcanic origins.

The formation of Auvergne and the Massif Central took place in three main stages. The first occurred some six hundred million years ago when what is now Europe lay under the sea and convulsions of the Earth's crust forced great blocks of granite mountains up above sea level. In the hot and humid climate of that era the mountain slopes became covered with luxuriant vegetation, with forests where even the ferns grew as tall as modern trees. There were no birds or mammals but the forests were alive with nightmare insects and monstrous reptiles. Over millions of years erosion wore down the mountains into a vast undulating plateau. Rotting vegetation filled the troughs and fissures in the landscapes, became covered with layers of alluvial soil, and gradually decayed to form coal deposits.

The second great upheaval took place about thirty million years ago when more violent movements of the Earth's crust threw up the mountain chains of the Alps and the Pyrenees. The thrust and counter-thrust of this enormous shock cracked the old granite plateau of the Massif Central in numerous places, and changed the relief around its southern and eastern edges. In some areas highlands, such as the Forez and Livradais mountains, remained in relief; in others new valleys and depressions were formed. In these lower areas, the Limagne and the Ambert plain, for example, sediments collected and fertile soils accumulated. But the most dramatic changes in this period occurred where the old granite crust had been cracked and weakened. Molten material from the Earth's interior burst up through these fissures and weak points. These eruptions formed the numerous volcanoes of the Monts Dore and Cantal and, farther south, the Cévennes.

The third stage began about three million years ago at the start of the present geological age, during which Mankind has developed. In this period the Chaîne des Dômes in the Clermont-Ferrand area were formed.

This chain, which is said to have 112 volcanoes (though estimates of the total number of volcanoes in the Auvergne vary wildly), has mountains of classical shape. The older mountains of the Monts Dore, though higher, are more eroded and less clear cut. The peaks of Cantal, such as Puy Mary, Puy Violent, Puy Girou and Plomb du Cantal, are what remains of one vast volcano, which was the largest in France, 100km in circumference and more than 3,000m high.

Some of the laval flows produced during these periods of volcanic activity are unrivalled except in parts of New Zealand and Alaska. At Pas de la Margeride in Cantal a fossilised forest lies buried beneath deep layers of ash. There are many places where the rock of these lava deposits is phonolithic (literally 'sounding stone'), so that when you stamp your foot the ground resounds strangely like an empty barrel, and the sound of a galloping horse is like the beating of a distant drum. In other places, they say, if you poke your finger into the lava ash, you can sense the gentle bubbling of the lava far beneath. Perhaps, but I do not think I believe that one.

But the old granite plateau of the Massif Central was by no means completely buried under the lava. Walkers in the Cantal uplands often come across squat buildings, huddled against the mountain side, too big to be just shelters, too small for permanent habitation. They are called *burons,* often roofed with turf but with walls built from huge stones hewn from the primeval granite of pre-volcanic times. The farmers lived in them in summer while they grazed their cows on the rich grass of the uplands, milked them on the spot, and made their Cantal cheese by hand in the *burons.* A few of them still do so.

Regional Parks

These three volcanic regions, the Chaîne des Dômes, the Monts Dore and the Monts du Cantal now form the Regional Nature Park of the Auvergne Volcanoes (Le Parc Naturel Régional des Volcans d'Auvergne) which extends 120km north to south through the départements of Puy-de-Dôme and Cantal. This Nature Park, proposed in 1970 and established in 1977, is the largest in France covering 346,000 hectares.

The Parc des Volcans (for short) lies to the west of the fertile corridor known as the Limagne. To the east of this corridor lies the second largest Regional Nature Park in France, the Parc du Livradois-Forez, 100km from north to south and covering 297,000 hectares. This huge area includes only two small towns, Thiers and Ambert, and has few roads. More than half of it consists of thickly forested mountain slopes.

These two Nature Parks together occupy 40 per cent of the administrative area of Auvergne. They share the same purposes, to preserve the natural and cultural heritage of their region, and to stimulate the local economy.

The Parc des Volcans (Administrative address: Château de Montlosier, Randanne, 63210 Rochefort-Montagne) is well organised to encourage tourism, and already has a number of centres which, in summer, welcome visitors and students to exhibitions of local interest. Near Riom-ès-Montagnes, for example, the Maison de la

Gentiane has a botanical garden specialising in mountain plants and herbs. Other centres describe the cheese industry in Auvergne, the production of honey, and the quarrying of lava stone at Volvic. The administration of the park also concerns itself with the preservation of such typical aspects of Auvergne life as the stone-tiled roofs, old bread ovens, and traditional furniture and farm implements, as well as the preservation and development of wild life.

The Livradois-Forez Nature Park is a more recent creation than the Parc des Volcans, not having been set up until 1984. Its stated objectives include specific reference to improving the income and standard of living of its farmers, the development of forestry and industries based on wood, as well as the promotion of the area as a tourist attraction, but at the time of writing its actual administration is still in a rather amorphous state.

Immediately south of Auvergne, though not strictly part of it, the Cévennes Mountains, the most southerly part of the Massif Central, contain another huge nature park. Unlike the two regional parks already mentioned, the Parc National des Cévennes is a National Park. It covers 84,200 hectares and is entirely surrounded by a protective zone of another 236,000 hectares. This extremely wild and mountainous area is more than one-quarter covered in forest, but also includes the deserted, treeless uplands of the Lozère mountain complex, 1,200m above sea level.

These great open spaces of Auvergne and the Cévennes are rich in wild life. In Auvergne there are fewer badgers and polecats than formerly, but the squirrel-like marmot, mountain sheep and chamois have been introduced in the Cantal mountains and are beginning to thrive. The eagle owl, once rare, is now more common in the valleys, and peregrine falcons are increasing on the escarpments. There are wild boar and roe deer in the forests, as well as many rare birds. The last wolf was killed on the plateau of Aubrac only ten years ago, and it is not planned to reintroduce them.

In the Cévennes National Park red deer, chamois and beaver have been re-introduced, and grouse and vultures will be added in the near future. The climate of this park is as varied as its scenery, from Mediterranean-facing valleys where mimosa and lemons flourish, to the mountain tops of Mt. Lozère and Mt. Aigoual where snow may linger long into summer. Founded in 1970, the Park now has more than a dozen information centres, some permanent, some seasonal. During the season they are used as bases from which day-long guided tours can be made. The administrative headquarters is at Florac.

The Spas

The unusual character of Auvergne is further enriched by the numerous hot springs and mineral waters, the existence of which it owes to the volcanic nature of its sub-soil. Some of the springs surge from the depths of the earth at high temperatures (the record is at Chaudes-Aigues, 82°C). Others are much cooler and owe their health-giving properties to long filtration through rocks with different mineral content.

Hot springs and mineral waters are

for the most part unstable and begin to lose some of their properties from the moment they come out of the earth. To get the most benefit from them they must be used at source and this is why spas and a health industry have developed on the sites of the most effective springs.

Because cures can last several weeks, and because the actual medical treatment occupies only a small part of the day, the spas have gradually taken on the characteristics of holiday resorts, offering their visitors a range of sport and leisure activities, excursions and entertainments which altogether make them very agreeable places, so that nowadays most of them attract as many tourists as they do unwell people. At Vichy this anomaly has been carried even further, and the town is now so well-equipped for sporting activities of every kind that it has become the sports capital of France and is used by various French Olympic teams for training in their speciality.

Though their chemical composition varies considerably the majority of Auvergne springs are rich in carbonates and are mildly radio-active when they first leave the earth. These qualities help to stimulate the human system, particularly the digestion.

Over the years different spas have established reputations for the treatment of different illnesses. Vichy treats the digestive system; Royat, the heart and arteries; Châtelguyon, the intestines; Le Mont-Dore, asthma and the respiratory system; St. Nectaire, the kidneys; Bourbon l'Archambault, rheumatism and fractures. The list is long and it is not, perhaps, too much to say that, with few exceptions, whatever your complaint an Auvergne spa will offer a treatment. Sceptics point out that many spas are treating different illnesses today from those they treated a hundred years ago. Enthusiasts reply that, of course, they have learned from experience where they get the best results.

The curative properties of the hot springs were known to the earliest inhabitants of Auvergne, long before the Romans arrived. This was discovered in 1818 when a new thermal establishment was being built at Le Mont-Dore. Workmen, digging deep for solid foundations, came across the remains of a Celtic bath big enough for fifteen people to use at once. The remains of two similar baths were found nearby. As there were so many hot springs, it is unlikely that those at Mont-Dore were the only ones known to the Celts. But unlike the Romans, who enjoyed bathing for its own sake and would often loll about in the baths for hours gossiping and greeting new arrivals, the Celts, like small boys, avoided washing and only took a bath when they hoped to be cured of something.

Though the spas were known so early and though the Romans expanded their use and encouraged the local population to enjoy their benefits, archaeologists believe that they fell completely into disuse about the 7th century AD. They base this opinion on the fact that no coins of later date than that have been found in excavations on the sites of old spas. In other words, once the Romans had gone, the local inhabitants slowly relapsed into their former dirty habits.

During the 16th century the spas slowly began to come into use again. Henri IV, who is said to have washed only once a year in order to preserve his 'delicate aroma', nevertheless appointed the first superintendent to administer the spa at Vichy. In 1641, when he was 56, Cardinal Richelieu wrote to a friend (he did have one or two) that he meant to go to Vichy to restore his failing health. As effective ruler of France he was too busy to do so, and died a year later.

The reputation of Vichy was strengthened by several visits from the Marquise de Sévigné in the 1670s and 1680s. In correspondence with friends, France's most famous letter writer gave detailed descriptions of the treatment as it was practised at the time. Apart from drinking the water, the taste of which she found revolting, her treatment consisted of being hosed all over with a stream of hot water by a woman attendant, and at some length. As she found it long-winded and boring, she made a local doctor sit behind a curtain and talk to her while the treatment continued. Much as she complained about it the treatment so relieved her rheumatism that she wrote that she felt she was cured for life. The house she stayed in is today a hotel, the Pavillon de Sévigné, reckoned by many to be the best in Vichy.

Other great and famous people who visited spas in Auvergne included Françoise Athenaise de Rochechouart, Madame La Marquise de Montespan, mistress (one of the many) of Louis XIV. Her preference was for Bourbon l'Archambault, and she happened to be there once at the same time as the Marquise de Sévigné. The King's mistress did not, and could hardly, go unnoticed. According to Madame Sévigné's letters '... we tell each other everything she does, what she eats, how she sleeps ... She goes about in a coach drawn by six horses, followed by another harnessed in the same way and with six women in it, and two wagons, six mules, and about a dozen men on horseback ... Altogether she has more than forty people with her ...' Madame de Montespan liked Bourbon l'Archambault so much that she went annually for thirty years, and eventually died there in 1707.

The famous French foreign minister, Talleyrand, the 'Slippery Sam' of early 19th-century French politics, spent every August for thirty years, from 1801 to 1832, on holiday at Bourbon l'Archambault, taking the waters, playing whist, gossiping with the locals, and no doubt nurturing his talent for deserting sinking ships. He lived to be 84 and always said that he owed his physical vigour and liveliness of mind to his annual stay in the spa.

But it was the visits to Vichy, in the 1860s, of the Emperor Napoleon III, who suffered from kidney and intestinal troubles, which really established that spa and made 'taking the waters' a more fashionable practice. Numerous improvements were made in Vichy which, until then, had been a rather unattractive little town completely lacking in style.

In the 18th and 19th centuries 'to take the waters' remained the privilege of a rich and leisured class but today the French health authorities recognise the effectiveness of many spa treatments, and the cures are often chargeable to the Social Security, which brings them within reach of everybody.

Apart from Vichy the spa towns which have contributed most to the solid reputation of Auvergne in this field are Royat, Châtelguyon, La Bourboule and Le Mont-Dore. La Bourboule, specialising in the treatment of children, and Royat where serious research on arterial disease is carried out, both get more than 20,000 patients a year. But it seems that the number of doctors and patients who believe in spa treatments is not only limited but more or less fixed. Considerable promotional efforts have not succeeded in increasing the number of visitors who go to Auvergne spas for health reasons only to more than about 115,000 a year.

Vichy is inclined to be and can afford to be nostalgic about its great days as a spa. Its very progressive administration has succeeded in turning it into a stylish and popular resort, which with the realisation of new plans announced late in 1987 will become the sports and leisure capital not only of France but of Europe.

When to Go

The climate of the Massif Central like that of many mountain regions is changeable. There are glorious summers and there are others when the rain never seems to stop, but the normal year is very satisfactory.

There are fewer rainy days than in many parts of Britain but when it does rain the quantity that falls, particularly in summer storms, varies from considerable to the almost incredible.

It is often said that Auvergne stays green all summer, watered by storms and cooled by its elevation. This is often true but by no means always. In three of the past four years the hills have turned golden brown everywhere and several of the most famous rivers in France were shortened by a few kilometres.

So Auvergne also gets plenty of sunshine, most of it towards the end of summer and in autumn. In winter the higher slopes of the mountains are covered in snow, and in many places there are large snowfields where winter sports resorts have been established and are becoming steadily more popular. Like the sunshine in summer the snowfall varies from year to year. In abundant years the new ski resorts match their Alpine rivals in the sport offered and have the advantage of being cheaper and less crowded.

In spring the snow lingers in the hollows, while a few metres away sunshine falls on green grass, daffodils, violets and irises. But it is a short season, really just the month of May. Summer comes suddenly and in the valleys it is warm or very warm, though sometimes more cloudy than on the coasts.

In general the best time of year to visit Auvergne is autumn. The farmers refer to it as 'shirt-sleeve time' and it is often calm, warm and sunny. The countryside is even more beautiful as the forests take on their first autumn tints. In the woods there are mushrooms of all kinds, as well as wild raspberries and strawberries — the deliciously scented tiny *fraises des bois* which cost a small fortune from the dessert trolleys of the smart Paris restaurants.

Opening Hours

Despite the steady improvement in tourist amenities in the past few years the administration in Auvergne still moves at its own rustic pace, and I think it is true to say that many town councils have not yet understood the full potential. It is a region very much tied to the French habit of taking holidays at fixed times, notably the latter half of July (mostly wives and children) and the month of August (when Papa joins in). The result is that many tourist offices, museums, exhibitions, even some churches, and some hotels and restaurants are firmly closed outside these periods.

Many churches and religious buildings are closed between 12 and 2. There is also no consistent rule for opening times of museums. In general they are closed on Mondays and at lunch times. Some make an entry charge, others are free.

Even in the summer season many tourist attractions close at midday and may not open again until four o'clock. So before you drive off to see a particular castle or church, check at the local Tourist Office, to make sure you will not arrive just in time to wait two or three hours for it to open.

When visiting sites, such as the Gorges du Tarn, it is advisable to get there as early as possible, especially in high season, to avoid the considerable crowds that build up later in the day.

If you plan to lunch out, except in large towns, make sure that you arrive at your chosen restaurant soon after midday. You will certainly get a better table. At half-past twelve you will probably be squeezed in with someone else, and at quarter to one you may not get one at all. Early arrival is especially important if you are a fan of Relais Routiers, the excellent café-restaurants used by lorry drivers. The best thing on the menu here is always the speciality of the day, and the lorry drivers know what it is for every day of the week for every Relais on their route and they make for it early. By half-past twelve it's 'off' and you may be left with dubious steak and chips, or omelettes, or perhaps something quite nice but if, in retrospect, the speciality would have been just what you fancied, it will almost certainly be too late.

Of course, not all the hotels and restaurants close outside the summer season. The spring or autumn tourist is that much more welcome in those that are open and finds them in their true colours, catering for their habitual clientele of discriminating French businessmen and workers.

And outside there is fresh air, freedom, room to move. The great open spaces, never crowded even in the height of summer, are even more themselves, timeless and unchanged.

Conversion Tables

km	miles	km	miles	km	miles
1	0.62	8	4.97	40	24.86
2	1.24	9	5.59	50	31.07
3	1.86	10	6.21	60	37.28
4	2.48	15	9.32	70	43.50
5	3.11	20	12.43	80	49.71
6	3.73	25	15.53	90	55.93
7	4.35	30	18.64	100	62.14

m	ft	m	ft	m	ft
100	328	600	1,968	1,500	4,921
200	656	700	2,296	2,000	6,562
300	984	800	2,625	2,500	8,202
400	1,313	900	2,953	3,000	9,842
500	1,640	1,000	3,281	3,500	11,483

ha	acres	ha	acres	ha	acres
1	2.5	10	25	100	247
2	5	25	62	150	370
5	12	50	124	200	494

kg	lbs	kg	lbs
1	2.2	6	13.2
2	4.4	7	15.4
3	6.6	8	17.6
4	8.8	9	19.8
5	11.0		

°C	°F	°C	°F	°C	°F
0	32	12	54	24	75
2	36	14	57	26	79
4	39	16	61	28	82
6	43	18	64	30	86
8	46	20	68	32	90
10	50	22	72	34	93

The Best Museums

Aurillac

La Maison des Volcans, in St. Étienne Château. Interesting explanation of the Volcanoes of Auvergne, France, and the rest of the world. Jul–Aug, 10–12, 2–7, exc Sun am; Sep–Jun, 9–12, 2–6, exc Sun.

Clermont-Ferrand

Musée du Ranquet, near Cathedral. Good general collection relating to life in Auvergne and Clermont: art, furniture, arms, agriculture. 10–12, 2–5 or 6 exc Mon and national holidays.
Musée Bargoin, bd la Fayette. Good general collection. 10–12, 2–5 or 6, exc Mon and national holidays.
Musée Lecoq, near Jardin Lecoq. Mineralogy. 10–12, 2–5 or 6, exc Mon and national holidays.

Le Mas Soubeyran

Musée du Désert. The story of the Camisard revolt, arranged in the original home of one of its leaders. Mar–Nov, 9.30–12, 2.30–6.

Montluçon

Musée de la Vielle (hurdy-gurdy museum), in Château. Fascinating musical instruments from 17th century onwards. 15th Mar–15th Oct, 10–12, 2–6, exc Tues; 16th Oct–14th Mar, 2–6, exc Mon and Tues.

Le Puy

Musée Crozatier, Jardin Vinay. General collection, including lace and early stonework. 10–12, 2–4 or 6, exc Tues and Feb.

Riom

Musée Régional Auvergne, rue de l'Hôtel de Ville. Very well displayed collection of traditional life in Auvergne. 10–12, 2–4.30 or 5.30, exc Tues; closed end Oct–early Nov.

St. Jean-du-Gard

Musée des Vallées Cévenoles. Fine general collection relating to life in the Cévennes, including silk industry and importance of chestnut tree. 15th June–15th Sep, 9.30–12.30, 3–7, exc Mon and Sun am; 16th Sep–14th June, Sun only 2.30–6.30.

Thiers

Maison des Couteliers (Cutlery House), 58 rue de la Coutellerie. The making of knives from Middle Ages onwards. June–Sep, 10–12, 2–6.30, exc Sun; Oct–May, 2–6, exc Sun and Mon.

Terms Used in the Massif Central

VOLCANOES **Puy** or **Dôme** — a volcanic peak in northern Auvergne
Truc — a volcanic peak in Aubrac
Suc — a volcanic peak in Cévennes
Basalte — basic lava rock with less than 45 per cent silica
Phonolithe — lava rock which occurs in layers only a few centimetres thick and which resounds when struck (*lauzes*, the tiles used for roofing in parts of Auvergne, are cut from phonolithic rock)
Planèze — Plateau of lava divided by radiating valleys, e.g. Planèze de St. Flour

OTHER GEOGRAPHICAL TERMS **Massif** — a mountain system as a whole
Versant — mountain slope
Causse — limestone plateau
Limagne — fertile plains between the mountains, especially La Grande Limagne, watered by the Allier and the Dore
Couzes Rhues Boraldes Gardons — regional terms for fast-flowing mountain streams or torrents, often subject to violent floods
Source — mineral spring with therapeutic value
Source thermale — the same at a temperature above 35°C

AGRICULTURE **Draille** — drovers' road, especially routes by which cattle or sheep are taken up to or down from summer pastures. Some have been used for more than a thousand years
Transhumance — the seasonal movement of sheep and cattle from valley to mountain pasture and back
Buron (Auvergne)
Jasserie (Velay)
Mazuc (Aubrac) — Regional name for a small dairy in mountain pasture. Cows were milked on the spot and the cheese made by hand in these dairies, where the cowherds lived throughout the summer
Fourme — a firm cheese of cylindrical shape, e.g. Fourme d'Ambert

CHURCHES **Roman** — Romanesque or Norman (nothing to do with the Romans)

2
History

The discovery of stone weapons used for hunting indicates that men lived in Auvergne as long as 15,000 years ago, and archaeologists have found many fragments of domestic pottery suggesting that by about 5,000 years ago they sometimes lived a more settled life in small communities.

It was about 800BC that the region was invaded by a Celtic tribe, the Arvernes, from whom its name is derived. These people were nomads who lived by grazing cattle, moving them from place to place as necessary. Their first settlements were in the plains of the Allier river and on the lower slopes of nearby mountains.

About 125BC they became imperially minded and succeeded in conquering a number of neighbouring tribes, extending their influence over the whole of the region. Their power was short-lived. Only four years later they were defeated by the Roman general, Fabius Maximus, and their territorial ambitions came to an end.

But they resented being subject to the Romans. In 52BC their chief was a young man named Vercingetorix. His ambition was to liberate Gaul from the Romans and, in retrospect, French historians like to see him as the first French patriot. He succeeded in rousing the ordinary people with inspiring words: 'Let us take up arms to gain our freedom. Let us call upon all the peoples of Gaul to join with us in our struggle so that together we will chase the Romans from our soil. Do not believe that they are invincible, despite their great victories in the past. No one is invincible. Our ancestors defeated them. Why not us? Are we less courageous than our fathers? Have we fewer reasons to conquer?'

Noble words, and Julius Caesar did not much like the sound of them. He decided to show Vercingetorix who was boss. Surprisingly, for once, Caesar got beaten. There was more to Vercingetorix than a silver tongue.

It happened like this. Gergovia, the Arverne capital, was situated on a plateau in a naturally strong defensive position. Caesar besieged it for weeks without success. Every schoolboy knows, or at least there was a time when every schoolboy knew, that Caesar was a great general whose victories were due not only to the courage and discipline of his soldiers but also to his strategic and tactical skills. Gergovia was one occasion where he got it all wrong.

Realising that his siege was not going to succeed, he decided to take the stronghold by a method of military sleight of hand. There was a small pass on the west of the plateau, the only weak point. Caesar moved his troops there, letting the Arvernes see that he was about to attack. Vercingetorix, well aware of the weakness, rushed his men to defend it. But Caesar's real attack came from the most unexpected quarter, the eastern side, where the slope was steepest. At first he was successful, taking three camps inside the 2m stone wall which encircled the site and going on to attack the town gate with a battering ram. But the noise of the attack and the alarmed cries of the population massed inside the town alerted Vercingetorix who turned his soldiers, led by horsemen, back to its defence. The Roman troops, exhausted by the climb up the steep slope, were attacked on the flank and fled in disorder. Caesar, by his own account, narrowly escaped capture by the Arvernes.

A bronze Vercingetorix still fiercely challenges his enemies in the place de Jaude in Clermont-Ferrand, but in fact his hour of glory was quickly past. He was soon obliged to surrender. When this day came, he took up his most prized weapons and, on a splendidly caparisoned horse, rode out of the town to where Caesar, seated in state, awaited him. With a last display of bravado Vercingetorix put the horse through its paces in front of the Emperor. He then dismounted, walked up to his conqueror and sat at his feet in silence. He was made a prisoner and was later crucified by Caesar's orders.

In the centuries that followed Vercingetorix and his battle were forgotten. Today, nobody knows for sure where Gergovia really was, though thousands of tourists every year think they visit the site (see box on page 106).

After the battle the Romans colonised the region, developed the spas, improved agriculture, established mines, and began to make a road system. They also set up potteries which exported goods to Britain and throughout the Roman Empire. They replaced Gergovia by a new capital which they called Augustonemetum, on the site of which Clermont-Ferrand stands today.

When the Roman, Sidonius Apollinarus, Bishop of Clermont, died towards the end of the 5th century AD, the Roman Empire had already fallen into decay, and Auvergne had been invaded by Visigoths led by Alaric the Bold.

It was Sidonius Apollinarus, a poet as well as a cleric, who wrote in a letter in AD 454 describing the Auvergne he loved . . . 'mountains enclose it in green pastures, vines flourish on the hillsides, farms are scattered through the countryside, castles stand on rocky heights flanked by deep forests, crops fill the plains, clear streams sparkle in the valleys, and rivers cascade over precipitous cliffs . . . in short, once strangers have come to know this place, the memory of their own country fades away . . .' (My free translation of his letter, which is reproduced at the entry to the Regional Museum of Auvergne in Riom.)

After the end of the Roman occupation there followed centuries of anarchy in which the only islands of stability were provided by the Church with its network of abbeys and monasteries throughout Auvergne.

This period of European history has been called the Dark Ages and it was certainly nowhere darker than in Auvergne. All the same, occasional figures emerge from the general chaotic gloom. In the 6th century Gregory of Tours — he was Bishop of that town, although he came from Clermont — the first French historian, left lively accounts of the corruption of the Church at the time of aristocratic life in the countryside.

In the year 614 the self-governing Duchy of Aquitaine was formed, taking in the whole of Auvergne. But this dubious and disorganised Duchy was replaced towards the end of the 8th century by a confused and corrupt kingdom, when Pippin the Short, the first Carolingian king of France, defeated the Prince of Aquitaine, Gaifier, in 768.

Up to this time France had consisted of the kingdom of the Franks, a much smaller territory than the France of today, although it did include some western parts of Germany. The acquisition of Aquitaine and Auvergne represented a great increase in size, but it was to prove the kind of gain made by modern financiers who make a great deal on paper but have not got much in the bank. Even after this doubtful acquisition France was still small, not including Brittany, or Roussillon, or Burgundy, which extended from the Burgundy of today all the way down the Rhône valley to the Mediterranean.

Pippin the Short was clearly a small man but, according to legend, so powerful that he could fell a lion with one blow of his fist. The legend makes no mention of where he found the lions. In any case he had a more positive claim to fame in that he was the father of Charlemagne.

This extraordinary man combined irresistible qualities. As big as his father was small (his mother was known as Bertha Big Foot, so perhaps he got his size from her), he was the ideal chief to his Frankish warriors. He was jovial but commanding, with flashing blue eyes and an aquiline nose. He was fearless but never rash, genial but precise, well-loved and yet formidable, a man whose leadership was accepted without question. He was more than a warrior. He had the gift of statesmanship, was able to take a broad view, had a flawless memory, strong common sense and a tenacious will. He had a rich and diverse character, loving to hear and join in the old Frankish songs, keeping to the traditional dress, enjoying festive occasions but eating and drinking little himself. With all this, Charlemagne was a devout Catholic and a defender of the established Church. The chief purpose of his fifty-three campaigns, fought on all fronts from Spain to Denmark, was to defend Christianity in western Europe against the enemies who attacked it from all sides.

It was a part of Charlemagne's talents that he would not attempt the impossible and asked no more of his followers than he thought they could achieve. He built a Frankish empire that extended from the Pyrenees to Poland but when he died in 814 that empire soon broke up without his forceful, guiding personality.

Aquitaine, including Auvergne, was given in succession to various offspring of Charlemagne's family (one of whom, his son-in-law, is said to have had a summer palace in our local village of Casseneuil, a few hundred metres from where I am writing) but their influence was never strong, and the real power in Aquitaine was gradually seized by the Counts of Auvergne, the most powerful of whom was William the Pious, so-called from having founded the great Abbey of

Cluny, in Maconnais. In addition to Auvergne and Maconnais, William the Pious held lands in Berry, Velay and Lyonnais, and gave himself the title of Duke of Aquitaine.

It was quite common at the time for those who had a castle and some armed followers to announce that they were now Count of Something or Duke of Wherever, and to run up a few forged papers to back their claim. It was not often disputed unless the number of their armed retainers was really too few.

William the Pious was sufficiently powerful to conduct his affairs on equal terms with the royalty of France. But when his dynasty came to an end in 927, with the death of his nephew, Alfred, the power in Aquitaine passed to the Counts of Poitiers. They left things in Auvergne in the hands of lesser nobles who followed the example of William the Pious in enriching themselves and assuming false titles. They did little else and under them the central power steadily disintegrated and Auvergne became once again a territory fought over by robber barons.

Such social order as there was, and it was very little, was parallel with the feudal system in Britain, being centred on a lord who exercised real power by force through armed followers on foot and horseback, policing the land around his stronghold and protecting his serfs who, in return, supported him in kind and through taxes.

More and more fortified strongholds were built. The economy of the region was paralysed by the constant petty wars between these noble villains who, except that they were dealing in vast tracts of countryside instead of drugs and gambling in New York or Chicago, behaved very much like modern gangsters, 'rubbing out' their enemies in order to acquire their property and incomes.

At the beginning of the 13th century armed expeditions organised by Philippe Auguste, King of France, were successful in Auvergne and led to the region becoming part of the Kingdom of France. At least that was the French view of things. In reality nothing changed. Auvergne remained a country torn apart by the private wars of landowning nobles, and where bands of horsemen led by soldiers of fortune raided farms and villages, and where the roads were infested by highwaymen. Important travellers would make long detours to avoid stretches of country where all classes of society were engaged in brigandage, where lords of the manor did not hesitate to pillage and burn even the churches, where priests were often smugglers and sometimes assassins, and where false money was as common as the real thing. Even today it is not unusual to find place names which recall this long period of lawlessness — Cutpurse Pass, Deadman's Cross, Rock of the Hanged Men, Cutthroat Wood, are translations of just a few of the names on modern maps of Auvergne.

Most lawless of all were the nobles from whom example should have come. In his spired and crenellated castle of Nonette which stood in Riom on the site of the present Law Courts (the chapel still stands), Jean, Duc de Berry, lived in the sumptuous style of an eastern potentate. While his brother Charles V was more seriously occupied in trying to get the English out of France, Jean maintained his own architects to work on his sixteen other castles in Auvergne, Berry and Poitiers.

He had a permanent train of musicians, poets, courtiers and jesters, and his own painters, the Limbourg brothers, who produced several Books of Hours, including the famous *Très Riches Heures du Duc de Berry*.

In the great ducal hall of Nonette two hundred guests could sit down to feast, and often did, while Jean de Berry presided in gorgeous robes trimmed with jewels and furs. He kept a menagerie of wild animals, possibly the earliest European version of a stately home game park, as well as aviaries of exotic birds, and packs of hounds.

To maintain this magnificent style he exacted heavier and heavier taxes and sent his soldiers far and wide to collect them by force. When the town clerks of Riom, St. Flour and Montferrand tried to use some money, legitimately gained, on behalf of their towns, he threw them into prison.

Oppression of this kind was repeated on a smaller scale by lesser nobles throughout Auvergne. The victims often appealed to the King's justice, but very little was done. Safe in their castles, the nobles simply ignored the few judgements made against them. In the wild mountain country the lesser bandits had countless hideaways.

Normal life was impossible in such conditions and many of the ordinary people began to leave the more populated areas to escape the tyranny of these landlords. They went either to more remote districts, creating settlements for the first time in the uplands of Auvergne, or placed themselves under the protection of the abbeys and churches. These religious institutions thus acquired a stronger labour force which they used to improve farming standards in the region.

In the year 1400 Jean, Duc de Bourbon, married Marie de Berry, the heiress of Jean de Berry; they founded the Bourbon dynasty which was to give eight kings to France, and which linked Bourbonnais to Auvergne.

During the 15th century things began to improve slightly. The country became more peaceful and, as a result, the economy took an up turn. New industries were started, among them cutlery in Thiers, the making of lace in Le Puy and other towns in Velay, the weaving of woollen cloth in the mountains, and the manufacture of paper in mills scattered throughout Auvergne. One of these, at Ambert, still exists and makes superb paper by the old methods.

Conditions were improved further by King Louis XI who made military expeditions against Bourbonnais and Auvergne in 1465, 1471 and 1476, reducing the power of the Duc de Bourbon and capturing the Comte d'Armagnac, both of whom had refused to recognise the royal authority. In his great fortress at Carlat in southern Auvergne, Jacques d'Armagnac withstood the siege by royal troops for eighteen months before yielding. He was put in a cage and transported to Paris where he was beheaded in Les Halles, the old market.

But it was more than another hundred years before the full weight of royal authority was felt in Auvergne and a more ordered society established. In the 16th century the towns began to grow steadily larger and richer, yet still the barons disregarded or failed to recognise the drift of events. They remained a law unto themselves, ignoring the government or actively resisting it.

At the same time France entered a period of religious upheaval in which Auvergne was deeply involved. From about 1530 Protestantism began to gain ground in France, largely due to the teachings of John Calvin who led the Reformation from his base in Geneva. Calvin was a Frenchman of the upper middle class, very well connected, highly educated, with an especially clear mind and lucid powers of expression. Many of the French Protestants (Huguenots) were people of influence, including about one-third of the nobility, top-ranking army and navy officers, and many of the richest merchants and bankers. They were strong but they were far outnumbered and were often persecuted, and this persecution reached a bloody climax on St. Bartholomew's Day (24th August) 1572 when between 3,000 and 4,000 Huguenots were slaughtered in Paris and thousands more in towns throughout the country.

There were violent reactions. Many Huguenots had died but those who were left had no intention of lying down. In Auvergne the town of Issoire was captured by the Huguenot, Captain Merle, a cruel and fearsome soldier of whom one of his officers said, 'With him I would attack Hell itself, even if fifty thousand devils were defending it'. Catholics were put to the sword and their houses destroyed. In 1577 the Catholics under the Duc d'Anjou recaptured and burned Issoire, killing thousands of Huguenots. In the same campaign 400 Auvergne villages were attacked and Protestants were killed everywhere.

After the accession of Henry IV in 1593 and the Edict of Nantes in 1598, which gave the Huguenots rights of worship in certain places, the religious situation became less tense.

In Auvergne the tyranny of the nobles and their complete disregard for central government and the consequent social insecurity and disorder continued. In the towns the influential traders and officials had repeatedly appealed to Cardinal Richelieu to break the power of the nobles. In 1632, when he discovered that some of these nobles were plotting against him, he acceded to the demands of the townsmen and gave orders for the destruction of the fortresses throughout Auvergne. Not many escaped his fury.

Richelieu's strong action against the barons was reinforced later in the same century when Louis XIV sent his law officers to bring the worst of the nobles to justice. These trials, known as Les Grands Jours de Justice de l'Auvergne, took place in 1665. The townspeople rejoiced, saying that this was 'a last judgement when the great would be made small'. Similar legal forays had been made to Auvergne several times in the past with little effect, but this time the judges meant business. They began with a sensation. They arrested the Vicomte de la Mothe-Canillac, who was considered by the people to be much the least offensive of several horrible Canillacs, as he had murdered only one person. Nevertheless, the Vicomte was judged, condemned and executed on the same day.

The speed and finality of this action set off an 'every man for himself' panic among the nobles. Those who had tyrannised the poor tried to redress their wrongs by dashing about handing out largesse right, left and centre.

Others whose crimes had been of a more bloody nature made off into hiding in the mountains. They included the Seigneur de Massiac, who had

Kings and Queens of France*

Capet Dynasty

HUGUES CAPET, born 938 (?), came to throne 987; married (i) Adelaide d'Aquitaine and (ii) Constance de Provence, died 996.

ROBERT II (the Pious), born (?), came to throne 996; married Rozala of Flanders; died 1031.

HENRI I, born 1008 (?), came to throne 1031; married Anne of Kiev; died 1060.

PHILIPPE I, born 1052, came to throne 1060, married Bertha of Holland; died 1108.

LOUIS VI (the Fat), born 1081, came to throne 1108; married (i) Lucienne de Rochefort and (ii) Adelaide de Savoie; died 1137.

LOUIS VII (the Young), born 1119, came to the throne 1137; married (i) Eleanor of Aquitaine and (ii) Adèle de Champagne; died 1180.

PHILIPPE II (Philippe-Auguste), born 1165, came to throne 1180, married (i) Ingeborg of Denmark and (ii) Agnès de Méranie; died 1223.

LOUIS VIII (the Lion), born 1187, came to throne 1223; married Blanche de Castile; died 1226.

LOUIS IX (Saint Louis), born 1215, came to throne 1226; married Marguerite de Provence; died 1270.

PHILIPPE III (the Bold), born 1245, came to throne 1270; married Isabela de Aragón; died 1285.

PHILIPPE IV (the Handsome), born 1268, came to throne 1285; married Jeanne de Navarre; died 1314.

LOUIS X (the Battler), born 1289, came to throne 1314; married Marguerite de Bourgogne; died 1316.

JEAN I (posthumous), born 1316, came to throne 1316; died 1316.

PHILIPPE V (the Tall), born 1294, came to throne 1316; married Jeanne de Bourgogne; died 1322; uncle of Jean I.

CHARLES IV (the Handsome), born 1294, came to throne 1322; married (i) Blanche de Bourgogne and (ii) Marie de Luxembourg; died 1328; brother of Philippe V.

Valois Dynasty

PHILIPPE VI (Philippe de Valois), born 1293, came to throne 1328; married Jeanne de Bourgogne; died 1350; nephew of Philippe IV.

JEAN II (the Courageous), born 1319, came to throne 1350; married Bonne de Luxembourg; died 1364.

CHARLES V (the Wise), born 1337, came to throne 1364; married Jeanne de Bourbon; died 1380.

CHARLES VI (the Mad, or the Well-beloved), born 1368, came to throne 1380; married Isabeau of Bavaria; died 1422.

CHARLES VII (the King of Bourges), born 1403, came to throne 1422; married Marie d'Anjou; died 1461.

LOUIS XI, born 1423, came to throne 1461; married Charlotte de Savoie; died 1483.

CHARLES VIII, born 1470, came to throne 1483; married Anne of Brittany; died 1498.

Valois–Orléans Dynasty

LOUIS XII (the Father of the People), born 1462, came to throne 1498; married (i) Jeanne de France and (ii) Anne of Brittany and (iii) Mary of England; died 1515; descended from 1st son of Louis d'Orléans, brother of Charles VI.

Orléans–Angoulême Dynasty

FRANÇOIS I, born 1494, came to throne 1515; married Claude de France; died 1547; descended from 3rd son of Charles d'Orléans, brother of Charles VI.

HENRI II, born 1519, came to throne 1547; married Catherine de Médicis; died 1559.

FRANÇOIS II, born 1544, came to throne 1559; married Mary Queen of Scots; died 1560.

CHARLES IX, born 1550, came to throne 1560; married Elizabeth of Austria; died 1574; brother of François II.

HENRI III, born 1551, came to throne 1574; married Louise de Vaudement; died 1589; brother of Charles IX.

Bourbon Dynasty

HENRI IV (Henry of Navarre), born 1553, came to throne 1589; married (i) Marguerite de Valois and (ii) Marie de Médicis; died 1610; descended from 6th son of Louis IX.

LOUIS XIII, born 1601, came to throne 1619; married Anne of Austria; died 1643.

LOUIS XIV (the Sun King), born 1638, came to throne 1643; married the Infanta Maria Teresa; died 1715.

LOUIS XV, born 1710, came to throne 1715; married Marie Leczinska; died 1774; great grandson of Louis XIV.

LOUIS XVI, born 1754, came to throne 1774; married Marie Antoinette of Austria; died 1793; grandson of Louis XV.

Republic and Empire until 1815

LOUIS XVIII, born 1755, came to throne 1815; married Marie-Joséphine de Savoie; died 1824; brother of Louis XVI.

CHARLES IX, born 1757, came to throne 1824; married Marie-Thérèse de Savoie; died 1836; brother of Louis XVIII.

Bourbon–Orléans Dynasty

LOUIS-PHILIPPE, born 1773, came to throne 1830; married Maria Amelia of The Two Sicilies; died 1850; descended from Philippe d'Orléans, brother of Louis XIV.

*Unless otherwise stated, each King is the son of his predecessor.

poisoned his completely innocent wife and castrated and tortured to death her supposed lover; and the Marquis de Montboissier-Canillac, who kept a gang of a dozen desperadoes whom he called his 'apostles' ready for any evil, who beat or put to the sword anyone who opposed the Marquis.

In four months the judges dealt with thousands of cases, civil and criminal (certainly the fastest that French justice has ever moved, before and especially since). Murder, adultery, incest, infanticide, robbery, fraud, all were dealt with in the same express fashion. The curate of Saint-Babel who had murdered a peasant who had denounced the curate's misconduct was despatched without delay to make his own explanations to his Maker. The judges handed out death penalties, banishments, whippings and fines, by the hundred, and, for variety an occasional branding with a red hot iron with the mark of the fleur de lys. Some nobles escaped punishment, through influence, evasion or sheer luck but more and more of their castles were destroyed.

Though the merchants of Clermont were very pleased with the way things went at the trials, they found that, as usual, there was a fly in the ointment. It took the form of Madame Talon, mother of the Procurator-General, and surely one of the great busybodies of all time. She held reunions of the most important women in the town, explaining to them how to be more devout and do more for charity and manage their homes more efficiently; she told the nuns how they should be running their hospital; she exposed all the Town Hall scandals; and in church, if she did not like the way the priest was conducting the service, she would interrupt and finish it herself. In the course of her shopping she discovered that an Auvergnat pound (characteristically perhaps) weighed only 13½ ounces instead of the 16 usual in other parts of France (this was before the introduction of the metric system). She had it changed, and to make sure that she was really getting value for money gave herself a discount on everything she bought, knowing that the shopkeepers would not dare to protest.

Not surprisingly, the judges began to weary of this feast of justice, and occupational indigestion and boredom with provincial life set in. It was time to get back to the smart society of Paris and their friends at Court. Thus Louis XIV's 'Great Days of the Auvergne' came to an end and a sharp lesson to the wrongdoers it was.

Almost overnight the fortresses which had so dominated and frightened the people became picturesque ruins which look today as if they have been specially arranged and sited for the benefit of tourist photographers. Among the more photogenic of them are Tournoël, Busséol, Alleuze, Léotoing and Murol.

With the fear of oppression at last removed and royal support behind them the cities became larger and more prosperous. The richer merchants and officials began to build themselves gracious town houses with ornate façades and inner courtyards with statuary and fountains. The castles were gone; the mansions arrived.

Even so, there was still trouble. Towards the end of the 17th century there were more religious disturbances and persecution of the Huguenots. The pressure built up and exploded at the beginning of the 18th century in the revolt of the Camisards (the name comes from the Languedoc word *camisot* which means 'shirt', and it was given to them because many of them fought in their shirtsleeves).

It started when the Abbé François de Chayla, the Catholic Inspector of Missions in the Cévennes area, arrested a group of religious fugitives in July 1702 and put them in prison at le Pont-de-Montvert in the Lozère département. He had been especially cruel to the Huguenots, the men had been tortured, broken on the wheel, sent to the galleys, and he allowed the wives and daughters left behind to be raped with impunity. The fugitives he arrested were Huguenots trying to join up with others to emigrate and start a new life in England or America.

Fifty peasants armed with guns, swords, pikes, knives and pitchforks decided to set them free. They forced the gates of the prison, released the prisoners, set fire to the building and then the Abbé de Chayla's house. They allowed him time for a prayer and then shot him, and each man stabbed him as he died.

I shall not try to improve on the words of Robert Louis Stevenson who gives a full account of the Camisard revolt in his *Travels with a Donkey in The Cevennes*, including the death of de Chayla. 'The Camisards dragged him to the public place of the town, raging and calling him damned. "If I be damned," said he, "why should you damn yourselves?" Good reasoning [says Stevenson] but in the course of his inspectorship he had given many stronger which all told in a contrary direction; and these he was now to hear. One by one, the man they called Spirit Seguier first, the Camisards drew near and stabbed him. "This", they said "is for my father broken on the wheel. This for my brother in the galleys. That for my mother and sister in your cursed convents." Each gave his blow and his reason; then they all kneeled and sang psalms around the body until dawn.'

Spirit Seguier was captured a few days later, and went to his death with dignity. His judges asked 'Have you no remorse for your crimes?' He answered, 'I have committed none. My soul is like a garden, full of shelter and fountains.' On 12th August 1702, his right hand was struck from his body and he was burned alive.

Up until this incident most of the atrocities in the new wave of religious disturbance had been committed by the Catholics. Now the Huguenots followed the same pattern, burning, torturing and killing. The peasants of Auvergne supported the revolt of the Camisards and paid for it dearly, often with their lives.

The Camisards were inspired by ardent leaders, the most famous of whom were Jean Cavalier and Roland. Cavalier was a baker's apprentice who became their military leader at the age of eighteen. He showed great tactical ability, once defeating a force of 250 regular soldiers with fewer than half that number of poorly armed peasants. In the end it took thirty thousand regular soldiers led by three Marshals to contain the revolt of the four thousand Camisards, and the final solution was arrived at only by negotiation. Marshal de Villiers offered the Huguenots the right to emigrate, if they would lay down their arms. Cavalier accepted on their behalf, only to be accused of treachery by his associates. He went to England where he made a successful career in the army, ending as Governor of Jersey. Some others accepted the emigration offer. Roland fought on with

The Best Romanesque Churches

From north to south

Châtel-Montagne, Allier
Notre-Dame-du-Port, Clermont-Ferrand, Puy-de-Dôme
St. Saturnin, Puy-de-Dôme
Notre-Dame d'Orcival, Orcival, Puy-de-Dôme
St. Nectaire, Puy-de-Dôme
St. Austremoine, Issoire, Puy-de-Dôme
Notre-Dame-des-Miracles, Mauriac, Cantal
St. Julien de Brioude, Haute-Loire
Cathedral of Notre-Dame, Le Puy, Haute-Loire

Other Important Churches

Cathedral of Notre-Dame, Moulins, Allier (Gothic and 19th Century; fine stained glass)
St. Pierre de Souvigny, Souvigny, Allier (part Roman, part Gothic; tombs of early Bourbons)
Cathedral of Notre-Dame of the Assumption, Clermont-Ferrand, Puy-de-Dôme (early Gothic)
Abbey of St. Robert, La Chaise-Dieu, Haute-Loire (Gothic)

total fanaticism, but when he was betrayed and killed in 1704 the revolt of the Camisards came to an end.

Roland's house still exists just as it was at the time, at Le Mas-Soubeyran between St. Jean-du-Gard and Anduze. It is now the Musée du Désert and contains documents of all kinds recalling the Huguenot struggle, the Camisards, and the eventual triumph of tolerance, as well as personal souvenirs of Roland, including his Bible.

After his death the peasants returned to their burned villages and rebuilt their houses, often taking the stones from ruined castles to do it. The religious struggle went on in non-violent conditions, ending only when Louis XVI, 'convinced by the uselessness of a century of persecutions, and rather from necessity than sympathy', signed an Act of Tolerance in 1787. The villages that had been Protestant a hundred years before were still Protestant, and were Protestant a hundred years later when Stevenson walked through them, and are still so today.

Following the destruction of the castles and the breaking of the power of the nobles, Auvergne was governed by a succession of royal stewards called 'Intendants'. Throughout the 18th century they did much to improve conditions. New roads were opened up, marshes were drained, and in Aurillac and Clermont the town ramparts were demolished and replaced by wide boulevards to improve traffic circulation. Until then Clermont had the reputation of being the filthiest and most foul-mouthed town in France. None of the streets was wide enough to allow coaches and wagons to cross each other, so that infuriated coachmen, when they were not striking each other with whips, swore with a range of obscenity startling to passers-by. There was no sanitation in the houses and these same narrow streets were full of filth and rubbish of all kinds. No wonder that the plague had struck several times over the years. In 1631, forty per cent of all the heads of families in Clermont died of it. It was said that the inhabitants would willingly have burned their own town, if there had not been so many fountains ready to put the fire out.

In 1693/4 and in 1709/10 the cereal harvest throughout France was disastrous, especially in Auvergne, where there were many deaths from starvation. For many landowners this was a turning point. Land which yielded so little was more trouble than it was worth to them, and gradually, during the 18th century, more and more land came into the hands of small peasant farmers. By the eve of the French Revolution peasants already had control of a large part of the land in Auvergne.

If there was any spirit of revolt in Auvergne immediately prior to the Revolution, it was not observed by visitors, although its absence *was* remarked. While it cannot be said that the Revolution by-passed Auvergne, it is true to say that it was met there with general apathy and occasional resistance.

The Revolution was violently active against the Church. Holy effigies and church furniture were burned, sculpted statues, however beautiful, smashed with hammers. Belltowers were destroyed and the bells sent to be melted down. Many churches were converted to warehouses or covered markets. None of this went down well with the God-fearing peasantry who several times demonstrated in favour of 'God and the King'. Many priests became active against the Revolution and continued to carry out their work in secrecy. Many went into hiding in the mountains. Jean-Baptiste Roques, canon of Monsalvy, dressed as a woman during the day and pretended to be mad but when night fell he put on his priest's robe, visited the sick and held Mass in secret.

Since the farms could not survive without the labour of the young men, there was active resistance to the government's conscription order for all men between 18 and 40. At St. Pardoux, near la Tour-d'Auvergne, they met as ordered in the main square but only to shout that they were not going to be conscripted as a group, or by numbers drawn by lot, or in any other fashion, and that anyone who argued the point would have his head cut off. The few representatives of authority present were not inclined to debate the issue. Similar disrespect for the government's plans was shown in other villages in Auvergne.

So, all in all, there was not much fondness for the Revolution in the region. The peasants had enough on their hands making a living from day to day off their ungenerous land. They had nothing against Napoleon but he was not going to make the cows give more milk. When the monarchy was restored after the Emperor's downfall, it, too, was greeted with apathetic approval.

Towards the middle of the 19th century two quite different things happened which were to have a considerable effect on the future of Auvergne. It does not seem likely that British raincoats have much to do with the history of Auvergne but it was the Scot, Charles Mackintosh, who discovered that rubber was soluble in benzine and made the first waterproof coats, lined with rubber. By chance, his niece married a Frenchman named Édouard Daubrée, a demobilised cavalry officer with nothing to do. Also by chance, Daubrée had a cousin, Aristide Barbier, who had made unlucky investments and had lost most of his money. Hoping to make more money, they founded together a small factory in Clermont to make agricultural machinery. A good idea, but not as good as one that Madame Daubrée had.

One day, remembering Uncle Mackintosh's experiments, she made a few rubber balls to amuse her children and their friends. They were greeted with such enthusiasm that the partners decided to manufacture them commercially. The factory expanded and began to make pulley belts and rubber tubing but, after a very successful period, went into decline and in 1886 was on the point of closing down. To save it the grandsons of the founder, Aristide Barbier, agreed to take it over. Their name was Michelin.

These two brothers, Édouard and André Michelin, were men of business and innovative genius. Aided by the advent of the motor car, they laid the foundations of the great industry which was to make Clermont-Ferrand one of the world's great rubber centres, and the successful industrial town which it is today.

The second important change in the middle of the 19th century was the arrival of the railways in Auvergne. Clermont-Ferrand was reached in 1855 and Aurillac in 1868. By 1885 the system was already well advanced and was further extended by the construction of the Garabit Viaduct by Gustave Eiffel in the 1880s. It was here that Eiffel learned the techniques he was to use a few years later in building the Eiffel Tower.

The railway, it was thought, would bring more goods and people to Auvergne. Certainly the spa towns and the few industrial centres did benefit but the record shows that many of the Auvergnats, especially the poorer peasants, looked at this new development differently. To them the railway meant an opportunity to escape, to get away. The temptation was great and many did not resist.

The exodus which began in the latter half of the 19th century and which has continued ever since seemed to the Auvergnats logical enough. There was already a long established tradition of seasonal emigration to find work in other parts of France or even in Spain. The emigration now became permanent and most of it was directed towards Paris.

It is often said that Paris is the largest city in Auvergne. In a sense it is true. There are more than 300,000 Auvergnats living in Paris, at least as many as in Clermont-Ferrand with all its agglomeration. In Paris they have their own newspapers, clubs and societies; their own unions; their own insurance companies. They are feared in the business world, not only for their astuteness but because they stick together, helping and protecting each other.

When they first came to Paris, they had to start in a very small way. They had no qualifications for city work, just their toughness. They were obliged, like the Arabs and negroes of today, to do the dirty, unrewarding jobs that no one else would tackle. In the 1870s, for example, most Paris water came from street fountains supplied by unfiltered water from the Seine. The police made an order that every family must have a constant reserve of up to fifty litres, according to the number of rooms, as a precaution against fire. Instead of going for water only when they needed it, each family had to refill its tank every day. The nearest fountain might be a couple of hundred metres away and the living quarters up many flights of stairs, and water is heavy.

The Auvergnats, never afraid of hard work, became the water carriers. For three sous, then the price of a loaf of bread, they would bring a family its daily water supply. It had to be done early in the morning and by afternoon they were free. So they started hawking coal through the streets. They did well because their rivals dumped the coal outside and let the client take it in, while the Auvergnats delivered it exactly where it was wanted. It was thirsty work so they washed the dust down with their own wine, sent from home. They found that other Paris manual workers liked its sharp, thirst-quenching qualities. They began to open little bars from which they sold wine, coal and wood, and where the women would provide the famous Auvergne cabbage soup 'like mother made'. When the bar began to prosper, they would add another room at the back and once a week they would have a dance, Auvergne style with their own traditional instruments, the bagpipes which they call *cabrette* or *musette*. And so began the famous *bals-musette*, so much a feature of popular Paris life for so many years, though now it is accordion music.

But they were not all small traders. One well-known French writer, Alexander Vialatte, said that 'Auvergne produces cheeses, volcanoes, and Ministers ...' and it is a fact that Auvergne has produced a long succession of important politicians.

In the Middle Ages they were often the right-hand men of kings. In recent times they have been ministers, prime ministers, and Presidents of France. Every town in France seems to have an avenue or a place Gambetta; many have a rue Doumer; avenues and places Pompidou are common. No doubt there will be many rues d'Estaing and places Jacques Chirac. President Gambetta, one of the founders of the Third Republic, came from Cahors, on the edge of the Massif Central, Doumer from Aurillac. Georges Pompidou, prime minister under De Gaulle and later President, was born in the village of Montboudif, Cantal, grandson of an Auvergnat peasant. Former President Valéry Giscard d'Estang comes officially though distantly from one of the great noble families of Auvergne. Jacques Chirac comes from Corrèze on the edge of Auvergne and still has a family home near Ussel.

So in latter years Auvergne has not lacked support in the central government and this has helped the economic development of the region.

Another French President who was an Auvergnat was Pierre Laval, chief of the Vichy government during the 1940–1945 war. Laval was the son of the owner of a small café in Châteldon. He was always ambitious for power though he followed no particular political doctrine. The purchase of the oldest established newspaper in the region enabled him to further his career in politics and in 1935 he was elected senator for the département of Puy-de-Dôme.

In 1940, Vichy became the seat of government in Unoccupied France. At first Marshal Pétain and Laval were welcomed in Auvergne, but Laval soon discredited himself by his pro-German speeches. In 1942 some officers in the feeble and servile Vichy government decided to offer resistance if the demarcation line between Occupied and Unoccupied France was crossed. Together with members of the faculty of the University of Strasbourg, they stored arms, and met at Gergovia, under the cover of archaeological digs, to plan their organisation.

The resistance movement became active and important in the Massif Central. Just as the wild and deeply forested countryside had offered shelter to countless brigands over the centuries, it now provided scores of bases for resistance groups who carried out numerous acts of sabotage as well as attacks on German troops.

In April 1944 an important group of the Maquis, under the command of 'Colonel Gaspard', installed themselves on Mont Mouchet, a forested summit in la Margeride, in southern Auvergne. Signposts were erected reading 'Free France begins here'. A few days before D-Day three thousand Resistance troops confronted the German Forces. It was an unequal battle, the lightly armed Maquis fighters losing more than a third of their numbers. German reprisals were savage. Villages and isolated farms were burned and their occupants killed, twenty-seven in the village of Ruynes alone. But a few weeks later the Maquis forces regrouped and in July, aided by detachments from Limousin and Bourbonnais, succeeded in driving 20,000 German troops north, forcing them to surrender at Bec d'Allier.

On the summit of Mont Mouchet today there is a National Monument to the Resistance. The forest lodge in front of it, which was their headquarters, now houses a museum of the Resistance which is open from 1st May to 15th October.

Since the war the history of Auvergne has been one of economic development, a steady expansion of business and industry, and a marked decline of peasant farming.

Depopulation of rural Auvergne, i.e. 95 per cent of it, has been going on for a long time. The figures show, for example, that the population of Cantal dropped from 261,000 in 1846 to 173,000 in 1962. The trend continues. One Canton, Viverols, a long way from the towns, has lost one-third of its population in the past seven years.

As people, particularly the young, leave the country, the population of the towns has increased by more than ten per cent in the past twenty years. Clermont-Ferrand has grown from 30,000 in 1806, to 58,000 in 1906, to 108,000 in 1946, and is now well over 150,000 with as many more in its suburbs. The city is expected to double in size in the next thirty years.

Clermont already has 3,500 people to the square kilometre, while in huge areas of the uplands the figure is lower than ten. But whatever happens economically and historically in Auvergne in the future, nothing is going to alter its true nature. No one is going to fill in the countless gorges or level the mountains; the great lakes, foaming rivers and thermal springs are not going to run dry; the wind will continue to sigh through the deep forests and over the deserted plateaux; every spring will see carpets of flowers on the grasslands.

But what is changing is life in the small villages whose history in the past was so violent. The young people are going, true, but every year those who are left welcome more and more holidaymakers attracted by the inexhaustible space and beauty, and the great variety of things to do.

Tourism is bringing a new peace and a little prosperity to these places for so long poor, isolated, and scarred by time.

3
Food and Wine and Bread and Water

There is a story that during the Roman invasion of Auvergne the Gauls were forced to retreat to the slopes of the Puy de Dôme where they were besieged for some time by Caesar's troops. So far, this is all true. One day the Gallic chief, symbolically thumbing his nose to Caesar, sent him an old, dried up cockerel. Caesar was vexed but being, as history shows, a man of considerable resource, he decided that the insult could be turned to his advantage. He declared a truce and invited the Gallic chief to a *dîner à deux* the following evening.

At the meal the Gaul was served a wonderfully flavoured dish swimming in a rich, red sauce. Being well-mannered and also Gallic and unable to resist talking about food, the chief asked politely what was this speciality. Caesar replied that it was the superb chicken which he had been kind enough to send across the day before, cooked very slowly, and very long, in the wine of the region. The Gaul recognised that the tough, old cockerel had been transformed by Caesar's chef into a gastronomic masterpiece and, swallowing his pride with another glass of wine, he managed to say so.

Caesar brushed aside the compliment lightly. It's nothing, he said, just one of the many things the Romans can teach the Gauls.

That, so they say in Auvergne, was the very first coq au vin. A dubious assertion, perhaps, but as good as the claims of many other French regions, including Bordeaux and Burgundy. Better in some ways, since the great chefs say it is a mistake to use too rich a wine, which will dominate instead of enhancing the flavour of the chicken. The light red wines of Auvergne are ideal (see recipe, p. 34).

If you were to show a set of Scottish bagpipes to the average Auvergne farmer, he would at least recognise it as a close relation to his own traditional musical instrument, the *cabrette*. He might after a few trial runs even be able to play it. Give a pig's stomach and one of its feet to his wife and she will turn it, with a few other magic ingredients, into a close, if ennobled, relation of a good Scottish haggis.

For centuries the food of the Auvergne farmer was based on what he could find within walking distance outside his own door, and many of their favourite dishes of today are the same as they have been for generations.

It is enough to list a few of the things commonly used in Auvergne cooking which are unfamiliar to British or

American palates to understand that the visitor will have every opportunity to extend his experience of good eating. Take for example, bilberries (blueberries), walnut oil, wild boar, pumpkin, home-cured hams, carp, snipe, chestnuts, crayfish, venison, and more than two dozen kinds of mushrooms.

The average Frenchman thinks of Auvergne as a region where one eats well enough and copiously. The dishes which the farmer's wife prepares are meant to satisfy the hunger of a man who has worked hard all day in the open air in any weather, and who needs his health and strength to do it again tomorrow, and every day, all his life. So, many of the recipes are rich, the sort of dishes that are prescribed in winter in Britain 'to keep the cold out'. The famous 'potée Auvergnate' is typical, a thick stew based on salt pork and home-made sausage with a variable blend of vegetables, always including carrots, potatoes and cabbage. The equally well-known cabbage soup of Auvergne sounds simpler, but is as much like ordinary cabbage soup as barley water is like a good glass of wine. At its most elaborate and best it contains chicken, veal, rib of beef and leg of pork. It should be understood that dishes like these were made in huge iron pots and were meant to last a week or more, being reheated from day to day, and improving in flavour as the days went by. At meal times they were often served as two courses. First the liquid would be poured over pieces of bread in the bottom of a bowl, then the meat and vegetables with the cabbage at the bottom. You might think that this would satisfy any appetite but, if there was any more warm liquid left they would pour it into their empty bowls and add a dash of red wine. The French for this habit is *faire chabrol* and as far as I know there is no English equivalent. Its effects are beneficial, helping the circulation and so the digestion. It is also considered to prevent infections of the throat or stomach.

Auvergne is rich in all kinds of raw materials for first-class cooking. Apart from those already mentioned there are pigs and poultry in every farmyard, and flocks of sheep and cattle in the pastures. There are ducks on the lakes, hares and partridges on the mountain slopes. There are vegetables of all kinds, fruit in great variety, and herbs and medicinal plants grow wild in the woods and on the hillsides.

Even in ordinary restaurants you are likely to come across some unusual and appetising dishes, such as braised partridge, jugged hare, rabbit in white wine, gratin of crayfish. Almost every village has its own way of producing home-cured hams, and pork, duck and hare pâtés. When it comes to desserts Auvergne is well known for its raspberry and bilberry (blueberry) tarts, its pumpkin pie, and its delicious cakes made with local fruits and walnuts.

Cheese

In France, of course, before you come to the puddings you come to the cheese. It is not without reason that Paris restaurateurs refer to Auvergne as 'the cheese-board of France'. Cheese has been made in Auvergne for much more than a thousand years and was praised by writers even in Roman times. The best known today are Cantal, St. Nectaire, Bleu d'Auvergne

Three Characteristic Auvergne Dishes

Coq au Vin d'Auvergne

INGREDIENTS

1 cockerel about 3.2 kg
3 bottles Châteaugay
(or any *light* red wine)
6 carrots
6 onions
200 g lard
200 g small onions
parsley (the Auvergne recipe calls for 3 roots of parsley, if you can find them)
300 g small mushrooms
300 g green streaky bacon
10 cl marc
bread for croutons
4 cloves of garlic
salt, bouquet garni, pepper grains

METHOD

Cut the cockerel into 16 pieces (collecting the blood in a bowl in which you have put a spoonful of vinegar) and marinate them for 48 hours in the three bottles of red wine with thyme, bay leaves, a clove of garlic, 3 onions, 3 carrots cut in pieces, and parsley.

When ready, take the pieces from the marinade, dry them and brown them gently in a pan in lard. Place them in an iron pot on top of three carrots and three onions cut in large pieces and browned lightly, two cloves of garlic, seasoning and a bouquet garni. On top of the chicken pieces spread 200 g of small onions, 300 g of small mushrooms and 300 g of green bacon lightly fried. Flame the chicken with 10 cl marc, then cover with the wine used in the marinade. Cover and place in a slow oven. Remove the trimmings as they cook — mushrooms, then onions, then bacon — and set aside.

When the chicken is cooked, after 2½ to 3 hours, take out the pieces, arrange them in a dish and add the trimmings. Reduce the gravy gently, adding 20 cl of the blood. Check the seasoning then pour the gravy over the chicken, finally adding some croutons. Serve with boiled potatoes.

This dish is *not* improved by using a richer red wine. It should be light.

Salmon in Flaky Pastry

A traditional recipe from the Brioude region — enough for six people, but which can be adjusted proportionately for any number down to one.

INGREDIENTS

six escalopes of salmon
about 100 g each
two rounds of flaky pastry, rolled out, one 30cm and one 20cm in diameter
½ litre fresh cream
150 g butter
2 lemons
pepper and salt
1 chopped shallot

350 g of fresh salmon (skin and bones removed)
1 whole egg plus two egg whites
1 soupspoon each of chives, tarragon, chervil, chopped fine and mixed

METHOD
Put the escalopes of salmon to marinate for one hour in the juice of the lemons with the chopped shallot and one soupspoon of the herbs. Place the larger round of pastry on an oven tray or at the bottom of a shallow pie dish and put it to cool.

Put the fresh salmon in a mixer, mincing it while adding the three whites of egg, one at a time (keep a yolk to brush on the pastry). Add the cream little by little and the pepper and salt. Mix for a few seconds to form a mousse and leave to cool for an hour. Then take out the large round of pastry and spread the mousse on it, leaving enough pastry around the edge to turn up. Arrange the marinated escalopes neatly on the mousse. Cover with the smaller round of pastry, turn up the lower pastry all round, wet with a brush and seal the edge carefully. Make an opening in the centre. Brush the top with yolk of egg and make a few light cuts in it. Cook for about 40 minutes in an oven at 190 to 200 degrees.

Serve with melted butter in which the rest of the herbs and a little lemon juice have been stirred.

Baked Wild Rabbit

INGREDIENTS

1 young rabbit (in Auvergne it would be from the upland pastures)
200 g of butter
1 kg of small potatoes
sprig of rosemary
chopped parsley
pepper and salt

METHOD
Cut the young rabbit in two halves lengthwise. Season each half with salt, pepper and rosemary, and spread all over with softened butter. Wrap each half in greaseproof paper and then enclose in aluminium foil. Bake in the oven for 30 to 40 minutes.

Peel the potatoes, slice thinly, wash, and dry on a cloth. Fry to a golden brown, seasoning with salt when half-cooked. Cover to help the cooking but turn frequently to brown evenly.

Serve the rabbit in one dish, and the sautée potatoes in another, sprinkled with parsley.

Could serve six but so good it may not go that far.

(sometimes called Bleu de Laqueuille) and Fourme d'Ambert.

Cantal and St. Nectaire are uncooked cheeses made from cows' milk. In the past Cantal was made during the summer when the cows were on the mountain pastures. A team of three men lived all summer in the mountains with their cattle. Their small stone houses, called *burons* in Cantal, had a deep cellar where the 36kg hand-made cheeses were stored for three months to ripen. Some Cantal is still made in this way in the Salers region but most comes from modern cheese factories in the villages. The *burons* are mostly in ruins or have been converted to tourist attractions which may sell the factory-made Cantal, as well as postcards, cow bells, and what are called *bouffadous*, which are made from straight branches about 5cm in diameter and about 76cm long with a small hole bored down through the length. They are used for blowing up the embers of a dying fire. They do the job well, with less fuss than a bellows. If you have log or coal fires at home, they make useful souvenirs.

But to get back to our cheeses. The hand-made Cantal, from the milk of Salers cows, is reckoned to have the best flavour and to keep longer than that made in the modern factory-dairies.

St. Nectaire is a flat, round cheese, much smaller than a Cantal, and weighs only about 900g. A lot of it is still made by farmers, as well as the factory production, so it is a cheese of variable quality, some is quite good and some is superb. If you find a piece of straw sticking to the rind, it may well have been ripened as it should be, on a bed of rye straw. The same cheese exists with a hole in the middle and is called Murol after the village of that name near St. Nectaire.

Roquefort is not in Auvergne but it is in the Massif Central, or at least on the edge of it, and deserves mention because it is available throughout the region and is, undoubtedly, one of the world's great cheeses.

It is said to owe its origin to a rustic love story. A shepherd was about to have his lunch of bread and ewe cheese in one of the grottoes — he wanted to get out of the sun — at the foot of Mount Combalou. Suddenly, he saw a girl he was in love with paddling in a nearby stream. He forgot his lunch, leaving it on a rock shelf in the cave, and made off after the girl. The story does not say what happened next, though apparently he met with some success, because it was three months before he returned to the cave. His lunch was still there, the bread covered in blue mould, the cheese veined in the same colour. Noticing that the cheese had not dried up and being hungry, he gingerly tasted it and found it delicious. He did not know it but he had just discovered Roquefort.

Today, thousands of these cheeses are ripened in the same Grottes de Combalou near Roquefort-sur-Soulzon. They are carefully tended by women who brush them, turn them over, and regularly puncture them with needles to help the formation of the mould, which is a kind of penicillin. Men with highly developed 'noses' sniff the cheeses from time to time, deciding which are ready to be packed.

The cheeses called Bleu des Causses and Bleu d'Aveyron are made in similar fashion except that ewes' milk is mixed with cows' or goats' milk. Fourme d'Ambert is an excellent cheese made in the shape of a cylinder. It should be cut in horizontal slices rather than vertically, and is said to be better towards the bottom.

Bread

The natural accompaniment to cheese is bread. The earliest tourists to Auvergne, nearly always distinguished people from Paris, were frankly astonished at the great quantities of both which were eaten. Even nowadays the farm worker or artisan in central and southern France often eats a whole loaf with his midday meal.

It is difficult for anyone who has always had enough to eat to think of bread with reverence but this is exactly the traditional attitude of the Auvergne peasant towards bread. It was an old saying in the countryside there that 'an empty stomach attracts illness'. The important thing was to be sure that it was never empty. The basic answer was bread. In the harshest times they would be obliged to eat barley bread as dark and tough as tree bark. In those parts of the mountains where the chestnut tree would grow, especially in the Cévennes, and where there were no cereal crops, they made their bread from chestnuts. The tree was even called 'l'arbre de pain' — the bread tree. No bread was ever thrown away; even mouldy it was put in soup.

So their respect for bread was almost religious. The farmer's wife would never make a loaf without marking the dough with the sign of the Cross with her knife. The baked loaf was always put on the table with the Cross uppermost. It was considered sinful to waste bread, or to walk through a field of ripening wheat. White bread was a treat; a sure sign of good times.

Depending on the size of her family, the farmer's wife would have a baking day at least once a fortnight. The children would be there helping and watching, and waiting, knowing that their mother would have put aside a little ball of dough for each of them which they would be given as it came from the oven, warm and golden brown. This little loaf was known as a *michou*. For many of those children it must have remained in their memories as a symbol of home and happiness because it is not unusual to see it in the name of a house — Clos de Michou in the country, or Notre Michou in a neat little suburban road.

The high standard of the country cooking of Auvergne owes a lot to a particular class of women. They belonged to a religious order known as the Daughters of St. Agnes which was created in the 17th century by the Jesuits of Aurillac. These women took a vow of celibacy and obeyed the rules of their order but instead of entering a convent they lived in the world, in general as cook/housekeepers in the bourgeois homes of Aurillac, Murat, St. Flour, Pleaux and Salers. They had been trained in household management and knew their trade well, providing well-cooked meals at reasonable expense, and were ingenious in improving and varying recipes.

They were called *menettes* and in time it became the habit to use this word to describe any of those old women and widows to be found in every village who knew better than most how to make the most of the local raw materials and were expert in the old kitchen traditions. They were called upon for help in all festive and special occasions. As they were always in and out of other people's houses they invariably developed the defects of their merits, meddling in everybody's business and retailing gossip from one house to another.

Whatever their faults, it was certainly true that they had a high degree of skill. Some were said to be able to name the flour from wheat grown on different farms, even water from different springs, simply by taste. As a result of their fine palates, their innovations, and the traditional methods they handed down, Auvergne cooking has developed over the years from the simplest peasant standards to a cuisine which often shows subtlety and refinement.

Wines

On the other hand it must be said that the wines of Auvergne are not much appreciated in other parts of France. They are said not to travel well and some unkind people say that it was Auvergne wine that made Orléans the French vinegar capital. This is because the wines used to be sent to Paris by barge by river and canal but it was a long, slow journey and either they reached their destination flat and tasteless or they had already turned to vinegar by the time they reached Orléans. In Auvergne they tell it differently. They say the boatmen were frequently held up because, in their own estimation, there was either not enough depth of water or it was flowing too fast and that, while they were waiting, the boatmen soon exhausted their own small supply of wine. They then turned to the excellent Auvergne wines they were transporting and drank those, topping up the barrels with water.

If long experience means anything Auvergne wines should have been good. Although the Druid priests forbade the growing of vines, the number of pieces of broken wine jars which archaeologists have found suggest that even in the time of Vercingetorix the people of Auvergne did drink wine. It was no doubt imported for the rich and influential, because as a race the Celts were beer drinkers.

In the third century AD the Roman rulers gave permission and even encouraged the local people to grow vines and make their own wine but, just as they gave up using the spas once the Romans had gone, the Gauls gave up producing wine and went back to beer drinking. It was not until the time of Charlemagne that the vineyards were replanted. From then on, under the influence of the monasteries, wine grew into an important industry. Following an extremely hard winter in 1709 the vineyards were replanted with new varieties more resistant to frost but the wines they produced were not as good as in former times.

Grapes have never been grown in the mountains, so the mountain farmers, who liked wine as much as anybody, made their own arrangements. When the time for the grape harvest and the making of the wine came around, these mountain farmers set off for the valleys, or even went as far afield as Quercy or Languedoc Roussillon. The richer and thirstier farmers took with them horse- or ox-drawn wagons loaded with empty barrels; the poorer or more modest drinkers contented themselves with mules loaded with wineskins. Several of them from the same general area would join up together in caravan, stopping on the way at small inns, which they felt was essential to refresh their palates and their taste in wine. When they set off again, they would give each of the animals a bowl of wine to encourage them, and often a musician with a fiddle or bagpipes would go ahead to lead the staggering caravan on its way. These happy processions were known as *vinades*, and apart from feast days they were the nearest thing to a holiday that the working farmer ever had.

These mountain people liked their wine strong and, despite 'refreshing their palates', they had an original way of judging it. Instead of tasting it they would let a few drops fall on the cleanest part of their shirts. If the stain was not dark enough, they assumed that it had been watered and refused it.

Being good Christians the peasants considered it their duty to be hospitable. If a neighbour called he would invariably be offered wine, while a stranger would also be offered bread, cheese, or sausage. Otherwise, wine was mostly reserved for feast days and fairs. Even when he was working fifteen hours a day in the heat of summer, the farmer would content himself with water or watered milk. But on Sundays many men would go to the local inn and would sit around drinking wine, gathering the local news and discussing prices.

On feast days a good deal of heavy drinking went on. It is said that in Salers the fountains ran with wine on the annual feast day, and as a result the holy revellers soon set about each other, settling old scores, often with cudgels. There were several deaths and a great many injuries until the authorities put a stop to it.

The patron saint of wine producers in Auvergne is St. Verny, whose statue is found in all the churches in the wine region, especially in the valley of the Allier. He was often carried in procession and anointed with wine to encourage his good offices but the respect for the saint had its limits. If he failed to come up trumps with a good harvest, they turned his face to the wall until the next year. If it was bad they stood him to the knees in cold water to teach him a lesson, and if it was awful, they threw him in the river. Being Auvergnat and thinking of the cost of a new statue they always fished him out again.

In the valley of the Allier some of the vineyards made an unusual 'straw wine'. The best bunches of well-ripened white grapes were laid on a bed of straw in a dark place and were left there until January or February before being pressed. The result was an amber-coloured, sweetish wine, richly flavoured and good for thirty years in the bottle.

In the latter part of the 19th century a great deal of wine was being produced in Auvergne. In 1885 the département of Puy-de-Dôme alone produced 1,600,000 hectolitres, making it the third largest producer of all the French départements. The phylloxera, which had already destroyed the vines in the Bordeaux region and the Midi, arrived late in Auvergne but by the end of the century had ruined the vineyards there as well.

In 1878, when Robert Louis Stevenson was staying in the village of St. Germain de Calberte in the Cévennes, he wrote, 'The phylloxera was in the neighbourhood and instead of wine we drank at dinner a more economical juice of the grape — La Parisienne — they call it. It is made by putting the fruit into a cask with water. One by one the berries ferment and burst. What is drunk during the day is supplied at night by water. So with ever another pitcher from the well and ever another grape exploding and giving out its strength, one cask of Parisienne may last a family until spring. It is, as the reader will anticipate, a feeble beverage, but very pleasant to the taste.'

After the phylloxera some replanting was done but the regrowth of the industry was cut short by the 1914–1918 war and since then there has been a steady decline. From 16,000 hectares of vineyards in 1920 there are now only 4,000 in Auvergne as a whole and much of that is planted by farmers solely for their own use.

There was a time when Auvergne wine producers got up to all sorts of tricks to sell their wine. When Bordeaux and the Midi had already been stricken, but the phylloxera had not yet reached their vines, the Auvergne wine-makers jumped on the band-wagon, increasing their production rapidly to fill the gap. If the wine was not fruity enough, they would flavour it with raspberry essence bought at the chemist; a little verdigris scattered on it would make good any lack of pungency; a feeble alcoholic content was increased by the generous addition of sugar.

In recent years the remaining professionals have concentrated on quality. There are now forty communes producing VDQS wines (*Vins Délimités de Qualité Supérieure*). Four of them are allowed to call themselves Côtes d'Auvergne; they are Clermont-Chanturgue, Coret, Châteaugay and Riom-Madargues. These light wines are often served in restaurants in Auvergne and also figure in typical recipes of the region.

In addition to wines many apéritifs and liqueurs have been made in Auvergne. Fruit grown there is renowned for its excellent flavour, which seems to derive from the volcanic soil. Add to this the great variety of herbs and wild flowers to be found in the countryside, which the monks discovered long ago could be used to flavour drinks of all sorts, and you have all that is required for the making of liqueurs and apéritifs. In the past it was common practice for innkeepers to make their own liqueurs and give them appropriate local names. There have been drinks called 'Liqueur of the Flowers of Puy-de-Dôme', 'Liqueur de Pic de Sancy', 'Prunelle d'Auvergne' and so on. Most of these old specialities have disappeared but an apéritif based on gentian, which grows freely in the uplands, is still made.

The tastiness of the local fruits also led to the setting up of a confectionery industry in Clermont-Ferrand and Vichy. This reached its height in the 19th century as the increasing number of visitors to the spas provided a ready market. Chief products of the industry, still active today, are candied fruits, especially apricots, barley sugar and the well-known pastilles of Vichy.

Water

No account of cuisine in Auvergne could be complete without a mention of water. The soups of the region are famous and the local chefs insist that it is the extreme purity of the water which enables the full flavour of the vegetables and other ingredients to emerge. One of the best known of the bottled waters, Volvic, is medically pure enough to be given to babies as it is, without boiling or any other treatment.

Eating Out — Value for Money

One final point: I am sure that a lot of readers will be experienced in the ways of French restaurants but for the few who may not be, I would like to suggest one or two tips for getting value for money when eating out in France. Unless you are celebrating, always take the house wine, which has to be good value, if they want regular customers who are not tourists. Named wines are normally marked up two and a half to three times on shop price, and I have seen them up to six times as expensive. Do not bother with cheese or pudding. They are sometimes good, though nothing is more difficult to maintain than a good cheese board. They are always overpriced. If you do not see exactly what you want on any of the menus, do not hesitate to ask for a substitution of whatever for whatever; if they are about the same price, and you can tell from the *à la carte* list, there will be no problem. Two people eating together can work out any combination they fancy. For example, one can take a three course menu and the other one dish *à la carte,* and one has the starter and the main dish from the menu, and the other what they chose *à la carte* and the cheese or whatever from the menu. I have never known a restaurateur to object.

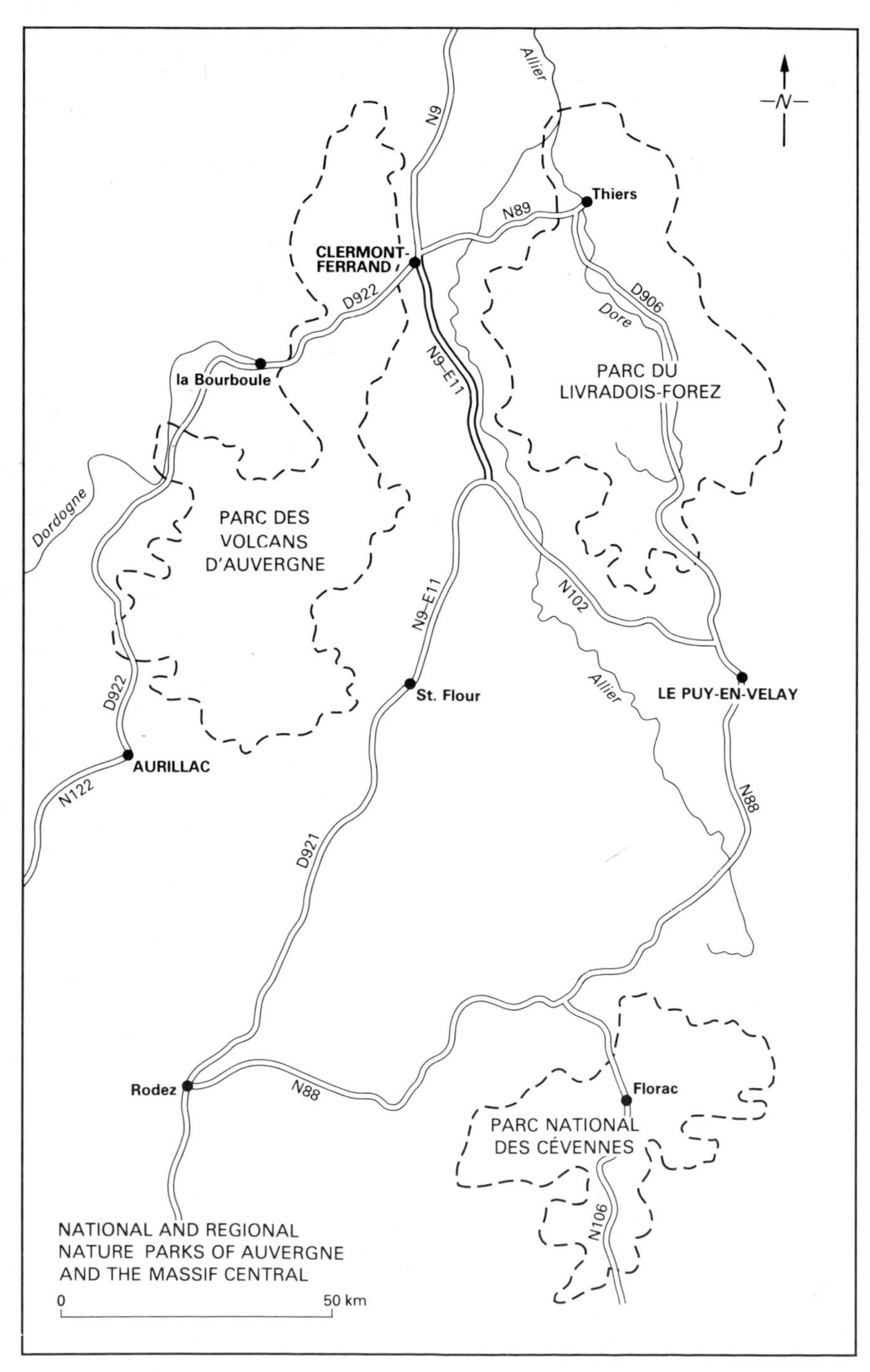
N
Allier
N9
Thiers
N89
CLERMONT-
FERRAND
D922
D906
Dore
N9–E11
PARC DU
LIVRADOIS-FOREZ
la Bourboule
Dordogne
PARC DES
VOLCANS
D'AUVERGNE
N9–E11
N102
Allier
LE PUY-EN-VELAY
St. Flour
D922
AURILLAC
N122
N88
D921
Rodez
N88
Florac
PARC NATIONAL
DES CÉVENNES
N106
NATIONAL AND REGIONAL
NATURE PARKS OF AUVERGNE
AND THE MASSIF CENTRAL
0
50 km

4

Touring the Auvergne

It is as impossible to see the whole of the Auvergne and the Massif Central in one visit as it would be to see the whole of countries like Scotland, Wales or Denmark. The aim of this book is to provide enough information of all kinds to enable visitors travelling by car to choose the places and routes most suited to their own tastes. It is more for people who think of themselves as travellers rather than as tourists; people who thought as children, as I did myself, that it must be exciting to be an explorer. They may well be spending their lives doing more mundane things, but they still feel the attraction of other cultures, other places. They like to get the interest out of things. It is not really for people who want to rush from A to B and do nothing much in either place. In any case, rushing is impossible in Auvergne, which is one of its charms.

The region covered by the book divides naturally into five sub-regions, some of which differ considerably from others. They are the Bourbonnais, on the northern limits of Auvergne, and practically synonymous with the département of Allier, and which includes Vichy. Then, going south, the département of Puy-de-Dôme, and then the département of Cantal. These two départements form the land of the volcanoes and the heart of Auvergne. To the east of Cantal is the fourth region, Velay, a large part of the département of Haute-Loire, and the town of Le Puy. Finally, almost 320km south of the northern limits of Allier, the département of Lozère and the Cévennes mountains.

Geographically, the Bourbonnais is the gentlest of these regions, an open, charming countryside of rolling hills with occasional pretensions to being mountains, of wooded slopes and plains where sometimes the woods become splendid forests. A countryside of rippling streams, forest lakes, and where some of the great rivers of France, the Loire, the Cher, the Allier, are young but already impressive.

If charm is the keynote of the Bourbonnais, Puy-de-Dôme is a land of extremes, at once dramatic and serene. In the west the great chain of the old volcanoes of Monts Dôme and Monts Dore stretches from north to south. In the south-east are the Monts du Livradois and the Monts du Forez, picturesque and empty, one of the least populated areas of France. Between these mountain ranges lies an entirely different countryside, the valleys through which flow the Allier and Dore rivers. These valleys, where the rich black alluvial soil is as much as 3m deep, are warm and very fertile, rich with orchards, vineyards and prosperous farms. The same word *limagne* is used to describe this sort of valley wherever it occurs in Auvergne, but the usual reference is to this valley between the mountain ranges of Puy-de-Dôme, the Grand Limagne.

The volcanic chain of the Monts Dore continues southwards to the Monts du Cezallier, really a plateau, then into Cantal where it becomes the Monts du Cézallier, really a plateau, of the eastern half of the département. These mountains, several of them approaching 1,700m high, with their great variety of form and the picturesque valleys between them, offer some of the finest scenery in Auvergne. The Monts du Cantal merge with the plateau of Aubrac, the most southerly of the volcanic uplands of Auvergne. The western flanks of these mountains slope down towards a landscape not unlike parts of Bourbonnais, open but partly wooded. Aurillac, the capital of Haute Auvergne, is already a thousand metres below the mountain heights.

Velay consists, for the most part, of the broad valley of the Loire itself, bounded on both sides by hills and in the south by the mountains of Mézenc and Gerbier-de-Jonc, where the Loire rises, and the first slopes of the Cévennes.

It is enough to say that Florac, one of the main towns and a sous-préfecture of Lozère, has barely 2,000 inhabitants, to show that this département is one of the wildest and emptiest in France. It includes the spectacularly beautiful, often forested, slopes of the Cévennes, which also spread into Haute-Loire, Gard, Ardèche and Aveyron, as well as the majestic gorges of the Tarn and similar but smaller gorges of several other rivers.

The climate of these regions varies comparatively little. The Bourbonnais with few mountains is drier. In other regions the controlling factor is height above sea level, the higher up the more rain and the cooler the temperature. The difference is very noticeable when coming down into the valleys on a hot summer day. The sheltered valleys of the southern slopes of the Cévennes face the Mediterranean and enjoy its climate. Palms, mimosa, bananas, lemons grow easily here, though a few kilometres away and higher up, they would die in their first winter.

So every one of these regions has its own character, its own attractions, its own charm. Clearly the 320km between north and south means that it is likely to be slightly warmer in the south, but in summer and autumn there is really nothing in it.

But there is more to the whole region than the inexhaustible variety of its wild and wonderful scenery. Auvergne is also a superbly illustrated history book written in stone, a story of fanatical religious faiths, of private wars, pages of Machiavellian plots and counter-plots, of feuds and greed and murder, chapters of ruined castles, soaring cathedrals, simple country churches, the châteaux and mansions of the great, the solid farmhouses.

I have mentioned as many points of interest as there is room for. There are many, many more that you can discover for yourself.

One practical point which motorists may find helpful. Off the beaten track in Auvergne, and that means most of it, petrol stations can be few and far between. It is advisable to keep your petrol tank well filled. This is always true, but even more so on Sundays

Driving through France

The **Michelin Red Guide** is extremely useful, especially for the opening and closing times of hotels and restaurants.

The **Michelin Road Atlas** which covers the whole of France is recommended for ease of use when on the road, particularly for those who drive regularly in France, and is remarkably cheap when you add up the number of maps you get for your money. The **Road Atlas IGN** (Institut National Géographique) is also excellent value but is somewhat more difficult to read — a lot of fine print.

The individual Michelin yellow maps numbers 73, 76 and 80 cover the whole of the area described in this book: 73 for Allier and Puy-de-Dôme, 76 for Cantal and Haute-Loire, 80 for Lozère, Cévennes and Gorges du Tarn. Map 239 covers almost the entire area except for the Gorges du Tarn and Cévennes which comes in Map 240.

Maps of the French national signposted footpaths (the Grandes Randonnées), a superb system which offers some of the best walking in Europe, can be obtained from good map shops. If you mean to do serious walking, they will be a great help. They tend to disappear quickly from the shops in France and are better obtained in Britain or the USA, even if you have to order.

when, even in towns, most of the petrol stations are closed.

There is just one other little thing I would like to say. A motor car is in itself an environment, small but big enough to insulate its occupants from the world outside just a little. It is fine to drive across these open spaces admiring the views but it will mean a great deal more if, from time to time, here and there, you stop the car and walk, if only for a few minutes. Get the feel of the ground, the fresh air on your face, the particular smell, the sound of the breeze in the trees, between the rocks, even over the long grass. In recent years I have driven over 161,000km in the French countryside. The places I remember best are often those where we left the car to itself for a while.

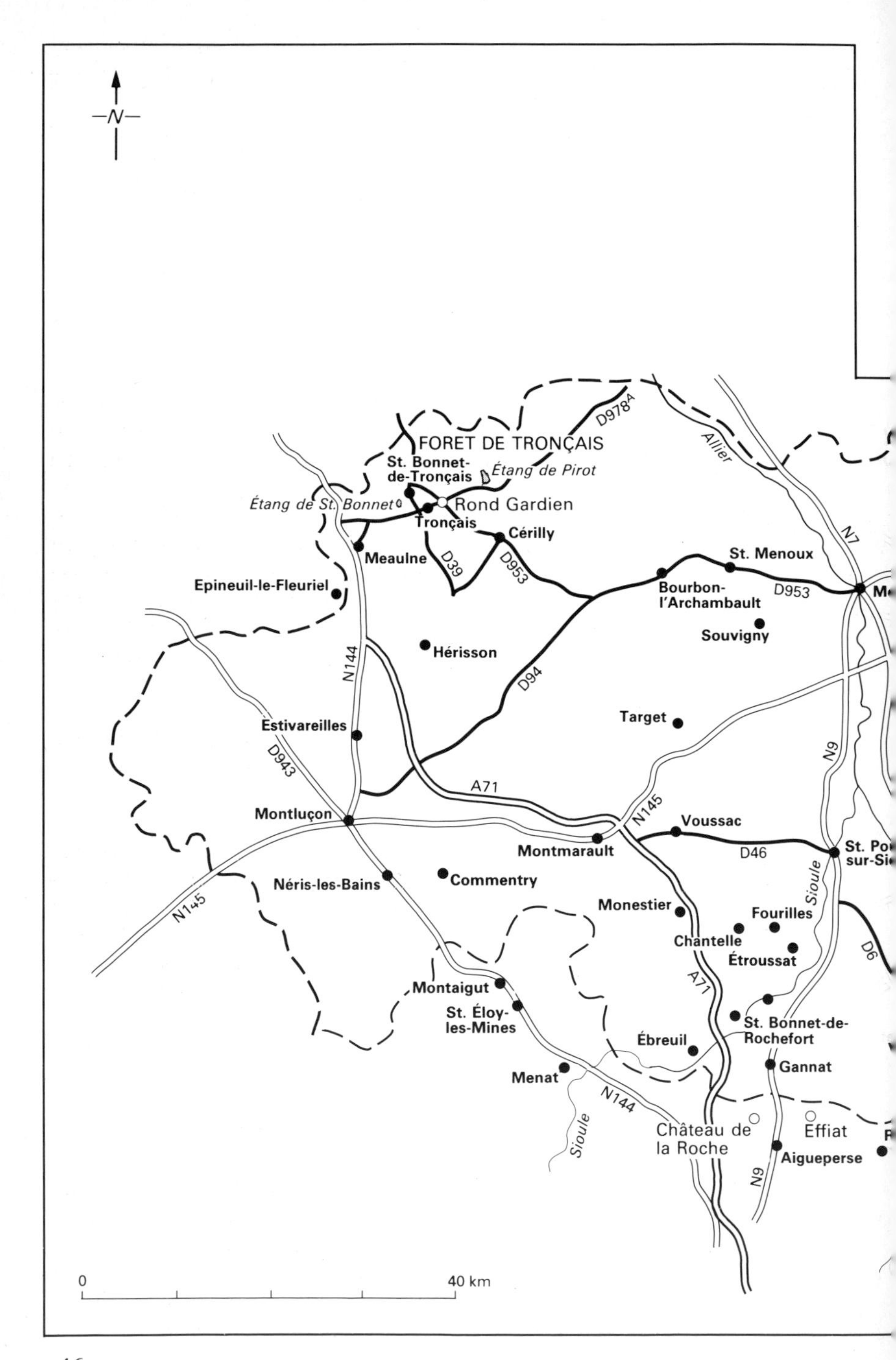
N
FORET DE TRONÇAIS
D978A
Allier
St. Bonnet-de-Tronçais
Étang de Pirot
Étang de St. Bonnet
Rond Gardien
Tronçais
Cérilly
Meaulne
D39
D953
St. Menoux
N7
Epineuil-le-Fleuriel
Bourbon-l'Archambault
D953
Souvigny
Hérisson
N144
D94
Target
N9
Estivareilles
D943
A71
Montluçon
N145
Voussac
Montmarault
D46
Néris-les-Bains
Commentry
N145
Sioule
Monestier
Fourilles
Chantelle
Étroussat
D6
A71
Montaigut
St. Éloy-les-Mines
St. Bonnet-de-Rochefort
Ébreuil
Gannat
Menat
N144
Sioule
Château de la Roche
Effiat
Aigueperse
N9
0
40 km

5
Bourbonnais

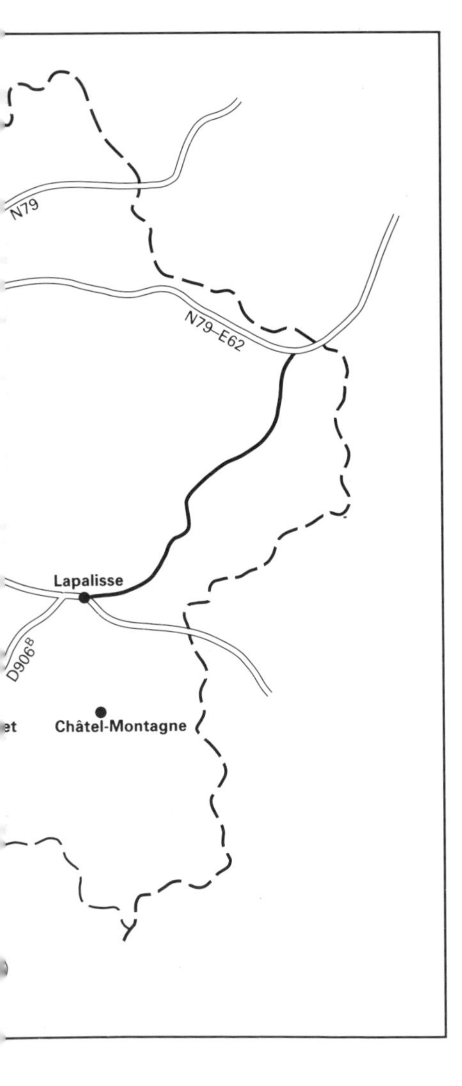

To the visitor from Britain driving down from the north, much of the Bourbonnais, with its green fields, its neat hedges, its occasional hedgerow trees, its low hills crowned with small woods, is reminiscent of the English shires. It is the kind of countryside that forms the background in sets of hunting prints. But away from the main roads there is a lot more to this little-known region of France. It has splendid forests, lakes, hills higher than the Cotswolds, even a few modest mountains, and old towns redolent with history.

It was this fertile land which first made the fortunes of the Bourbons, a family whose influence spread over the whole of Europe, giving eight kings to France, and many rulers and princes in other countries. Even today the kings of Spain and Belgium, and the Grand Duke of Luxembourg, are Bourbons.

Moulins, once the capital of the old Duchy of Bourbon, now the Préfecture of the département of Allier, the most northerly administrative division of the modern Auvergne, is a charming, sleepy old town of 25,000 inhabitants. Its sous-préfectures, the go-ahead Vichy and industrial Montluçon, have both passed it by. Indeed, Montluçon is twice the size of Moulins.

There are several things of interest in Moulins itself and the town makes a good base from which to explore the Bourbonnais. The most important of the sights is the Cathedral of Notre Dame, a strange building consisting of two adjacent halves, one old, one new, with nothing in common except that together they form one cathedral. The older part, which includes the choir, was built between 1474 and 1507 in the Flamboyant Gothic style. This part of the cathedral is remarkable for the magnificence of its stained-glass windows, a whole series of them dating from the end of the 15th and the early 16th centuries. Among the subjects are the crusades of Louis IX (St. Louis), and Duke Pierre II of Bourbon and his wife, Anne of France, venerating St. Catherine. Bearing in mind that the ordinary people of the time saw no books, and in any case could not read, and that, apart from the few of them who were indoor servants of the very rich, they saw no works of art, no advertising, and, of course, no films, no television, in other words no pictorial images of any kind, it is easy to imagine how impressive these lovely windows with their simple stories must have seemed to them. They were, in fact, the earliest strip cartoons.

The choir also has a chapel with a Black Virgin said to be a copy of the one in the cathedral at Le Puy. This is a slightly cloudy point since the one at Le Puy is itself a 19th-century copy of the one that used to be there but was burned during the French Revolution. Both Moulins and Le Puy were on the pilgrim route to St. James of Compostella.

The Cathedral, Moulins, famous for its 15th-century stained glass

From the beginning of April to the end of October there are guided visits to the Cathedral treasure which includes one of the great works of art of the Middle Ages, the Triptyque of the Maître de Moulins. This remarkable work was painted towards the end of the 15th century for Pierre II, Duke of Bourbon, and his wife, Anne of France. It shows, in the left-hand panel, Pierre de Bourbon in full ducal regalia, and in the right-hand panel, his wife wearing a purple cape and a surcoat embroidered with gold and huge pearls and other precious stones. The centre panel depicts the Virgin and Child. The Virgin is also splendidly clothed, though somewhat less richly than the ducal pair and, where they are crowned, her head is bare.

It is not known who the artist was though most votes go to Jean Prévost, a painter from Lyons. The work is exceptional in several ways, none more so than in the painting of the faces; the heavy and enigmatic Pierre who might be a close relation of Holbein's Henry VIII; the meditative, or is it calculating, Anne; the maternal but rather puzzled-looking Virgin; the extraordinary, Churchillian baby.

Not far from the Cathedral, in the Place de l'Hôtel de Ville, there is an interesting old belfry called the Jacquemart, originally built in 1232. The city's time is kept by a family of four automatons. The father, in the uniform of a grenadier, and his wife strike the hours, and the two children sound the halves and quarters. The upper part was burned in 1665 and again in 1946 when fireworks were being let off from the platform. The people of Moulins immediately raised a voluntary subscription enabling it to be rebuilt without delay.

Just around the corner from the Jacquemart there is a Folklore Museum in a 15th-century house (restored in the 17th) which includes an important collection of antique dolls.

Apart from an extremely ugly keep, restored in the 15th century, which blocks any overall view of the front of the cathedral, nothing remains of the original castle. But a later addition known as the Pavillon d'Anne de Beaujeu, still survives (Anne de Beaujeu is often given this name, but is more correctly called Anne de France, as she was the eldest daughter of Louis XI). It is a charming building considered by some to be the first in France to show the influence of the Italian Renaissance. Today it houses the city's Museum of Art and Archaeology.

From Moulins it is a short drive west on D945 to **Souvigny**. This little village, still very rustic, was the starting point of the Bourbon fortunes. In 916 Aymard, an officer in the forces of the Duke of Aquitaine, gave his land at Souvigny to the monks of the Abbey of Cluny. The monks established a priory at Souvigny which became famous following the deaths there of two saints, St. Mayeul in 994 and St. Odilon in 1049. They were buried in the same tomb and the priory and its church became a place of pilgrimage.

The barons of Bourbon, descendants of Aymard, gradually built up a great estate around Souvigny. It took them three hundred years, and they did it by taking advantage of their situation between the Royal domains and the independent duchies of Aquitaine and Auvergne, and by steadfastly taking the King's side in his disputes with these duchies. Archambaud IX of Bourbon accompanied Louis IX of France on his crusade to the Holy Land, and in 1276 Beatrice de Bourbon married Robert de Clermont, the sixth child of Louis IX. This royal marriage, after their long alliance with the Court, led to the Bourbon estates being recognised as a duchy. It also enabled the Bourbons, nearly three hundred years later, to gain the throne of France, when Henry of Navarre, who was descended from Robert de Clermont, became Henry IV of France.

The power of the Duchy was considerably increased in the 14th century by Duke Louis II who built the castle of Montluçon, and improved and enlarged the castle of Bourbon-l'Archambault. Both he and Charles I of Bourbon made the priory church of St. Pierre of Souvigny their burial place.

Virgin and Child in the priory church of St. Peter at Souvigny, where Bourbon dukes are entombed

This church, much of which dates from the 11th, 12th and 15th centuries, with minor additions in the 18th and 19th, is exceptional in a number of ways. It surprises first by its great size, 87m long by 28m wide. Then due to the influence of Cluny, its style is strongly Burgundian. The façade and the northern flank and the three chapels radiating from the deambulatory date from the 11th and 12th centuries. In the 15th century the height of the nave was increased and the Romanesque towers were joined by a gable.

Unlike the majority of churches in Auvergne, St. Pierre de Souvigny is built in a light-coloured golden stone which makes the interior seem almost cheerful by comparison with some of the severe Romanesque churches farther south. Inside the entrance, on the left, is the tomb of St. Mayeul, finely carved but worn with age. At the end of the nave on the right, the Old Chapel contains the tomb of Louis II of Bourbon and his wife Anne of Auvergne. On the left, the larger New Chapel holds the tomb of Charles I of Bourbon and his wife, Agnès de Bourgogne. Near the Old Chapel there is an unusual reliquary cupboard with wooden doors painted with scenes from the lives of St. Mayeul and St. Odilon.

Opposite the north side of the church of St. Pierre, the disused church of St. Mark now houses a museum of local history. The most interesting exhibit is a 12th-century calendar, an octagonal stone with a carving for each month showing the work the monks would be doing at that time of year, and also showing the signs of the zodiac.

From Souvigny it is a pleasant drive through farmland to the little town of **Bourbon-l'Archambault**. Though no longer as fashionable as it was in the 17th, 18th and 19th centuries, when the Marquise de Sévigné, the Marquise de Montespan, mistress of Louis XIV, and Talleyrand, France's powerful Foreign Minister, regularly took the waters there, Bourbon-l'Archambault is still an active spa. It has a number of small and very reasonably priced hotels catering for *curistes*. The Hôtel des Thermes has a restaurant to which the Michelin Red Guide gives one star. The thermal establishment is set in a park next to a small lake, and it is from the far corner of the park that you get the best view (and photograph) of the picturesquely ruined castle, across the end of a much larger lake. Nothing remains of the once princely residence except the three towers of the northern side. Admission to the ruins, open from

Bourbon L'Archambault, the 14th-century castle of Louis II, Duke of Bourbon, destroyed during the French Revolution

Priory of St. Pierre at Souvigny, burial place of the early Bourbons

mid-April to mid-October, is free, a fairly sure sign that there is not much to see. It is possible to climb to the top of a tower, which gives broad views over the town, the lake, and the country-side. In short, Bourbon-l'Archambault is a place for the casual visitor to stop for lunch or coffee and a stroll around, but probably not to stay longer.

Instead of going directly from Souvigny to Bourbon-l'Archambault there is a slightly longer route by way of the village of **St. Menoux** where there is an interesting 12th-century church. The interior has a very fine choir enclosed by pillars with carved capitals supporting a series of arches which are separated from a higher level of arches by a carved stone frieze.

This church also has a curiosity which I am sure must be unique. The remains of St. Menoux are kept behind the main altar in a sarcophagus which has a fairly large hole in the side. In the past St. Menoux was credited with the ability to cure simple-minded people who had difficulty in speaking clearly. The French for 'to mumble' is *bredouiller,* and in Bourbonnais people afflicted in this way were called *bredins.* Such people were brought to the church of St. Menoux, to be cured by putting their heads through the opening in the side of the tomb, that is

The 14th-century castle at Bourbon L'Archambault, destroyed in the French Revolution

to be *débridiner,* and this sarcophagus was called the *débridinoire.* If the local Syndicat d'Initiative is to be believed many people are still brought to St. Menoux for this purpose.

Bourbonnais is one of many regions in and around Auvergne where everyday realism is tempered by a readiness to accept the supernatural. Many of the local castles have one or more ghosts; werewolves are said to roam the forests; sorcerers abound; such things as warts and shingles are more likely to be treated by a healer than a doctor; the parish priests are asked to keep storms and hail away from the crops and to exorcise the possessed; that calendar at Souvigny is also carved with fabulous animals, demons and mysterious people. It is a countryside where the devil is in the shadows, and fairies can spoil your harvest. So why not a hole in a tomb to cure the simple-minded?

No one who is a lover of Nature and has the time to spare should miss visiting the **Forêt de Tronçais**. Not only is it probably the finest hardwood forest in Europe, it has a number of country inns which make ideal places for a stopover of a day or more.

The forest covers 10,600 hectares but it is not its size which makes it so remarkable — there are ten larger forests in France — it is the fact that, apart from one period during the 17th century, it has been properly managed for more than three hundred years.

There has always been a forest here. In 1327 the villagers of the fourteen parishes of the forest abandoned it to the Dukes of Bourbon, who held it for two hundred years. By the early part of the 16th century, Charles III, the 9th Duke of Bourbon, ruled over a vast princely estate, including all Bourbonnais and extending far beyond. It was not yet part of the Kingdom of France. As a result of his dash and bravery in battle, in alliance with the monarchy, Charles III had been honoured with the title, Constable of Bourbon. But relations between him and Francis I of France deteriorated to the point of open hostility. In retrospect it seems simply that Francis was jealous of the power and splendour of the Bourbons and the last great independent Duchy. Apart from falling out of favour, the Constable of Bourbon does not seem to have done much at this stage to merit the harsh treatment he suffered. He was accused of treason, unjustly condemned, and some of his possessions and lands were confiscated. In this situation he turned to the Emperor Charles V, the great rival of Francis I, who appointed him Lieutenant-General. As such he fought against the French at Rebec, Pavia — where Francis I was defeated and taken prisoner — Milan and then Rome. He took part in the attack on Rome on 6th May 1527, wearing a white tabard, making him easy to pick out, and was killed in the first attack.

When Francis I was returned to France, after a spell as a prisoner, he at once confiscated almost all that remained of the Constable of Bourbon's estates, and Bourbonnais became attached to the crown of France in 1531. The Forest of Tronçais was among the lands taken and has belonged to the State ever since. For more than a hundred years it was neglected. Peasants and nobles alike took what they wanted from it. Trees of any age were cut down thoughtlessly, no replanting was done, no regard was paid to future needs, and by 1670 three-quarters of the forest had been ruined.

It was Louis XIV's great minister, Colbert, a man of phenomenal drive and efficiency, who saved the forest. Colbert devoted a working lifetime to increasing the power of the monarchy and the glory of France. It was a key part of his policy that France should have more ships to enable her to dominate European trade. Ships had to be built of hardwood, and Colbert, who seemed to have had his eye on everything going on in France, had an inspection made of the Tronçais forest. As a result of his decisions new trees were planted and proper management of the forest was established. Colbert knew very well that it takes more than two hundred years for hardwood trees to reach maturity, and that his own plans would never benefit from his reorganisation of the forest. This abstemious, water-drinking minister may have been, as the Marquise de Sévigné described him 'as cold as the North Star', but he cared about France. France would need the wood from the forest one day and, for Colbert, that was reason enough. A few of the trees he had planted remain today. The forest now provides wood of the highest quality, for veneers, for the barrels in which brandy is matured, and for construction. Seventy per cent of the forest is oak — not the squat, twisted English oak, but a close relation called Turkey oak, which grows taller and straighter. The rest of the forest is beech, with a small area of pine.

D978^A runs through the forest from east to west, and D953 from south-east to north-west and at the cross roads where they meet there is an Information Office, and from this point, called the Rond de Gardien, eight signposted footpaths radiate to other parts of the forest. Farther west, D39 crosses the forest from north to south. The meeting points of forest roads or footpaths are called *ronds* and each one is named and signposted to others, so it is easy to find your way about.

The charming Romanesque church at Fleuriel, near Pourçain-sur-Sioule

The Forest of Tronçais is rich in wild life. There are many deer of different kinds, as well as wild boar. Coursing hunts are arranged at regular intervals. Smaller animals include hares, stone martens, pine martens and polecats, and many varieties of birds and water fowl.

Overleaf: *Street market in Montluçon*

CHARCUTERIE · ROTISSERIE
POBEAU Traiteur

RUE
SAINTE ANNE

There are five small lakes among the trees, and several ponds. The largest of the lakes, Étang de Pirot and Étang de St. Bonnet, both have bathing beaches with lifeguards (during July and August), and both offer excellent coarse fishing for carp, tench, roach and pike. Étang de St. Bonnet is also equipped for sailing, windsurfing, and has some pedalos.

There are a number of picnic spots among the trees, equipped with tables and wooden benches. If you want to have a good look at the forest without necessarily staying overnight, take the D111 from Cérilly towards the village of Isle-et-Bardais and then turn off left for Étang de Pirot and follow the road which runs beside the lake. This joins the D978ᴬ at the Rond Gardien, where you can pick up a brochure and map of the forest, and then carry on to the village of Tronçais. Then turn right for the village of St. Bonnet-Tronçais and Étang de St. Bonnet. Near the village a footpath leads from the Rond de Vieux Mourat to the Stebbing Oak, the largest tree in the forest. It is more than 300 years old, stands 38m high, and is almost 4m in circumference. Another pleasant walk is along the footpath which encircles the 70 hectares of the Étang de St. Bonnet.

From this village return to the D978ᴬ and continue as far as the Rond de Montaloyer, where there is a picnic site, and then left down D28 to **Meaulne**. It was from this village that Alan Fournier took the name of the hero of his book *Le Grand Meaulnes*, one of the classic novels of modern times.

Other key places in the novel are in this region. La Ferté Angillon where the hero lived with his mother is the real La Chapelle d'Angillon, north of Bourges. Much closer, just across the Cher from Meaulne, is the village of **Épineuil-le-Fleuriel** where the hero (and Fournier himself) went to school and which in the novel is called St. Agathe. The book was written just before the 1914–1918 war but the village has hardly changed. In the school where Alan Fournier dozed through his lessons, there is now a miniature museum with relics of this young man whose death in the First World War was surely a great loss to world literature.

The best holiday centre in the forest is the village of St. Bonnet-Tronçais. Apart from the watersports facilities of its lake, bicycles can be hired (also at the Étang de Pirot), and it is equipped for archery. There is a riding school at Cérilly.

There are a number of small and charming inns in and around the forest, the largest of which is the Tronçais in St. Bonnet-Tronçais, which has only 12 rooms. There is a 3-star camping site by the Étang de St. Bonnet and another by the Étang de Pirot.

Probably the best time to make a short stay would be during the month of June or early July, or just after the end of September. I must admit that I have seen the forest only in late autumn when the leaves glowed with every shade from gold to dark reddish brown, but the deserted villages appeared to have been struck by some paralysing power from outer space.

There is a direct road south to Montluçon by N144 but if there is time to spare there is a more attractive road up the valley of the Aumance from Meaulne, where it joins the Cher, by D157 to the medieval town of Hedgehog — at least that is the English translation of its actual name — Hérisson. It is a dozy little place with narrow streets, old houses, towers and doorways, and yet another artistically ruined Bourbon castle on its hill beside the village.

From Hérisson take D3 to Estivareilles where it joins N144 a few kilometres north of **Montluçon**. This industrial town is a centre for the production of chemicals, rubber and furniture. One large factory site by the river still has the name Dunlop painted on the walls but it is now owned by a Japanese industrialist.

Montluçon is not a place of major interest for the tourist but the old quarter has been carefully restored and is worth looking at. The road from Moulins, N144, brings you into the town near a garden square, the Jardin du Président Wilson, next to which there is a fair amount of parking space. The old quarter is just a short stroll away on the slopes of the hill on which the castle stands.

This is yet another Bourbon castle, but this one is not in ruins, having been restored and maintained by the town. It was built during the Hundred Years' War by Louis II, Duke of Bourbon, and his heirs. On the way up to it the narrow streets are lined with 15th-, 16th- and 17th-century houses which have been restored to a point where the original builders would surely not recognise them. The design remains in period and they look picturesque, but with new roofs, doorways and shutters like new housing estates, and walls with hardly a lichened stone, it will be another hundred years before they suggest anything of the real past. Some are lived in, some are smart shops. If the climb to the château and the return has given you an appetite or a thirst, you will find a charming café-bar on a corner on the right, as you make your way back to the Jardin du Président Wilson.

The 14th-century castle of the Dukes of Bourbon in Montluçon, which now houses the city's museums

The promenade and gardens around the château give good views over the town. Inside the château there are two museums, one fairly run of the mill; the other, I think, is unique. The first, on the ground floor, is a folklore museum with a section illustrating the life and industry of Montluçon in the past. The second, on the first floor, is a museum of the hurdy-gurdy, one of the two traditional musical instruments of the Auvergne peasant. The other is the *cabrette* (called *musette* in Bourbonnais), a simple form of bagpipes, with a goatskin bellows. The hurdy-gurdy is a very ancient form of stringed instrument which was favoured by wandering musicians all over France, and by beggars who wanted to do something rather than just ask for alms. It became

very popular in Auvergne. Unlike the bagpipes, which took all the musician's breath, the hurdy-gurdy allowed him to sing an accompaniment, and the two instruments together were all that was needed to get up a country dance or to make music for a wedding feast.

On summer evenings, dancing to these simple instruments was the chief relaxation of the peasant farmers after their hard day's work. As long ago as 1665 a visiting abbot noted in the diary of his journey '... as soon as spring has arrived all the ordinary people spend every evening in this way. You can hardly find a street or a public square that is not full of dancers, so much so that even the children are soon able to take part without every having been taught ... When there are dances on more formal occasions, the actual dance is always the same, the "bourrée" ... perhaps because it is permitted to touch and kiss the lady (though she does not reciprocate) which is not at all the case in other dances ...'

The abbot was also struck by the wild steps and the great energy shown by the dancers, but supposed, correctly, that after working all day using only certain muscles, the more general exercise of the dance was relaxing and banished fatigue. The music of the *bourrée* is in three-time, faster than a waltz, and strongly syncopated.

The great days of the hurdy-gurdy were the late 18th and the 19th centuries. Its popularity was spread throughout Auvergne by a farmer named Jean Pajot, of Jenzat, near Aigueperse in Bourbonnais. It was his hobby to make them and he encouraged his sons to do the same. Until recently generation after generation of the Pajot family continued to make hurdy-gurdies. It is a highly skilled craft in which twelve different kinds of wood are used and more than three hundred pieces have to be assembled before the ten-stringed instrument is completed. This does not include the decoration which, in marquetry of ebony, ivory and mother of pearl, was sometimes very elaborate.

In the latter part of the 19th century the hurdy-gurdy began to be rivalled and was eventually superseded by the accordion which was more suited to popular modern songs. But in recent years traditional music has enjoyed a revival and new craftsmen have appeared to make the *cabrette* and the hurdy-gurdy. One of the best known of them is Gaston Rivière of Montluçon. His work is so much admired that he has sufficient orders to keep him busy for the next twenty years. The clients have to be patient because, once finished, the instrument has to dry out for a year before it can be used. There are always a dozen or so hanging from the ceiling of Rivière's workshop like hams in a farmhouse kitchen.

It may seem surprising but the rough and tough peasant of the Auvergne mountains was very found of songs. Though he was often his own master, he had much in common with the negro in the cotton fields of the American south, trapped on a never-ending treadmill of hard work, trapped in social isolation, trapped in obligations to the seasons and the soil, and, like the negro, he often found escape in song. There were simple work songs for different crafts; songs and lullabies

Montluçon: part of the folklore museum in the château of the Dukes of Bourbon

for children; sad, nostalgic songs called *regrets*. The most characteristic are the pastoral songs, the songs of shepherds and shepherdesses, teasing songs of love. There is a simplicity and a yearning about them which clothes hard lives and a hard land in Arcadian grace. A few years ago the great soprano, Kiri Te Kanawa, recorded a collection of songs of Auvergne with the English Chamber Orchestra. Anyone interested in pure song would enjoy listening to them. One of them, called 'Bailero', which was sung from shepherdess to shepherd and back, across the valleys, is hauntingly beautiful.

Montluçon has rather fewer hotels and restaurants than might be expected in a town of this size but it does have one out of the ordinary restaurant for those who do not mind expense. The Hostellerie du Château de St. Jean has a restaurant very agreeably installed in a 12th-century chapel on a former estate of the Knights of St. John of Malta. It also has seven luxurious and proportionately expensive bedrooms.

The second sous-préfecture of Allier, Vichy, is today one of the most interesting and progressive towns in France. There are two possible routes from Montluçon. The most direct is due east on N145 to Montmarault and just beyond this town turn right on to D46 for **St. Pourçain-sur-Sioule**, then south on the Clermont-Ferrand road, N9, for 5km and then left on to D6 to Vichy.

But if you have time take the trouble to stop in St. Pourçain, one of the oldest wine centres in France. Its first vineyards are said to have been planted in pre-Christian times and to have been much expanded by the Romans. Its prosperity continued throughout the Middle Ages until at the end of the 18th century there were more than 8,000 hectares of vineyards in the region. Nowadays quality is preferred to quantity and there are only about 800 hectares producing red, white and rosé wines, of which the best is possibly the dry white. Hugh Johnson in his comprehensive *World Atlas of Wine* places them on the map, but has nothing to say about them, and this is probably a more objective assessment than that usually made in the region itself.

St. Pourçain is an old town with a good deal more charm than might be supposed from the main road through the middle of it. It is attractively situated on the Sioule, one of the prettiest and most varied rivers in central France and well known for its excellent trout fishing. There is an old quarter on an island in the river, and old houses here and there in other parts of the town. The abbey church of St. Croix is a sort or architectural paella, with bits of everything in it. Some of it, notably the interior of the porch, dates from the 11th century, and other parts from the 13th, 15th, 16th and 19th centuries. It is such a mixture that it could well be used for a condensed course in religious architecture.

A slightly different route from Montluçon to St. Pourçain adds a good deal of interest for those who have time to spare. After Montmarault follow D46 as far as Voussac, then turn right on to D282 for Target, Monestier and Chantelle.

Here you are on the edge of a strange countryside of picturesque but rather dilapidated villages most of which have given up the struggle against a poor, unrewarding land of steep-sided valleys — incidentally, they are called 'combes' as in southern England — scrubby slopes and pasture. During the 19th century there were one or two relatively prosperous mining towns, such as Commentry and St. Éloy. This industry has now ceased, but even in those days there was a steady emigration to Paris of both peasant and mining families. They settled down in the capital as coal merchants, water-carriers, proprietors of small café-bars, and never returned. Those who stayed struggled on, raising sheep and cattle, often Charollais, and that, with a slight impetus from tourism, is the picture still today.

Chantelle is an old village in a pretty site on an escarpment above the Bouble, a peaceful tributary of the Sioule. It has a Benedictine Abbey with a shop in which you can buy beautifully bound books, enamels, pictures and perfumes, all produced in workshops on the premises.

This abbey was built on the ruins of yet another Bourbon castle, originally built in the 11th century. At the end of the 15th century, Pierre de Beaujeu, Duke of Bourbon, and his wife Anne de Beaujeu, the same couple as shown in the Triptyque by the Maître de Moulins (see p. 49), transformed the castle into an agreeable residence. Its story is closely linked to that of the Constable of Bourbon. When her father, Louis XI died, Anne was a capable Regent during the minority of her brother Charles VIII, who came to the throne at the age of thirteen and died in 1498 aged twenty-eight. He was succeeded by Louis XII and he, in 1515, by Francis I.

Anne of France died at Chantelle in 1522. Anne's only daughter, Suzanne, had married the 9th Duke of Bourbon, better known as mentioned previously as the Constable of Bourbon, but had died a year before her mother. Between the two of them they left an enormous inheritance to the already extremely powerful Constable of Bourbon. This was too much for Francis I and he and other members of the royal family, notably his mother, challenged the inheritance. The dispute added fuel to the smouldering fire between Francis and the Constable de Bourbon and was another reason why the Duke left France to side with the Emperor Charles V. The destruction of the château of Chantelle was carried out at the same time as the confiscation of the rest of the Bourbon estates. As is so often the case in Auvergne and the Massif Central there is so much history in so little a place.

From Chantelle carry on via the villages of Fourilles, Étroussat, Barberier and Bayet, along the pretty valley of the Sioule to St. Pourçain.

There is another possible route from Montluçon to St. Pourçain which takes you through the Gorge of the Sioule. Take N144 south-east to Néris-les-Bains and from there via Montaigut and St. Éloy-les-Mines to the village of Menat. A couple of kilometres beyond this village, at Pont de Menat, D915 on the left follows the Gorge of the Sioule. Before taking this turning you can, if you want a photograph of yet another dramatically sited Bourbon castle which looks as if it has been ruined for the benefit of postcard producers and Sunday painters, cross the bridge and turn right, and after a short distance you will see the Château Rocher on the edge of a steep cliff in front of you.

The whole of the route through the gorge by D915 is very picturesque. In the little town of **Ébreuil**, where the river is more serene, there is an important abbey church, St. Léger, which has a Romanesque nave and transept and an early Gothic choir with radiating chapels. The church has some fine early frescoes, said to be from the 12th century (if you want to see them, you should ask at the presbytery), and behind the main altar there is a superbly carved and decorated reliquary of St. Léger, dating from the 16th century.

From Ébreuil you can take D998 direct to Gannat to rejoin the N9 for St. Pourçain, or you can take D35 to St. Bonnet-de-Rochefort and then D37 to Gannat. D37 is a pretty road which is crossed by the viaducts of Rouzat and Neuvial, the very first works constructed by the famous Gustav Eiffel.

If you arrive in St. Pourçain in time for lunch, you might like to try the restaurant of the Hôtel Chêne Vert, just off the main square, the Place Clemenceau. It has a good reputation, and is not too expensive.

For Vichy take N9 south from St. Pourçain for about 5km and then turn off on to D6.

Vichy lies about 28km south of St. Pourçain but on the other side of the Allier from D6. There are three bridges over the Allier, the first at Charmeil, near the airport. The second, a barrage bridge, is about 2km farther south, and the third, joining the suburb of Bellerive

Romantic ruins of the Château-Rocher (13th century) above the Sioule river

to Vichy proper, is about another 3km farther on. It is the last of the three bridges which brings you most conveniently into the centre of the town.

No serious tour of Auvergne should omit Vichy, if only for the sake of variety. There is no other town, not only in Auvergne, but in the whole of France, even Europe, quite like Vichy.

For starters, there is nothing old worth looking at in Vichy and that is a statement which can be made of very few other places in Auvergne. This is not to say that it is a new town. It was already known to the Romans as a spa, and in the Middle Ages, under Bourbon influence, it was a small fortified town which had a rough time during the religious wars, as did most of the towns in the Massif Central. In the 17th and 18th centuries its reputation as a spa was maintained by a number of distinguished visitors, who included the Marquise de Sévigné, and the daughters

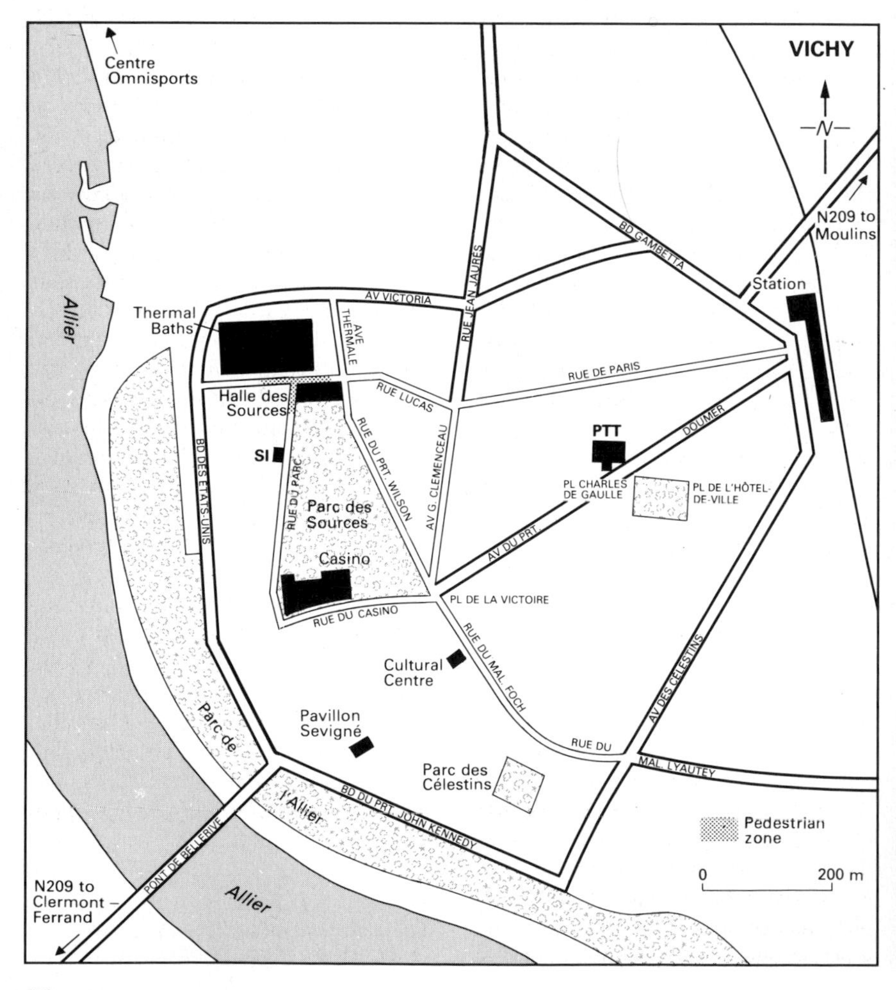

of King Louis XV. At the beginning of the 19th century the Emperor Napoleon signed the decree creating the Parc des Sources, probably because his mother told him to. Maria Laetitia Bonaparte had taken the waters there and liked the place.

In 1821 the Duchess of Angoulême laid the first stone of the old Thermal Establishment but throughout the early part of the 19th-century Vichy remained a small, rather dirty little town with a population of not much more than one thousand. It was not until the 1860s when Napoleon III took a series of cures for intestinal troubles (from which he eventually died) that it began to become a more important place. The Grand Casino was constructed at this time, and new parks were created on the banks of the Allier. When the railway from Paris was extended to Vichy from Moulins, more and more visitors arrived. Up until this time the majority had stayed in private houses, now more hotels were built. From being a resort of the noble and famous of France, Vichy became a spa for the richer middle classes from all over the world. In 1928 the income of the Grand Casino was the highest of any in Europe, including Monte Carlo, and in the few years before the Second World War the number of visitors annually reached 140,000.

After the fall of France, Vichy became from July 1940 until August 1944 the base for the so-called government of the independent State of France. It was chosen largely because of its hotel capacity, enabling it to receive numerous embassies and ministerial cabinets with all the paraphernalia of bureaucratic government. It was in effect an impotent and almost fictitious body, taken seriously only by its members, and hardly by them.

After the war, for about twenty years, Vichy was just another spa, no longer fashionable, and steadily losing many regular clients from the French colonial service, who had nursed their livers there, as France unloaded her colonies.

But the fortunes of Vichy changed from 1963, when a barrage was built across the Allier, transforming the section of the river by the town into a lake 3km long with an area of 120 hectares. This superb lake in the middle of the town, its level controlled by the barrage, has proved to be an ideal setting for watersports of all kinds, including world and international events. From this beginning Vichy has year by year added to its sporting facilities. To the Sporting Club, with its 18-hole golf course, 18 tennis courts and swimming pools, has been added the Centre Omnisports, covering 100 hectares. It is difficult to name a sport which is not catered for here with the most modern and spacious amenities. It includes, for example, an artificial river 3km long with a current of variable strength, controlled as required, for canoe and kayak training. There is an archery ground. There are seven football fields, a basketball stadium, a building with halls for specialised sports such as judo, karate and aikido. There is a large gymnasium, with weight-lifting rooms, and training halls adjoining. There are 18 more tennis courts, three squash courts, and facilities for table tennis, roller skating,

Overleaf: *Château de Chouvigny, near Gorges de Chouvigny; built in 1250, restored in 1960*

fencing and cyclo-cross. The Centre Omnisports has accommodation for 250 athletes in single or double rooms, each with its own shower.

There are 28 clubs for different sports in Vichy, but the Centre Omnisports is open to all: children and adults, beginners and experts, tourists as well as locals. Use of the facilities is based only on the purchase of a special 'passport' covering from one to three weeks, and from one to fifteen sports. Apart from one or two more expensive sports such as water-skiing and riding, and even for them the rates are advantageous, all equipment is provided free.

There is a good, sandy beach on the Allier by the Parc des Célestins, and there are indoor and outdoor swimming pools. On top of all this Vichy has one of the best racecourses in France, a show-jumping stadium, and several riding schools in and around the town. With all these amenities it is not surprising that Vichy is an official base for the training of several of the French Olympic teams.

So Vichy is really two towns, two different worlds. In the centre is the 'old' town, the original spa, where most of the visitors are middle-aged or old and have come to repair the damage caused by the stress of modern life or to find a new confidence against the uncertainties of advancing age. At its side there is the ultra-modern sports resort full of young people bursting with health, energy and aspiration. Oil and water, you might think, and laced with vinegar. Not at all, Vichy is a lively and cheerful town. The two groups do their own thing, but also mingle in the restaurants, at the concerts, in the cinemas and parks, and are increasingly joined by ordinary holidaymakers who are neither sick nor sporty but just like the place because there is always so much going on.

The 'old' Vichy is centred around the Parc des Sources, with its shady walks, neat gravel paths, its bandstand encircled by rows of elegant white-painted iron chairs, each one a work of art. Open-air concerts take place regularly throughout the season. At one end of the Parc des Sources is the mosque-like Thermal Establishment and the Halle des Sources. At the other end is the Grand Casino which, despite looking rather like a cross between a period railway station and a Kew Gardens hothouse, has a *fin de siècle* elegance about it.

This island of *belle époque* style and charm includes some of the town's best hotels and restaurants, and smart galleries of expensive shops, jewellers, fashion boutiques, leather goods, and so on, many with famous Parisian names.

Vichy is also a cultural centre. The Casino includes a splendid opera house where there is a programme of plays, operas, concerts and ballets during the season. There is another theatre for light entertainment, musical comedies and variety. There is an open-air theatre. At the last count there were twelve cinemas and fifteen night club/discos. Vichy has plenty of hotels. Michelin lists 30 and the town's own publicity brochures claim 150, as well as 900 furnished flats, and five excellent camp sites.

The most exclusive hotel is the Pavillon Sévigné, the much restored house of the Marquise de Sévigné. Five years ago it was twice as expensive as any other hotel there. Its prices were not quoted in last year's Michelin.

There are restaurants of all kinds and at all levels but only one which ranks a Michelin star, the Violon d'Ingres, in the Parc des Sources. 'Violon d'Ingres', incidentally is the French idiom for an artistic hobby. I do not know whether the artist played the violin but the existence of the phrase suggests that he did and that his neighbours preferred his painting. Perhaps the restaurant proprietor is a painter whose friends preferred his cooking?

I have not eaten in the restaurant of the Yacht Club but its position in the rotonda built out over the lake suggests that dinner there on a fine summer evening might well be a pleasant experience.

Vichy is such an unusual and complex place that it is really more suited to a stay than a short visit. It is worth at least a couple of days to absorb something of its special atmosphere. A morning or an afternoon could only leave a partial and probably false impression. Parking in Vichy at the height of the season is a particular problem. If you are not lucky within a reasonable time try the Place de l'Hôtel-de-Ville or the railway station. In provincial towns which have them, by no means all, railway stations are often a good bet, particularly if you are lucky enough to arrive in the interval between trains, which in most of them adds up to the major part of the day. Do not be afraid to park where, strictly speaking, you should not. Unless you do something really irresponsible such as blocking the entrance to a fire station or hospital, the authorities are indulgent towards tourists, either doing nothing or leaving a warning slip. In these days of on the spot fines this does not normally apply to speeding offences.

Although Vichy is a sous-préfecture of the département of Allier, which is administratively part of Auvergne, the people of Vichy (Vichyssois) do not like to be considered Auvergnat. They are, they say, Bourbonnais. But Vichy is on the northern limits of the real Auvergne and is a good base from which to tour both Bourbonnais and northern Auvergne.

One interesting excursion is to **Lapalisse** and Châtel-Montagne. Take N209 from Vichy over the railway line to the suburb of Cusset, about 3km, and in Cusset keep straight on to D906^{B} for Lapalisse, about 20km. There is only one thing to see in Lapalisse and that is the château, but it is well worth the short run from Vichy. Compared with the majority of Auvergne castles, noted for their rugged picturesqueness, the château of La Palice is a more refined building with many features of a Renaissance character. Part of it does date from the 11th century, but the main residence is late 15th-century and was constructed during the life of Jacques II de Chabannes, Lord of La Palice. He was a Marshal of France who had distinguished himself in campaigns in Italy and who brought back with him Florentine craftsmen to work on the building.

The old marshal was an impressive and daring soldier, popular with his men. He was captured at the battle of Pavia and was shot dead in the course of an argument between two of his captors. His soldiers are said to have remembered him in verse, the last two lines of which were:

Hélas, s'il n'était pas mort
Il ferait encore envie

which translates roughly as — Alas, if he were not dead, he would still be cutting a dash — but at some time the

last line was recopied as 'Il serait encore en vie' — which makes the couplet translate as 'Alas, if he were not dead, he would still be alive'. Ever since, crashingly obvious statements of this kind have been known in French as *lapalissades*, and Lapalisse likes to be known as the Cité des Vérités (Town of Truth).

The château is the property of a descendant of the Marshal, the Comte de Chabannes, who has kept the interior, with its rich furnishings, much as it was. There used to be six large Flemish tapestries of the 15th century, but three of them were stolen. Of the three left, one, of Charlemagne, hangs in the Italian Renaissance dining room, and there are two more in the Salon d'Or (The Golden Room) on the first floor. This room has a magnificent coffered and gilded ceiling.

The castle is open from Palm Sunday to the end of October; from the middle of July until the third week of August, a combined Son et Lumière and historical spectacle is produced every Friday and Saturday evening. There are fireworks, laser displays, period music, and many people in period costume. The shows are popular and there is parking for a thousand cars.

There is a bar restaurant in the 17th-century kitchens which is open throughout the season and where meals are provided at reasonable prices. The attractive grounds are also open to visitors.

From Lapalisse take D7 south for about 15km and then turn left on to

Vichy: the mosque-like dome of the Thermal Establishment

The 12th-century granite church of Châtel-Montagne, all that remains of a former Benedictine priory

D25 for Châtel-Montagne. It is a pleasant road winding down towards the valley of the Besbre.

Châtel-Montagne has an interesting 12th-century granite church, all that remains of a former Benedictine Priory. It is a solid looking structure but the two-storey Romanesque porch is well-proportioned and has a certain elegance. Those really interested in church architecture will find this one a blend of Burgundian and Auvergnat styles. The lofty nave, lit by small arched windows at the top of the side walls, and the transept, have little in common with the Auvergne style, but the deep choir with four radiating chapels is similar to many to be seen farther south in the region.

Châtel-Montagne is situated on the edge of country known as les Montagnes Bourbonnais. It is a district of high wooded hills and pastures, rather than mountains, though in one or two places there are heights of more than 1,000m. The capital of the region is Le Mayet-de-Montagne, a village south of Châtel-Montagne by the D207, from which there is a nice road back to Vichy by D176 as far as Arronnes and from there on D995 along the valley of the Sichon. A few kilometres south of Arronnes (i.e. going away from Vichy) on D995 is the hamlet of **Glozel**. This apparently insignificant place has been, and still is, the setting for one of the great archaeological disputes of this century.

In 1926 a local farmer, Émile Fredin, in the course of ploughing a field turned up a quantity of bones, pieces of pottery, and numbers of primitive bricks inscribed with what seemed to be letters of an unknown alphabet. What were they? Neolithic, hazarded the local schoolteacher. From him the discovery rapidly climbed the academic scale. First, a local doctor planned to write a paper in his name and that of Émile Fredin. 'No,' said a Parisian academic, having invited the local man to dinner. 'This is what we'll do. I have published quite a lot already. Let me do it. It will sell much better, er, in your name as well, of course, and we'll forget about the farm boy.' The local man refused to have anything to do with this proposition, whereupon friends of the Parisian scholar denounced the whole thing as a fraud. Other academics joined in, some on one side, some on another, and archaeology being a small world it became an international row. Accusations, insults, lies, jeers, sneers and outrage flew back and forth in cloistered academic halls. It was even suggested that Émile Fredin had made the mysterious alphabet bricks himself and buried them at night. But the bones?

In 1927, an international archaeological commission, loaded with 'antis' said the 'pros', ruled that the discoveries were not ancient. But many professors were not convinced and the row smouldered on until similar bricks were discovered in the mountains of Portugal by men who could not even read, when it flared up again. In 1972 a group of Scandinavian professors took samples from Glozel back to a Danish university and examined them, using dating equipment which did not exist at the time of the original find. Authentic, they said. The pottery was at least as old as 700BC and the bones could be much older. The alphabet remained unexplained.

There is a small museum in the hamlet showing some of these discoveries. It is open every day, except Sundays, during the summer season.

Another interesting château close to Vichy is **Effiat**. For me it is one of the most attractive of all those in Auvergne, though in its early history it was a setting for nothing but tragedy. It was built in the early part of the 17th century by Antoine Coeffier-Ruzé, Marquis d'Effiat, Marshal of France, and also Richelieu's Superintendent of Finance. Architecturally it has more in common with the châteaux of the Loire Valley than those of Auvergne, and Coeffier-Ruzé spared no expense to get what he wanted. In order to create a park which he felt would be appropriate to such a château, he moved the whole village of Effiat. All the houses were demolished. Each proprietor was given a piece of land farther to the east and enough money to rebuild his house. To confirm his feudal rights over the new village, the Marquis imposed an annual rent of two chickens from each householder.

After a brilliant political and military career, this close friend of Richelieu died suddenly at the age of 51 while leading an army against the Elector of Trèves, the modern Trier, in the Rhineland. He left a wife, two daughters and three sons. The eldest daughter married an eccentric, short-tempered cousin of Richelieu. He calmed his rages by eating candles. The second daughter lived to a great age in a Dominican convent. The eldest son died raving mad at the age of 32. The youngest son led a debauched and scandalous life and was eventually banished for conspiracy. The hopes of the family were focused in the second son.

This young man, the Marquis de Cinq-Mars, was both very handsome and highly intelligent. From the age of 13 he spent his life at the court. Louis

XIII, a strange, timid, pious man, never much interested in women, and subject to long spells of impotence, was completely infatuated by this beautiful youth. He made him his Lieutenant for the Bourbonnais at the age of 15. When he was 18 Richelieu made him Master of the Royal Wardrobe. Only a year later Louis XIII promoted him to Grand Equerry. If Cinq-Mars was absent from the Court, he was expected to write Louis two letters a day.

As one French writer put it, 'All this honey soon turned to vinegar'. The King, the Cardinal and the young Marquis finished in mutual hatred. All the favours had turned the head of Cinq-Mars, who demanded more and more. Richelieu became jealous and began to alienate him from the King. In retaliation Cinq-Mars launched a plot together with de Thou, the Duke de Bouillon, and his friend, Gaston d'Orléans, the King's brother. The object was to bring about Richelieu's downfall, but the plot was discovered. D'Orléans betrayed his associates, both of whom were executed on 12th September 1642. Cinq-Mars was just 22 years old.

When the news was brought to him, Louis took refuge in the royal kitchens, where it was jam-making time. He amused himself stirring the mixtures and when he was asked what he felt about the news, he continued stirring and is said to have muttered, 'The soul of Cinq-Mars was as black as the bottom of this pot'.

Châtel-Montagne (Allier): a superb example of a 12th-century Romanesque church

Today the château belongs to the de Moroges family, and is open every day from the beginning of June to the end of September. The gardens, designed by Le Nôtre, are also open to the public.

A few kilometres beyond Effiat, the village of **Aigueperse** straddles the N9 and is slaughtered by its traffic. It, too, has a colourful history. It was the capital of the Duchy of Montpensier, one of the domains of the Bourbon family. After the confiscation of Bourbon lands by Francis I, it passed to the Bourbon-Montpensier branch, and then to the family of d'Orléans. It became the property of Anne Marie Louise d'Orléans, the daughter of Gaston d'Orléans, the one who plotted against his brother, Louis XIII. This lady, Duchess of Montpensier, became known as 'La Grande Mademoiselle' and was famous for the number of times she failed to get married. Great hopes were raised but, perhaps due to some fault of her own, perhaps as a result of over-complicated machinations by Cardinal Mazarin, she failed in turn to become Duchess of Bourbon, Queen of Spain, Queen of France and Empress of Austria.

At the age of 54 she fell madly in love with the Duc de Lauzin, a favourite of Louis XIV. He was a man so unscrupulous that La Bruyère wrote of him 'It was not permitted to dream as he lived'. While the King dallied with his mistress, Madame de Montespan, Lauzun, who thought of her as his protectress, would hide under the bed to make sure she spoke as well of him as she claimed to do. La Grande Mademoiselle can be excused for not making a success of the marriage. Lauzun was unfaithful and she was jealous. She died in 1693. Two years

The Mother — Catherine de Médicis

This remarkable woman, destined to become queen of France and the mother of three French kings, was cursed by death and blood from the day she was born. Her mother, Madeleine de la Tour d'Auvergne, from whom she inherited great estates in Auvergne, died within two days of her birth. Her father, grandson of Lorenzo the Magnificent, died of tuberculosis within the week.

Catherine became the ward of a maternal grandfather, who soon died. Her uncle, Pope Clement VII, became her guardian. He moved her around from palace to convent, until he married her off, at 14, to the future Henri II of France, a political alliance. She bore Henri four sons and three daughters. He was accidentally killed in a friendly joust, and was succeeded by his son, Francis II, who was 15. He died of his grandfather's disease a year later. The second son, Charles X, followed on the throne. He was ten years old and died at 24. During most of his reign, and that of Francis, Catherine ruled France as regent, aided by her capable Chancellor, Michel de l'Hospital.

The third son, Henri, was 23 when he became king. He was a degenerate and treacherous fop, but managed to hang on for fifteen years before being assassinated.

Though herself a devout Catholic, Catherine strove for tolerance between Catholics and Huguenots, but there was constant bloodshed. In the end her patience ran out and she helped engineer the bloodbath of St. Bartholomew's Day, 24th August 1572, in which almost four thousand Huguenots were killed.

The compensations of Catherine's sad and bloody life were food — she was a glutton — and art, in which she had fine judgement. She died at 69, unregretted. On the surface she was agreeable enough, but she plotted, and never forgot or forgave an injury. Her youngest son called her 'La Dame Serpente'.

later, Lauzun then 62, married a Mademoiselle de Quintin who, at 15, expected soon to become a young and pretty widow. Lauzun died at 90, and she was 43 and never married again. You needed lucky cards to win in those days and Lauzun was the Ace of Spades.

There is not much to see in Aigueperse itself. Most of the church of Notre-Dame was built in the 19th century, though the 13th-century choir and transept still exist. In the chapel of the Sacré-Coeur on the left of the choir there is a Nativity painted on wood by Ghirlandaio in 1489, as well as a copy of Mantegna's St. Sebastien.

A few kilometres from Aigueperse by D12 is the Château de la Roche above the village of Chaptuzat. In appearance it is really more of a fortified manor house than a castle. It is reputedly the birthplace of Michel de l'Hospital, the courageous and competent Chancellor of Catherine de Médicis. After the early death of her husband, Henri II, in a friendly joust with the English soldier, Montgomery, Michel de l'Hospital helped her to maintain royal authority during the reigns of her feeble and tubercular sons, Francis II and Charles IX. He was a wise and tolerant man whose opposition to the persecution of the Protestants eventually led to his dismissal. He narrowly escaped with his life during the Massacre of St. Bartholomew, when Catholic fanatics invaded his home, the Château de Vignay, at Malesherbes, near Paris.

A room in the keep at Château de la Roche contains personal souvenirs, documents and portraits of Michel de l'Hospital. There is also a guard room with an interesting collection of 15th-century weapons, as well as rooms with 17th-century furniture and Aubusson tapestries. The château is open throughout the year except on Tuesdays.

Return to Vichy via Effiat or by the villages of Olhat and Bas on D223, then turning left near Randan on to D1093 which takes you through the Boucharde forest back to Vichy.

When you come to leave the worldliness and modernity of Vichy, going south, you will be on your way to the 'real' Auvergne, a more rugged country but one of supreme beauty, interest, and endless variety.

The Daughter — Marguerite de Valois

Marguerite de Valois, daughter of Catherine de Médicis, was the loveliest and liveliest of all the queens of France. Her exceptional beauty was celebrated in verse by the great poet, Ronsard. Alexander Dumas wrote a cloak and dagger novel about her. Even staid Montaigne described her as 'one of those supernatural beauties who from time to time glitter like stars in our mundane world'.

No wonder that her life was one long succession of love affairs. Almost the only man she had no time for was her husband, Henry of Navarre, the future Henri IV. She was cultivated. He was, by her standards, a peasant and, by all accounts, smelly with it. He consoled himself with women of all sorts, from servants to countesses. She was happy with men who could write and recite poetry, and who washed occasionally.

She ran away, riding for six days to her fortress at Carlat in Auvergne. Throughout the province there are towns where Queen Margot's house is proudly pointed out. Her acquaintance with them was usually of the 'Queen Elizabeth slept here' variety.

Her conduct was so outrageous, even for the time, that her brother Henri III put her under house arrest in the Auvergne castle of Usson, where she stayed for twenty years. But it was a strange prison. For every man ready to betray her there were ten bound by the spell of her charm and beauty. Usson was always crowded with musicians and men of letters, and lovers.

Soon after her husband became Henri IV, they were divorced. In time she was allowed to leave Usson to live in Paris, where she kept up the same style in a mansion in the Bois de Boulogne. Even as old age approached she liked her amorous pleasures and kept a lute-player as companion and lover. He was known as King Margot.

General Information

FORÊT DE TRONÇAIS Information: Kiosk at Le Rond Gardien, near the village of Isle-et-Bardais.
Where to stay: Le Tronçais (70.06.11.95), in St. Bonnet-Tronçais, is a small but pleasant inn in the Logis de France group.
Camp sites: One by the Étang de St. Bonnet, and another beside the Étang de Pirou.

LAPALISSE Information: Syndicat d'Initiative, pl Charles Bécaud (70.99.08.39, high season).
Where to stay: Hôtel Galland, 20 pl de la République (70.99.04.11).
Where to eat: The restaurant of the Galland offers good value. The Lion des Flandres, 40 rue Roosevelt (70.99.06.75), is also recommended, and has a few rooms.

MONTLUÇON Information: Office de Tourisme, 1 av Max-Dormoy (70.05.05.92) (just below castle).
Where to stay: Apart from the Hostellerie du Château St. Jean, rte de Clermont-Ferrand (70.05.04.65), which is really an expensive restaurant with a few luxurious rooms, the rest are a modest collection. Best bet is the Novelta (Logis de France) a few km out of town on the N145 towards Guéret (70.03.34.88).
Where to eat: For a special meal the Hostellerie du Château St. Jean. At a more ordinary level the restaurant at the Novelta is good. The Hostellerie du Théâtre, 1 rue de la Croix-Verte (70.05.07.27), is reasonably priced and good.

MOULINS Information: Office de Tourisme, pl de l'Hôtel-de-Ville (70.44.14.14).
Where to stay: Hôtel de Paris, 21 rue de Paris (70.44.00.58). In town centre. Not large, but very comfortable.
Moderne Hôtel (70.44.05.06). Sound hotel, nicely situated by pl Jean Moulin.
Two more modest hotels in town: the Parc (31 av Gnl.-Leclerc, 70.44.12.25) and the Dauphin (70.44.05.06) (by station), and one of the Ibis chain (70.46.71.12) 3km on N7 to Vichy.
Camp site: Municipal. On bank of the Allier near bridge.
Where to eat: The restaurant of the Hôtel de Paris is small (reservation advised) but very good; strong wine list. Another very good restaurant is the Jacquemart, 10 rue de l'Hôtel-de-Ville (70.44.32.58).

ST. POURÇAIN-SUR-SIOULE Information: Syndicat d'Initiative, bd Ledru-Rollin (the N9), near town centre (70.45.32.73, high season).
Where to stay: Hôtel Chêne Vert, 35 bd Ledru-Rollin (70.45.40.65). On the main road, so ask for a room at the back. Hôtel Les Deux Ponts, îlot de Tivoli (70.45.41.14) (Logis de France), also on main road. A few km away at Target, near Chantelle, the 17th-century Château de Boussac (73.68.43.03) has five guest bedrooms and a restaurant. Nice but expensive.
Where to eat: Restaurant of the Hôtel Chêne Vert. Good reputation. Local wines.

i

VICHY Information: Office de Tourisme, 19 rue du Parc (next to Parc des Sources) (70.98.71.94). They will make hotel reservations.
Where to stay: There are about a dozen luxury hotels in Vichy, headed by the very expensive Pavillon Sévigné, and many others at every level.
Camp sites: Four good ones, and a youth hostel.
Where to eat: Violon d'Ingres, 5 rue du Casino (70.98.97.70) has a Michelin star, well-earned, and prices to go with it. The Chateaubriand, rue de la Grange-aux-Grains (70.32.34.00), in the Marcotel, just across the river in Bellerive, has a good reputation. I like La Colombière (70.98.69.15) at Abrest on the road to Thiers (4km) which has a terraced garden by the Allier.
Leisure: Vichy has a remarkable range of top-class facilities for all sports, indoor and outdoor, all of which are available to foreign visitors at advantageous rates. Full details from the Office de Tourisme.

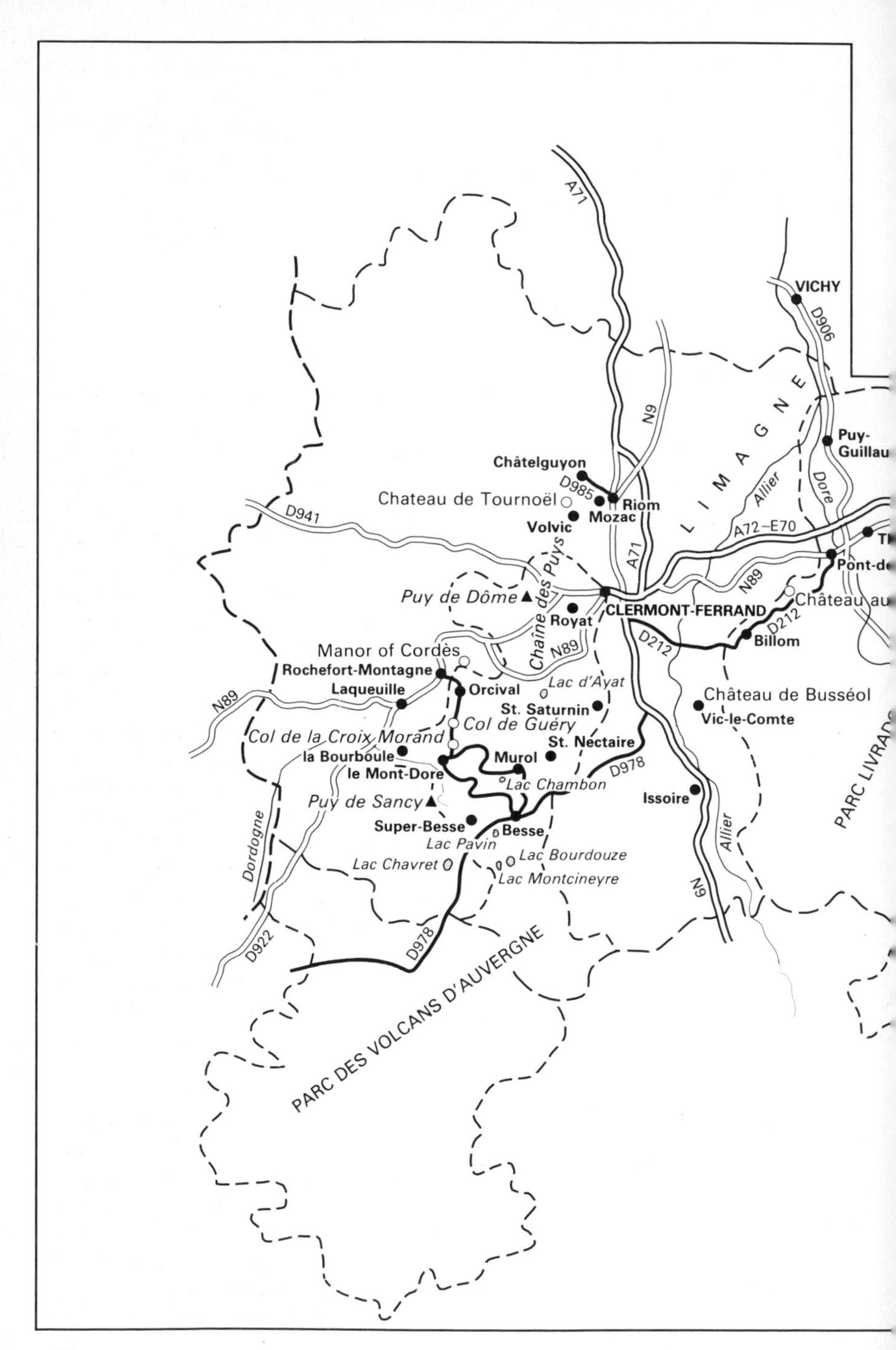
VICHY
D906
LIMAGNE
Puy-Guillau
Allier
Dore
A72–E70
Pont-d
Château au
D212
Billom
A71
N9
Châtelguyon
D985
Riom
Chateau de Tournoël
Mozac
Volvic
D941
Chaîne des Puys
Puy de Dôme
CLERMONT-FERRAND
Royat
N89
Manor of Cordès
Rochefort-Montagne
Laqueuille
Orcival
Lac d'Ayat
St. Saturnin
Château de Busséol
Vic-le-Comte
Col de Guéry
Col de la Croix Morand
St. Nectaire
la Bourboule
Murol
le Mont-Dore
Lac Chambon
D978
Issoire
Puy de Sancy
Super-Besse
Besse
Lac Pavin
Lac Bourdouze
Lac Chavret
Lac Montcineyre
Dordogne
D922
PARC DES VOLCANS D'AUVERGNE
PARC LIVRAD

6
Puy-de-Dôme

With Cantal, the département of Puy-de-Dôme forms the heart of the old historical region of Auvergne. The story goes that it is called Puy-de-Dôme because in 1790, when the old regions of France were organised into départements and renamed, it was suggested that Basse-Auvergne should become the département of Mont d'Or, as it was spelt at the time. With the typical hypersensitivity of the Auvergnat to anything to do with money — and at that time, of course, money consisted of gold coins — the deputy for Clermont, Gaultier de Biauzat, expressed fears that this very prosperous sounding name, Mountain of Gold, would attract the interest of the tax authorities and that his fellow citizens would suffer accordingly. He proposed Puy-de-Dôme instead, and his suggestion was adopted. I don't know whether his fellow citizens did benefit but he cannot possibly have done his own political career any harm.

The département has something of everything to be found elsewhere in Auvergne — mountains, lakes, forests, gorges, barrages, spas, picturesque villages, historic old towns, splendid churches, beautiful châteaux and romantic ruined castles. Two great regional Nature Parks, the Parc des Volcans d'Auvergne and the Parc

Livradois-Forez lie, for the most part, in the département of Puy-de-Dôme. In addition it has two things not found elsewhere in the region. Between these two great Nature Parks and their mountains is the wide and fertile valley called the Grand Limagne, watered by the rivers Allier and Dore. This degree of fertility is not equalled elsewhere in the Massif Central. Also, Puy-de-Dôme has the only large town in the Massif Central, Clermont-Ferrand, which with its suburbs has a population of more than a quarter of a million.

Puy de Dôme is the highest mountain of the Monts Dôme. The first settlers in Auvergne, Celtic tribes who made their homes in the fertile plains of the Limagne, were impressed by a mountain which dominated their horizon — a mountain which was green in spring, purple in autumn, and shining white in winter. They called it Dumia, meaning royal mountain. In the 17th century it was still known as the Puy de Doume. On the summit of Dumia these same Celts worshipped the greatest of their gods, Toutates, who was the god of war, as well as the protector of travellers and roads. The Celts did not build a temple. Their religion was Druidic and they held their services in the open air, offering as sacrifices, prisoners of war, murderers, sometimes innocent people whom the gods had chosen, or whom the priests did not like. They first had their throats cut and were then enclosed in coffins of wickerwork which were burned with their contents.

Volcanoes of Auvergne from below Puy Chavaroche, near Puy Mary

When the Romans came they too worshipped on the Puy-de-Dôme and made it a centre of the worship of the god Mercury. Unlike the Celts they did build a temple on the summit and a pretty luxurious one it was with sixty different kinds of marble brought from all parts of the Empire used to dress the walls and the floor, while the building itself was constructed from lava stones brought from the slopes of nearby volcanoes.

The Monts Dôme are also called the Chaîne des Puys, in which there are said to be 112 volcanoes, all, fortunately for mass tourism, extinct. They are the youngest of Auvergne's volcanoes, dating from about two million years ago and so are less eroded and have a greater variety of shape than the other mountain groups of the Massif.

South of the Chaîne des Puys are the Monts Dore (modern spelling). These are higher and older mountains dating from about sixty million years ago, and include the highest peak in Auvergne, Puy de Sancy, at 1885m.

To the east are the much older granite mountains of the Livradois, rising to 1210m, and separated from them by the valley of the Dore, the equally old granite Monts du Forez, with a maximum height of 1634m. Both these mountain ranges are characterised by high, undulating plateaux and deep valleys. The Monts du Forez link northwards with the Monts de la Madeleine and the Montagnes Bourbonnais.

These three different kinds of mountains, and vegetation varying from deserted upland pasture to forests of majestic pines, and, on non-limestone soils, forests of chestnut, and the intensely cultivated *limagnes* with vineyards, orchards and fields of cereals, make the scenery of the département very varied.

According to their natural resources different parts of the Massif Central have produced different kinds of town. Puy-de-Dôme, with its industry and larger fertile areas, is the only département of Auvergne to show a net increase in population in recent years. People have abandoned the hard life of the mountains all over Auvergne for the softer life of the fertile valleys of Puy-de-Dôme, and industry has brought in workers from all parts of France, and even as far afield as Turkey.

From Vichy, D906 leads south via St. Yorre and Puy-Guillaume to **Thiers**. Few places could provide a more vivid contrast with Vichy than this old, red-roofed town built on the steep side of a hill above the rushing waters of the Durolle, a tributary of the Dore. This wild little river, a free source of energy, is the origin of the industry which has kept Thiers prosperous for hundreds of years. Starting with a few artisans about five hundred years ago, Thiers gradually became the cutlery capital of France, a miniature French Sheffield. The fierce waters of the Durolle turned countless grinding wheels on which the artisans sharpened the knives. This was done in a horizontal position on a plank above the river. The workmen would lie there face down, while their dogs lay on their masters' backs to protect their kidneys from the cold and damp. I say masters, but old illustrations show that the work was quite often done by women.

Until the end of the 18th century and the beginning of industrialisation, Thiers was also a centre of paper production and was especially well known for the thin, supple card from which playing cards were made.

There were, at least until quite recently, and perhaps still are, a few tough looking men, reputedly at the disposal of the local tourist board (rather like the lacemakers near the Cathedral in Le Puy), prepared to lie down on planks and sharpen a knife or two in the old way. When sharp enough they could be flourished under the noses of tourists with the remark that tips were not obligatory. As far as I know, there has never been a Thiernois equivalent of Sweeney Todd, though in 1894 Président Carnot was murdered with a knife made in Thiers.

The picturesqueness of the town and the valley is rather spoiled by a number of abandoned, broken-windowed, crumbling old factories, which suggest that Thiers may be a town in decline. Though it would no doubt look better without them, the impression they give is misleading. The paper industry did not survive mechanisation, but Thiers still produces more than 70 per cent of the cutlery on the French market and has two hundred firms in this industry, about forty of them purely artisanal.

Shops near the Town Hall, in rue Nationale and in rue du Bourg scintillate with thousands of gleaming blades from pocket knives to vicious looking daggers. In the past twenty years the industry has diversified into allied areas, and the shops are also full of stainless or plated dishes and domestic utensils of all shapes and sizes.

Thiers is one of those steep-sided towns where there always seems to be more up than down. It is not an ideal place for asthmatics or people with dodgy hearts to walk for long. But otherwise it is a place that well repays an hour or two's exploration. It has to be done on foot because several of the most interesting streets are reserved for pedestrians, and others reserved for local traffic, so driving is impractical. Park somewhere in the upper town, in Place Duchasseint, perhaps, and walk down to the old town. The Office de Tourisme is in the Place du Pirou, reached by the rue Conchette and the rue du Bourg. If you should want to see a knife-maker at work in the old way you can ask there, and also pick up information on the town which will be useful as you walk around.

Though it is small, Thiers is industrial, and a good deal of architectural detail and interesting carving is masked by the grime that gave Thiers the name of the 'black town' in the past. But in recent years a policy of cleaning and restoring many of the fine 15th-, 16th- and 17th-century houses, with their splendid beamed and carved façades, has been in force and much has been done to improve matters.

Walk down rue Conchette, and then rue Bourg to Place du Pirou. The star of this attractive square is the 15th-century Maison du Pirou, much restored, which is now the property of the town. It is used for exhibitions in the summer. In adjacent rue du Pirou, No. 11 is called the House of the Seven Deadly Sins from the carvings on the ends of the seven beams which support the first floor. Farther on, the 15th-century buildings form a sort of gateway over the street and beyond it rue Durolle, lined with old houses and workshops, descends steeply to the river.

Return to Place du Pirou. On the other side in rue Grenette No. 8 is a 17th-century building called the House of Lauzun. Thiers belonged to the Dukes of Bourbon and was one of the places confiscated by Francis I after the 'treason' of the Constable of Bourbon. But it returned to the Bourbon-Montpensier family in the time of Charles IX and so to the 'Grande Mademoiselle', who gave it to her husband, the dubious Duc de Lauzun.

The church of St. Genès dates originally from the 11th century but had been almost totally rebuilt over the years and is of no great architectural interest. A little farther down, across Place de Lafayette, at 16 rue du Quatre Septembre, is the house where in the 1830s and 1840s Louis Daguerre perfected his process of making photographs with silver-coated copper plates.

Return up rue de la Coutellerie which has a number of old workshops and a 15th-century house at No. 21 now part of the museum and workshops of the Maison des Couteliers. Here the various stages in the making of a knife can be seen, as well as a collection of knives and daggers of all kinds going back hundreds of years.

Finish your tour with a visit to the Terrasse du Rempart from which there is an extensive view over the plain of the Limagne to the peaks of the Monts Dore and Monts Dôme on the other side.

Thiers does not have much in the way of hotels or restaurants but only 6km away by N89 there are three hotels, one of them rather up-market, and a good restaurant, Mère Dépalle at Pont-de-Dore.

From Thiers make for the capital of Puy-de-Dôme, Clermont-Ferrand, via N89 to Pont-de-Dore, and then by D212 to the little medieval town of Billom. This is not the direct route which is by N89 or the autoroute, but it is a lot more interesting.

D212 passes by way of two hamlets called Chez Cagnat and Chez Barriou. I think it is worth mentioning that this word 'Chez' in the name of a village or hamlet in this region has a rather stronger significance than it does in 'Chez Nous'. It indicates that this was the site of one of the collective farms which existed in Auvergne for more than a thousand years, long pre-dating the collective farms of Soviet Russia or the kibbutzim of Israel. These agricultural communities were formed originally to make the workload easier on land belonging to others, but as soon as they were able they acquired land for themselves. The first record of these communities is in a document of the year AD780 and refers to the community of Quittard-Pinon, near Thiers. It was still in existence at the end of the 18th century, when its master was awarded a red sash of honour by King Louis XVI for services to agriculture, and which he kept safe through the Revolution by wearing it under his clothes. It is in Thiers museum today.

The number of people in these groups varied from twenty to a hundred or more. Within them there were two classes, the joint proprietors of the land, who were called *personniers,* and the ordinary workmen who received a wage. It was all rather like a lay monastery. They lived apart in their own quarters but all ate in the same room. Their motto was 'one fire, one

Maison du Pirou, early 15th-century town house in Thiers, a place famous for centuries for its knives and cutlery

PARFUMERIE

Blaise Pascal

One of the most famous of French thinkers, Pascal was born in Clermont-Ferrand in 1623. He was both a remarkable mathematician and a brilliant writer, able to present a complex philosophical idea in a few telling words.

His mathematical genius showed itself at the age of 16 when he wrote an original treatise on conic sections. At 19, concerned at the hours his father, a business man, spent on his accounts, Pascal thought out and constructed the first calculating machine. In 1648 he initiated experiments on Puy de Dôme which demonstrated the variations in air pressure due to altitude, and then outlined the applications this discovery would have in thermometers, weather prediction and the calculation of altitude. He could have been a great scientist.

But Pascal was a religious mystic. At 31 he had visions which persuaded him to give up everything but God. He was deeply impressed by the writings of Bishop Jansen, and devoted the rest of his life to religious writing in support of the Jansenists, and attacking the Jesuits. The Jansenist view of Catholicism was essentially that of a Church open only to those who had been granted the grace of God, because they were worthy of it. To Pascal, the Jesuits, with their formidable ability to split hairs and make a case for (or against) anybody, were more concerned in increasing the size and the power of the Church than they were with the service of God.

The book for which he is renowned, his *Thoughts,* was made up posthumously from parts of an unfinished work in defence of the Christian faith. Pascal was an exceptional man but, in old-fashioned terms, more than a little 'touched'. All his life ill-health caused him constant pain but it was not enough; he also wore a belt studded with sharp nails to mortify the flesh. He died at 39.

pot', and this was often literally true. Some of the dining tables were made with a large bowl in the centre with smaller bowls hollowed out at intervals around the sides, and connected to the central bowl by channels in the wooden table top. At meal times a huge bowl of soup was brought in and emptied gradually into the centre bowl from which it ran into the side bowls, also connected by channels so that none would overflow.

The men ate together and the women apart with the children. The society was directed by a 'Master' and a 'Mistress' elected by the assembly of *personniers.* So that she would not be unduly influenced by him, the Mistress was never the wife, sister or daughter of the Master. As in a monastery different members had their own specialities. One might be in charge of the vineyard, another of the raising of the cattle, another of ploughing and preparing the ground for sowing.

The Master's authority affected all aspects of their lives. At meal times no one was allowed to serve himself with bread. The Master marked the huge loaf with the sign of the Cross with his knife, then cut it into portions and passed them round. His authority extended even to marriages which he arranged with as much regard for the interests of the little republic as for sentiments.

It was the responsibility of the Mistress to organise the kitchen, washing, mending, and to look after the poultry and other small animals. The education of the children, who were put to work as soon as they were strong enough, was also her responsibility rather than that of the mothers whose labour was always at the disposal of the Master. They both trained a successor whose appointment had to be confirmed by election. If their own administration was considered unsatisfactory they could be deposed by the assembly of *personniers*. The last of these groups was dissolved in 1875 in the village of Pions in the Montagnes Bourbonnais.

At the crossroads at Chez Barriou a short detour to the left down D223 to the Château Aulteribe is worth the trouble, especially for lovers of fine furniture. The 15th-century château, completely restored during the 19th, contains a very fine collection of period furniture and works of art left to the nation by a previous owner. The pictures include portraits of Henri IV, Richelieu, and the tragic Mademoiselle de Fontanges (see p. 145). There are also five superb Flemish tapestries based on works by Teniers.

Back on D212 not far beyond the crossroads at Chez Barriou there is a turning to the right to Bort l'Étang where there is an expensive, luxurious hotel, the Château de Codignat.

Not far beyond the turning to Bort l'Étang, a turning on the right, D10, and then right again brings you at once to the village of Ravel. A narrow and very steep road leads up to the impressive castle of the same name. Built at the end of the 13th century it was given by Philippe IV (the Handsome) to his Chancellor, Pierre Flotte. By inheritance and marriage it passed eventually to the d'Estaing family who extended and restored it during the 17th century. Though part of the original remains, most of what you see today dates from the 17th and 18th centuries. The spacious terrace, designed by Le Nôtre, gives extensive views of the Limagne and the Monts Dôme.

Billom is an old town well-restored and well-maintained. It was the site of an early university which in the 13th century had more than two thousand students. In 1556 the Jesuits set up their first college in France at Billom and it continued there with some interruptions until 1773. Today it is an active little town with several small industries and is the centre of a farming area famous for the production of potent garlic, much of which is exported to Egypt and Latin America. A good deal is also eaten by the local inhabitants with the result that their breath is often as sharp as the knives of Thiers; even other Auvergnats tend to stand at a respectful distance when talking to them.

The old town still has two of its medieval gateways and narrow alleys with many 16th-century houses, some leaning slightly inwards like mammoths about to butt each other. Do not miss rue des Boucheries and rue des Chanoines. The church of St. Cerneuf has some 14th-century murals said to be the work of English artists brought from Avignon. In the square near the

Overleaf: *The ancient castle of Bousséol has been rebuilt on its own ruins*

church is the Chapter House (1447) where the professors of the University met.

From Billom you can continue directly to Clermont-Ferrand by D212 or, if you have the time and the inclination, make a short but pleasant detour to see the attractively sited Château de Busséol. Just outside Billom take D229, a left turn off the D212, in the direction of Vic-le-Comte. At the hamlet of Laps, 11km, cross the stream, and take D4, a picturesque little road on the right, which leads to Busséol. The impressive château was restored from its own crumbled ruins in the 1960s. There is a magnificent view from the site.

From Busséol carry on northwards to rejoin D212 for Clermont-Ferrand.

Those tourists who have come to Auvergne for its mountains, rivers and unspoilt wilderness may well be tempted to give **Clermont-Ferrand** a

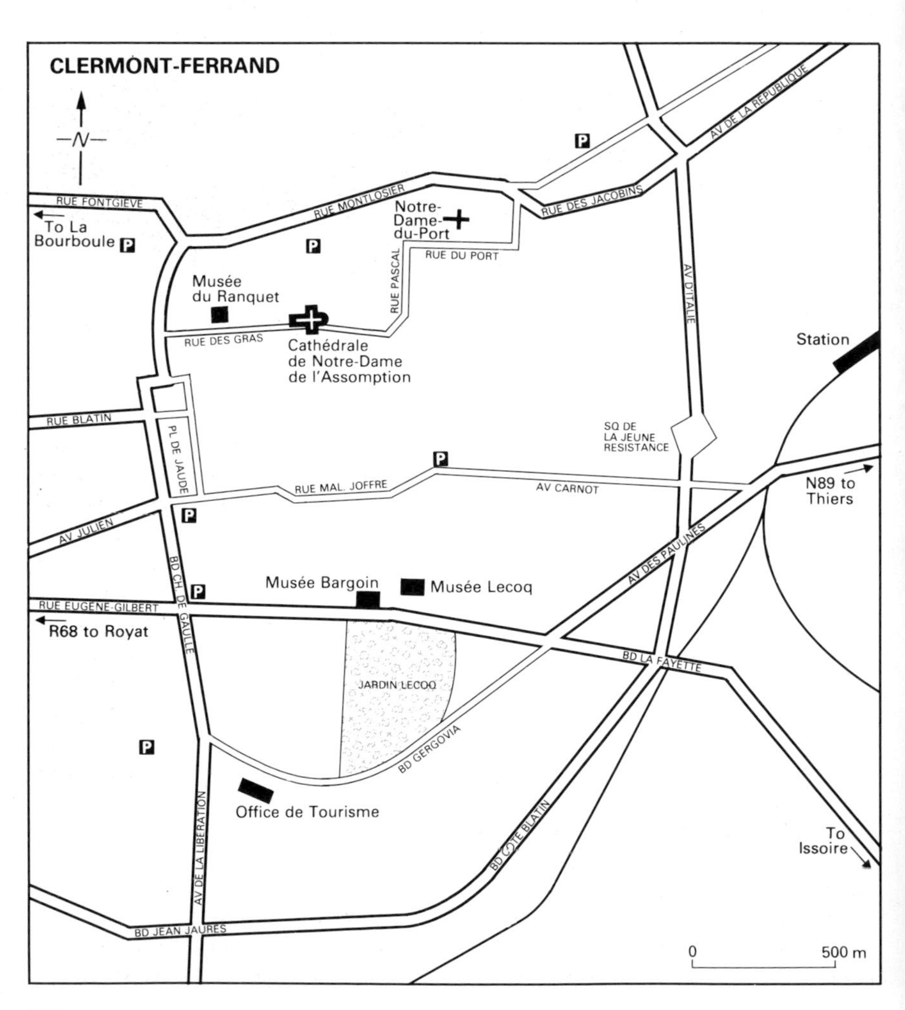

miss. But, though it is today an industrial town dominated by the enormous Michelin factories, it is also a very old town with several points of great interest. It is also a good base for excursions in the area.

It consists really of two towns, Clermont and Montferrand. In old Clermont there are two churches worth the attention of any alert-minded visitor, the Basilica of Notre-Dame-du-Port and the Cathedral of Notre-Dame de l'Assomption. Notre-Dame-du-Port is one of the five most beautiful Romanesque churches in Auvergne (the others are St. Nectaire, St. Saturnin, St. Austremoine in Issoire, and Orcival). The major part of Notre-Dame-du-Port dates from the 11th and 12th centuries and is built in the yellowish sandstone, grimy after more than 800 years, which was used for churches in Basse-Auvergne before the adoption of the lava stone from Volvic.

Its position, hemmed in by other buildings, makes it difficult fully to appreciate the exterior. But inside, bathed in a warm light from above, it is remarkable for its harmony and balance, and creates an atmosphere which is charming, almost in the literal sense of the word, spell-binding. According to recent research this harmonious and powerful effect is due to the fact that the church was built according to the rules of the Golden Number, 1618, and this can be demonstrated say the experts from measurements taken inside the church. I admit that I do not understand this, being able to do little more with figures than count my change in shops, but I mention it because architects and mathematicians may find it of interest.

The raised choir is particularly lovely, and the carved capitals, some

Notre-Dame-du-Port, Clermont: a superb example of the Romanesque style

of which date from about 1160, are among the finest to be seen in Auvergne. They can be lit to be seen to better advantage (1 franc) and the themes include the struggle of vice against virtue, the story of Adam and Eve, Joseph's dream, the announcement of the birth of John the Baptist, and the glorification of Mary, to whom the church is dedicated. Unusually for the time, the carving is signed, 'Rotbertus' — Master Robert of Clermont. He was also the sculptor of the renowned tympanum of the church of Ste. Foy, at Conques, showing the Last Judgement with more than a hundred figures, in near perfect condition.

In the 11th-century crypt of Notre-Dame-du-Port there is an altar with a small black Virgin, copied from an earlier one say some authorities, copied from a Byzantine icon, say others. There is an annual pilgrimage on the Sunday after 14th May.

The adjacent rue du Port has a number of 18th-century houses, and in the rue du Pascal, left at the top, No 4 is the late 18th-century mansion of M. de Chazerat, the last Intendant of Auvergne.

Coming from Notre-Dame-du-Port, which is a superb lesson in the art of the Romanesque church, the visitor will find a marked contrast in the Cathedral, a fine example of early Gothic architecture. It was started in 1248 and is believed to be the first building for which the almost black Volvic stone was used. The choir was finished in 1287 but the main part of the building was not consecrated until the 14th century and, in a sense, it was not finished until the 1860s when the famous architect of the day, Viollet le Duc, replaced the Romanesque towers by the twin spires which have been a landmark of Clermont ever since.

The use of the Volvic stone, both strong and resistant, enabled the pillars to be thinner and the whole construction to be lightened compared with earlier churches. This is the first impression of the interior, one of soaring grace and lightness, the lines sweeping almost uninterrupted up to the vaulted roof. The dark Volvic stone also brings out the full beauty of the richly coloured stained-glass windows in the choir and the chapels of the deambulatory. These magnificent windows date from the 13th to 15th centuries and are believed to come from the same workshop as the famous stained glass in the Sainte-Chapelle in Paris. This conclusion is based not only on the techniques used and the quality of the work but also on the fact that Louis IX, who was the benefactor of the Sainte-Chapelle, also had connections with Clermont, which he visited in 1262 for the marriage of his son, Philippe, to Isabel of Aragón.

The twin town of Montferrand, 2km from the centre of Clermont, has a remarkable old quarter which has been carefully restored over the past twenty-five years. Centred around the Carrefour des Taules — *taule* originally meant a market stall but in modern French its only use is as a slang term for prison, the equivalent of 'nick' — this old quarter contains about eighty houses, some of them dating back to the 13th century. It also has a church, Notre-Dame-de-Prospérité, built at about the same time as the Cathedral of Clermont.

On a corner of the Carrefour des Taules is the Maison de l'Apothécaire which has a pleasant little bar. This street has been lowered, so that what is now the bar used to be the cellar

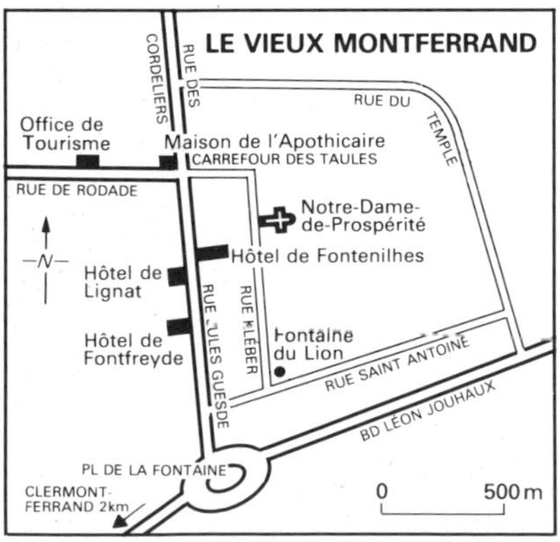

Stained glass in the cathedral at Clermont-Ferrand

House of the Apothecary, one of 80 15th-century restored houses in Montferrand

and what used to be the first floor is now the second floor. The result is that the carved beam ends, one showing an apothecary wielding a syringe and the other a patient offering an appropriate part of his anatomy for the injection, are now farther from the ground and more difficult to see.

A little way down rue de Rodade from the bar is the Tourist Office. If you call there and pick up a plan of the area showing the best of the houses, you will be able to wander at will. In any case you should see the Hôtel de Lignat, a lawyer's house at 18 rue Jules Guesde, the Hôtel Fontfreyde at 28 in the same road, and the Hôtel de Fontenilles at No 13. All three have interesting courtyards as well as architectural details of the 16th century.

Although it has a well signposted expressway encircling the town, Clermont remains an easy place to get lost in. If you plan to use it as a base for a few days, it is a good idea to arrive on Saturday night. This gives you the relatively traffic free Sunday to get an idea of the layout and to see the sites actually in Clermont. If you come from the north from Moulins and Riom, a convenient hotel is the Ibis, just off this road on the northern outskirts of the town, near Montferrand. This has the advantage of being easy to find, quiet, and of easy access to the centres of both Clermont and Montferrand. There is a good selection of other hotels, and as in most provincial towns in France, and often in England, there is one hotel more expensive and sophisticated than the rest. These hotels seem to exist to enable the successful businessmen of the area to demonstrate their prosperity when entertaining clients who, they hope, will make them more successful, and for the rich families to show their peers that they are as rich as ever. In Clermont-Ferrand this hotel is the Altea-Gergovia which, it must be said, has a high standard of comfort, marble, for example, in the bathrooms instead of the increasingly usual plastic. The restaurant of the hotel, la Retirade, serves a very good dinner at prices which look like provincial telephone numbers.

On Sunday morning also there is a chance that you may be able to park right in the heart of the town in the vast Place de Jaude, within walking distance of the old town and the Cathedral. Rather lost among the trees, the space and the high buildings of this great square there is a statue of Vercingetorix, the Auvergne hero who defeated Julius Caesar at the Battle of

Gergovie (see p. 106). It is the work of Bartholdi who was also responsible for the Statue of Liberty.

In the 1860s the average inhabitant of Clermont had probably never heard of Vercingetorix. A few academics felt the town should erect a statue to him, especially after Louis Napoleon's visit and official recognition of the site of Gergovia had revived their memories, but it took a long time to become a reality. In 1869 they had managed to raise two thousand francs towards it, and in 1870 a small model of the proposed statue was shown to the town council. It was received with polite interest and quickly forgotten. However, things changed a few years later when a drawing of the statue was used as a trademark for a popular make of gentian apéritif. The Clermontois understood this kind of reality and told Bartholdi 'We would like to have your statue, in bronze, of course, so long as it does not cost too much'. Bartholdi produced an estimate and the situation changed again, much more rapidly. 'On consideration,' said the Clermontois, 'we feel we were aiming too high. We will think of something else and manage on our own.'

What they thought of was three columns of Volvic stones fitted together rather like Lego. It cost almost nothing, and made a similar impression. But the academics still wanted their Bartholdi statue, and by the end of the century had raised enough money to talk to the sculptor again. He reduced the size of the monument and his estimate, and the order was given.

The long awaited statue was unveiled on 11th October 1903. The occasion was marked by what was called a 'democratic' banquet at which 4,500 places had been set out in the

Statue of Vercingetorix, the Auvergnat who defeated Caesar at Gergovia

contemporary equivalent of a department store. After the speeches, the banquet started, and for a high proportion of the guests finished at the same time. As the food arrived in minute quantities or not at all, tempers became as whetted as appetites. The more audacious guests left the tables and invaded the kitchens where they filled baskets and bags with food and departed. This infuriated the less bold who then set about smashing plates, bottles and glasses, until order was eventually restored by the police. As befits heroes, Vercingetorix never blinked an eye.

Whether or not you mean to do any walking in Auvergne, you should make the excursion to the top of the Puy de Dôme to see one of Europe's finest panoramas and to form an idea of the vast and wild region you are visiting. It can be done by car. A spiral road with a steady slope of 12 per cent winds around the mountain to the summit. It begins about 9km from the centre of Clermont, 5km from Royat, branching off N141A. The road replaces a little steam railway which, from the turn of the century until 1926, ran from Clermont to the summit. It was not a rack railway, the engine climbed the slope by means of revolving discs which exerted pressure on a central rail. The same company which built this railway and later the road now charges a small fee for the use of the road.

At the summit there are large parking spaces, souvenir shops, bars, restaurant and hotel. The Roman temple to Mercury was, according to experts, similar in appearance to the Maison Carrée in Nîmes, which still exists, but twice the size. The remains of the temple were discovered in the late 19th century when work was being done for the building of an observatory. The bottom of the huge walls and some of the steps of the grand staircase can be seen. Roman coins found by archaeologists cover the period from the Emperor Augustus to Constantine, indicating that the temple was in use at least until the 5th century AD. A miniature bronze statue of Mercury, now in the museum in Clermont, suggests that some of the coins were spent on souvenirs and that merchants had stalls around the temple.

Puy de Dôme: at 1465m the highest of the extinct volcanoes in the Monts Dômes range

Church of St. Léger at Royat, fortified in the 13th century

The summit of Puy de Dôme is shared between this ruined temple, a meteorological observatory, and the modern installations of the French radio and television service, including an 80m television tower. The large terrace at the base of this tower is freely accessible to the public. The views from it are truly impressive with more than sixty volcanoes visible, weather permitting, of course. The best time of day is late afternoon when the slanting light defines the varied contours of the mountains. It is said that in clear weather the view extends to eleven départements, one-eighth of the whole of France.

Puy de Dôme is subject to some strange weather phenomena. Sometimes, particularly in autumn, you can see scores of mountain tops in brilliant sunshine, while a couple of hundred metres below you nothing is visible but the carpet-flat, white top of cloud filling the valleys. During winter cold spells the temperature at the top of the mountain can be as much as 15°C higher than it is down below in Clermont. This happens when a mass of cold, heavy air slides down the mountain into the depressions. In summer the prevalence of hot air currents sweeping steadily up its slopes have made Puy de Dôme a favourite rendezvous for hang-gliders, probably the most important in Europe.

'Clermont the rich, Riom the beautiful' is an old saying in the region. Only 15km north of Clermont by N9 **Riom** is a dark, dignified and decorous place. Dark only in as much as many of its fine buildings are in the black Volvic stone, dignified from its attachment to its long and important history, decorous from an equally long association with the law — it is still the seat of the Courts of Appeal for Auvergne. It would never occur to the modern visitor that for centuries Riom rivalled Clermont for power and supremacy in Auvergne and, in some periods, was equally if not more important. But as Clermont-Ferrand grew, Riom did not. Most of the town still lies within the ring road which marks and replaces the old ramparts of the Middle Ages.

There are a number of things of considerable interest to see in Riom. Perhaps its greatest days were in the 14th century when Jean, Duc de Berry, one of the sons of King Jean II, was given the Duchy of Auvergne. He built a palace in Riom which became legendary for the sumptuous and grandiose style of the courts he held there (see pp. 19–20. When he died, an old man, he was bankrupt despite having owned a large part of France for most of his life, and having impoverished all the towns under his control through excessive taxation. This wonderful palace was pulled down in 1820 and the site is now occupied by the Law Courts (Palais de Justice). Only the Sainte-Chapelle, a copy of the one in Paris, remains. It has some good 16th-century stained glass, and can be visited by arrangement with the concierge of the Palais de Justice.

Around the corner in rue Delille, the Regional Museum of Auvergne occupies a fine 18th-century mansion. It has a superbly arranged collection showing all aspects of life in Auvergne prior to the Industrial Revolution, from the anti-wolf collars that the shepherds were obliged to put on their sheep to protect them, to the enclosed beds, the only place the peasants were ever warm in winter. The great variety of tools used in the traditional arts and crafts are also on display. The selection and arrangement of the exhibits is the work of the French ethnologist and museum specialist, Georges-Henri Rivière.

Nearby in rue de l'Hôtel de Ville, the Musée Mandet has an impressive collection of classical paintings from the 16th, 17th and 18th centuries, strong in Flemish and Dutch paintings as well as Italian, Spanish and French.

The Town Hall is installed in the early 16th-century mansion once the headquarters of the Intendants of Auvergne. It has an arcaded courtyard. On the first floor there is a small historical museum where you can see the original letter from Joan of Arc appealing to the generosity and loyalty of the people of Riom and asking them to supply gunpowder and arms. A little farther along on the opposite side of the road is another fine Renaissance mansion, called the Maison des Consuls, which has a splendid façade and an arcade along the street. At the Carrefour des Taules, with the Maison des Consuls behind you, rue de l'Horloge on the right has a number of old mansions with plenty of Renaissance detail, and also an old Clock Tower. Many of the ground floors are now occupied by shops, several with shop fronts which blend well with the period architecture.

On the opposite side to rue de l'Horloge, is rue de Commerce. On the left there is a pleasant little bar which offers snacks, *vin ordinaire* at very reasonable prices, and has modern toilets. At the other end of rue du Commerce is the Église Notre Dame de Marthuret, a 14th-century church which contains one of the great works of art of Auvergne. This is the statue known as the Vierge à l'Oiseau (Virgin with Bird) which was made to the order of Jean, Duc de Berry. It was saved from destruction during the French Revolution by the Butchers' Corporation who hid it in a cellar.

This tender and beautiful work shows the Virgin holding in her arms the child Jesus who is offering her a bird in his left hand. It illustrates a story from the Apocrypha. Jesus, about five years old, was playing on the ground making models of small birds from the mud. A Jewish passer-by stopped and criticised Mary for allowing the child to make models on the Sabbath. According to one translation Jesus clapped his hands and the birds flew away. In another version he blew gently on them, with the same result. The statue appears to represent the moment just before this happened, when Mary had picked him up, perhaps to remonstrate with him, and was immediately charmed by his offer of a bird. Unlike many statues of the Virgin and Child, where the two seem to have no connection with each other, this is quite clearly a mother and child and shows the love between them. On the central pillar of the doorway of the church there is a modern copy of this work. The original is inside on the altar of the first chapel on the right.

Less than 2km from Riom by D686, Mozac (sometimes spelt Mozat) also has a church of far from usual interest. The church of St. Pierre is what is left of an abbey which flourished throughout the Middle Ages. It was built in the 12th century and has been restored and in part rebuilt at various times. It is famous for its 44 carved capitals in the nave. Together with those of Notre-Dame-du Port, and those in the church of St. Nectaire Le Haut, they are considered to be the finest examples of Romanesque carving in Auvergne. The church was largely rebuilt in the 15th century, probably after an earthquake, and two of the capitals from the choir, destroyed at that time, have been placed on the ground at the entry to the nave. This enables one to appreciate at eye level the quality of the sculpture and composition. One shows the Holy Women at the Tomb of Christ after the Resurrection. Everything about it, the expression of the faces, the line of the silhouettes, the realism of the costumes, shows the work of a master. The second of these large capitals has a mysterious design for four men, kneeling with hands and feet apparently bound, with a decoration of vine branches and pine cones. No one seems to know what it represents.

There is another important artistic treasure in this church, the reliquary of St. Calmin, the man who founded the abbey of Mozac in AD680. This chest, 82cm long, is one of the best examples of Limoges enamel work in existence. It was made in 1168, and has fourteen panels of champlevé enamel. The church treasure includes another reliquary chest, of St. Austremoine, of painted wood, of much later date, probably 17th-century. It is one of the rare examples of this kind in France.

A few kilometres from Riom by D985 is a town of a different kind. **Châtelguyon**, which in Auvergne is always called Châtel, is built on a sunny, south-facing slope at the edge of the Monts Dôme. Though it is a spa town, it has none of the air of impending doom which lurks in some of them, but is cheerful, pleasant, full of gardens and flowers, parks and pine woods. It is crammed full of hotels and pensions from the most luxurious — the Splendide even has its own spa — down to the simplest family boarding house. If you do not want the hassle of Clermont-Ferrand, you might consider this as an alternative. All the sites mentioned in Riom, Clermont and Mozac can be seen with almost equal ease from here. Its church, St. Anne, makes an interesting change in that it has been decorated in modern style with windows in Baccarat crystal, and recent murals of Byzantine inspiration.

It is a pleasant cross-country drive from Châtelguyon to the small town of Volvic. Leave by D15 near the Parc de Chalusset. The road climbs for a few kilometres and then descends to the valley of the Ambène and the old village of Enval, where the river tumbles in little waterfalls out of a shady gorge. If you would like to see the End of the World (le Bout du Monde), it is just a ten-minute walk away along the side of this pretty stream.

From Enval the road follows the face of the mountain passing by the village of Crouzol, above which stand the ruins of the Château de Tournoël, probably head of the league of photogenic ruins throughout Auvergne. It is easier to reach from Volvic than from Crouzol.

Volvic itself is a place of limited and specialised interest. It is situated at the edge of lava fields created by eruptions of the Puy de la Nugère. This lava is the source of the Volvic stone — properly known as Andesite — which is today worked from open quarries. You can visit la Maison de la Pierre which, at the instigation of the Parc Regional des Volcans, has been installed in the first hundred metres of an underground gallery more than 5km long where stone was quarried for seven hundred years.

The stones were used in the construction of churches and other buildings for five hundred years before anyone bothered to find out what it was exactly. It was not until 1743 that a M. Jean-Étienne Guétard presented a paper before the Academy of Sciences establishing its volcanic origin. The famous Volvic mineral water, claimed to be the purest water in the world, comes from a natural underground reservoir in the heart of the Puy de la Nugère. Since it filters in its own time through 80m of porous volcanic rock, the claim is reasonable. The bottling plant is open to the public, and explanations of the methods of obtaining and bottling the water are given.

One kilometre from Volvic by a steep and narrow road are the ruins of the Château de Tournoël. There is still enough of this great, battered stone skeleton to evoke the life and spirit of the Middle Ages: enormous stone fireplaces that would have burned small tree trunks; a great reception room with vestiges of mural painting; the lord's chapel; a storeroom against times of siege with a water tank capable of holding 13,000 litres; a round keep with walls 4m thick and 32m high, from the battlements of which it would have been easy to see the slightest hostile move in the plains below; another square keep dating back to the 12th century. Tournoël was repeatedly captured and regained, battered and rebuilt. In easy imagination the banners wave above the walls, and the trumpets, the hoarse cries, the clash of metal on metal, echo faintly through the roofless, empty rooms.

The château was associated with some out-of-the-ordinary women. About 1500 it was the home of a pretty widow, Françoise de Talaru, who was only 21 and made it a centre for a free and easy life of hunting, parties and dances. But her brother-in-law, co-guardian of her daughter, did not approve of all the expense. She succeeded in turning him out of the castle but he went to the Sheriff of Montferrand who judged that Françoise was 'a sorceress, a magician, a Circe', and took away her rights over her daughter. It seems that the Sheriff judged her better than he realised at the time, because he turned out to be no match for her. First of all she persuaded the Sheriff's son to marry her daughter who was then only seven. Then, apparently she cast a spell on the Sheriff himself who promptly married her, but did not long survive the excitement.

In 1594 the chatelaine of the castle was a lady equally determined to have her own way but less subtly feminine. When the castle was taken by Catholic extremists opposed to the King, they

Where was Gergovia?

One of the important tourist sites in Auvergne is the battlefield of Gergovia, where the mighty Julius Caesar was defeated by the Gallic chieftain, Vercingetorix. You will find it a few kilometres south of Clermont-Ferrand, or perhaps on the hills a few kilometres to the north. Or possibly somewhere else. In the course of history the battlefield has been claimed by places as far apart as St. Flour and Moulins.

In the 16th century an Italian working for the Bishop of Clermont claimed to have found the true site after years of research. But had he? Nobody cared. Tourism was yet to come. It was three hundred years before his assertion received official support. The Emperor Napoleon III visited the site in 1862, gave official recognition to it, and changed the name of the local hamlet and plateau from Merdogne to Gergovie.

But years of archaeological digs have failed to convince scholars that the site really is that of the battlefield. But digs carried out by a M. Eychart on the hills *north* of Clermont have shown that *his* site was occupied from Neolithic until Roman times, and have revealed a small temple, and a ditch which, he says, linked the two Roman camps at the time of the battle. The debate continues with scholars favouring M. Eychart.

But as far as tourism is concerned Gergovia is where the Emperor Napoleon III said it was. It has been there now for more than a hundred years, and nobody is inclined to move it. Think what it would cost!

Anyway, it's a pleasant place, with a monument recalling the Emperor's visit, and splendid views over Clermont and in other directions. And if you are not actually at the real Gergovia, you could almost certainly see it from there. If only anyone knew for sure where it was.

turned out the chatelaine, Lucrèce de Gadagne, because her dead husband had been a royalist. She promptly organised a detachment of royal troops and attacked her own castle. The Catholics refused to surrender and the attackers had to bombard the castle with cannons and undermine the walls before they succeeded in retaking it. The lady Lucrèce knocked her castle to pieces but she got it back.

In 1632 it was captured by the normally unsuccessful Gaston d'Orléans, Cardinal Richelieu's bitter enemy, who hoped to use it in his armed struggle against the Cardinal. He ran true to form, failing again, with the result that it was one of the castles destroyed by order of Louis XIII and Richelieu.

Issoire, the third sous-préfecture of Puy-de-Dôme, is the old Protestant capital of Auvergne and had a bloody history during the religious wars between Huguenots and Catholics. Today it is a small but heavily industrial town, one of the few in Auvergne which has increased in size since the Second World War. It produces three-quarters of the aluminium products of France, heavily orientated towards the aircraft industry, as well as electrical goods and spare parts for cars.

It lies in the valley of the Allier on the N9 about 30km south of Clermont-Ferrand. Apart from the church of St. Austremoine, one of the most important Romanesque churches in Auvergne, and a few 15th-century houses in Place de la République, there is little to attract the tourist. The large and nobly proportioned church was so maltreated during the 19th century, when its steeple and façade were reconstructed, and its interior decorated in what might politely be described as extraordinary fashion, that it is a moot point as to whether it can be classed today as a work of art or a curiosity.

The riot of colour painted over the whole of the interior, pillars, capitals, arches, tribunes, vaulting, comes as a shock to the modern and northern mind accustomed to grey sobriety inside churches and cathedrals. But in the early Middle Ages it was quite usual to decorate church interiors in this way. The frescoes and stained glass windows were there to tell stories to the inquisitive but illiterate minds of the day, and the supplementary decoration paralleled that of illuminated manuscripts. What you see at St. Austremoine is a nineteenth-century attempt to recreate a medieval church interior, colourful, a touch mysterious, meant to inspire awe. It was the work of a man called Anatole Dauvergne who spent 60,000 gold francs and three years, 1857–1860, on the work. He may have succeeded in reproducing something that would have been exciting to the medieval mind, but that mind does not exist today, and the

How Giscard Became Giscard d'Estaing

The d'Estaings are one of the oldest and noblest families of Auvergne. Their fortunes were founded in 1214 at the Battle of Bouvines when a Pierre d'Estaing saved the life of King Philip Augustus. Over the centuries the d'Estaings provided many Bishops of Clermont, and a famous Admiral who was guillotined during the Revolution.

In 1790 Lucie-Madeleine d'Estaing married Guy, Comte de la Tour Fondue. In 1818, her daughter married a Barthélemy-Martial Giscard. Théophile Giscard, the son of this marriage, started a court action well over a hundred years ago seeking the right to add his grandmother's name, d'Estaing, to his own. The action went on for years and years, finally ending in victory for Théophile in 1922. He did not, however, a Giscard d'Estaing, for the good reason that he had already been dead for some time. The result was contested, presumably by members of the old d'Estaing family, but after three more years they lost their case.

So the Giscards became Giscards d'Estaing. The present Valéry Giscard d'Estaing, ex-President of France, is the great-grandson of Théophile, and despite the frequent snide remarks from his political opponents about his 'nobility', there is no doubt that he is entitled to the name.

modern visitor is likely to find the effect curious, but so unusual that it may well merit the journey.

Only the crypt escaped his attentions. It should be seen. It is as good as any in Auvergne and the noble simplicity and total absence of decoration provide a startling contrast with the rest. So, if by chance you like the painted church, the plain crypt will make it seem even better. If you do not like it, then the crypt will seem even finer than it is. The exterior of the choir, where the absidial chapels are decorated with a band of mosaics and a set of the signs of the zodiac, also merits attention.

In the valley of the Allier only 2km from Issoire by D996 is the Château of Parentignat. This is a more recent building than the majority of Auvergne castles. It is a classical 18th-century château built by the de Lastic family who still own it. It has been well-maintained and has never needed restoration. It merits a visit if only for the splendid interior decoration, the fine period furniture made in the best Parisian workshops, and the 20,000 volume library which includes some beautifully bound first editions. The paintings include Van Loo's portrait of Louis XV, a portrait of the Grand Dauphin by Rigaud, as well as works by Fantin-Latour and other well-known artists.

Distant view of Puy de Sancy, highest peak in Auvergne, 1885m

The drive from Clermont-Ferrand to St. Nectaire enables you to see two of the five most important Romanesque churches of Auvergne, two lakeside resorts, and takes you through majestic mountain scenery in the heart of the Parc Régional des Volcans.

From the ring road take N89 signposted to Le Mont-Dore and follow it as far as the village of Theix, about 15km, where you turn left on to D96 for **St. Saturnin**. After the village of Nadaillat this road climbs and for much of the way runs along the crest of the Montagne de la Serre, with panoramic views, before plunging into the valley of the Veyre. St. Saturnin is built on the ridge between the Veyre and the Monne. This ancient village with its time-worn houses nestled around the church, its Renaissance fountain in the square, and its feudal castle, is full of charm.

The castle was the home of one of the most influential families of medieval France, that of la Tour d'Auvergne. This family produced many people of destiny, cardinals, bishops, dukes, marshals, admirals, and the mothers, wives and mistresses of kings and princes. One of them was Madeleine de la Tour d'Auvergne who in 1513 married Lorenzo de Médicis and died in giving birth to a daughter, Catherine, who, by her marriage to Henri II, became Queen of France. Another was Louis XIV's most successful marshal, and one of France's greatest soldiers, known always just as le Grand Turenne. The family included the Viscounts of Turenne, the Dukes of Bouillon and the Barons of Murat.

The church, built about 1150, is not large and is very simple. But it is so well-proportioned that like Notre-Dame-du-Port it creates a powerful atmosphere of spirituality. Earlier churches were designed to make the worshipper feel that he was approaching God. In churches like this one the believer feels the presence of God around him.

From St. Saturnin take D213 up the valley of the Veyre through Ponteix and Rouillat-Bas, and 1km beyond this hamlet turn left on to D90 where it crosses D213. The road brings you at once to Lac d'Aydat. This pretty lake lies on the eastern flank of the Monts Dôme. It is a volcanic lake, though not a crater lake, and was formed when the Veyre filled in an irregular depression in the lava field produced by eruptions of Puy de la Vache. The stream flows in at one end and out at the other. The lake is surrounded by pine-covered slopes and is a kilometre long and up to a kilometre wide, large enough for most watersports. It is often the natural volcanic lakes which are best equipped for leisure activities because their water level remains constant, unlike that of the artificial barrage lakes. Lac d'Aydat has bathing beaches (supervised in season), waterside cafés with dancing in the evenings, canoes, pedalos and small yachts, good camping sites and holiday chalets. It is very popular with the inhabitants of Clermont-Ferrand, only about 25km distant, and summer weekends in season can be a scramble.

Even here there is ancient history. There is a small island near the north bank where Sidonius Apollinaris, the Roman poet, politician and Bishop of Clermont in the 5th century AD, had a holiday house.

A few kilometres north of Lac d'Aydat there is a similar but smaller lake, Lac de Cassière, and between them and in the woods around them there are several signposted footpaths for ramblers; green signs for long walks up to six hours, blue for the shorter ones.

From Aydat you can join the D5 south to Murol and then D996 for St. Nectaire, or find your way across country on narrow roads which call for a lot of caution in the high season.

Murol is a charming village set among open wooded hills on the banks of the Chambon stream with an impressive fortress standing guard above it. The castle is open to the public throughout the summer months.

The attraction of **St. Nectaire** is another superb Romanesque church in the upper part of the village. This is seen to advantage in the distance from several of the mountain roads in the neighbourhood, but its setting in relation to the village is rather spoiled by a large car park. As at St. Saturnin, the interior of the church seems larger than it is because of the harmony of its parts. The church has 103 carved capitals. Those on the 24 faces of the six columns of the choir provide an almost complete reference of Romanesque iconography. Among the themes treated are the apparition of the resurrected Christ to St. Thomas, the carrying of the Cross, scenes from the life and miracles of St. Nectaire, the Martyrs awakening to eternal life, and the misery of the damned. The capitals have been attributed to Rotbertus, the sculptor of those at Notre-Dame-du-Port.

Before leaving the church it is worth putting a coin in the time switch to illuminate the church treasure. The best item is a 12th-century bust of St. Baudime in copper chased with gold, and a Virgin in majesty from the same period carved in wood and painted.

There are hundreds of places named after saints in Auvergne, and at least a hundred different saints' names are used. Once you start wondering who they all were, all kinds of irreverent ideas come crowding in. It seems that in the early days of Christianity in Auvergne you were nobody if you were not a saint.

Certainly the last distinction that St. Nectaire would have expected would be to have a cheese named after him, though it was undoubtedly being made in his time, about the third century AD. Today, St. Nectaire is one of the best-known cheeses in France and is made in almost every village in the Monts Dore, except in St. Nectaire itself. The nearby village of Besse-en-Chandesse (new name, not much used, is Besse-et-St. Anastiase) is an important centre with a cheese market on Mondays.

Besse can be reached from St. Nectaire via Murol but you might first like to carry on for a couple of kilometres beyond Murol to Lac Chambon. This is another pretty volcanic lake formed in exactly the same way as Lac d'Aydat, and very much like it except that it has several little islands. It, too, is a summer resort with the same range of equipment as Lac d'Aydat, and several hotels with restaurants. Like Aydat it is popular with people from Clermont and becomes crowded on summer weekends.

Besse (D5 from Murol) is an old town which has increased its prosperity with the development over the past twenty years of the winter sports resort of **Super-Besse** on the large snowfields

Overleaf: *The spa town of La Bourbole, where the Dordogne is just a mountain stream*

between the Puy Chambourget, the Puy Pallaret, and the southern slopes of the massif de Sancy. Super-Besse is well-equipped both for alpine and cross-country skiing, and there is a cable-car linking it to the summit of Puy de Sancy. Besse has several hotels (one of which, the Mouflon, has a 1-star Michelin restaurant) open from the beginning of June to the end of September, and again for the winter sports season. Those at Super-Besse open in the summer only during July and August.

Within a few kilometres of Besse are several of the most attractive crater lakes in Auvergne. One of them, Lac Pavin, is a classical crater lake, almost perfectly round, and very deep, 92m. It is surrounded by thick pine forest. The ancients found something sinister and mysterious about it. The name is said to derive from the Latin *pavens* meaning alarming or frightening. It was believed that to throw a stone in it would unleash terrible storms. They say, too, that at certain times the sound of bells can be heard from a submerged church and that the original village of Besse lies drowned down there, swallowed up in some act of divine punishment.

The only authentic drowned villages are those beneath the water of the artificial lakes created by hydro-electric barrages, such as Naussac, near Langogne, in Lozère. From time to time when such reservoirs are emptied to clean them, the old houses are exposed, blackened by mud, their windows gaping, the low walls which surrounded their gardens still visible, sometimes the village bridge and a few skeleton trees. Grass begins to grow again, patches of green appear. One would think that the village was about to return to life. People out walking follow the old paths, but it is not long before the waters return, and the fish again swim in and out of the windows of the drowned houses.

Lac Pavin is a mecca for anglers who seek its enormous trout and that delight of French gourmets, the *omble chevalier,* which English dictionaries tend to describe as char, or hill trout. I wonder. The translation of the names of fish and plants from French to English and vice versa is in my experience a vague and rather haphazard business.

There are equally attractive, and less frequented lakes nearby, such as Chauvet, 12km on the road towards la Tour-d'Auvergne, D203, and the lakes of Bourdouze and Montcineyre on either side of D36 to Compains. Lac de Montcineyre is about a kilometre from the road. It is another favourite with anglers, being thickly populated with trout, perch and pike.

Between Besse-en-Chandesse and Le Mont-Dore you have a choice of two routes equally spectacular, steep and tortuous, and both offering panoramic mountain views. One is by D5 back to Murol, and then by D996 past Lac Chambon and on to the Col de la Croix Morand and down into Le Mont-Dore. The other is by D36 from Besse and perhaps this is the one to be preferred, especially if you have already been to Lac Chambon. D36 takes you to the Valley of Chaudefour, a wild and remote place closed at one end by the Cirque de Chaudefour and on both sides by steep slopes which rise 600m from the valley floor, already at 1,200 m. Both flanks are laced with waterfalls and here and there rough spikes of volcanic rock stand like petrified sentries waiting for a change of guard. The best part of a hundred years ago it was planned to set up a thermal establishment here but in this savage and, in winter, often inacessible place, the scheme was fortunately found to be impractical. One building, called the Chalet St. Anne, exists but the area is now a protected zone within the Parc des Volcans and no more will be built. An unsurfaced road leads into the valley as far as the Chalet St. Anne. If you are anxious about your shock absorbers, leave the car and walk a kilometre or so into the valley. It is a paradise for nature lovers with flowers throughout spring and summer, and it is one of the places where you may see mouflons, the wild mountain sheep, on the upper slopes.

From here the road continues to the hamlet of Monaux and on to the Col de la Croix de St. Robert at over 1,400m with superb views, then down into Le Mont-Dore.

This little town is one of the more active spas in Auvergne and is also a centre for winter sports. As a spa it specialises in asthma and other respiratory diseases and rheumatism. It is not uncommon to see patients padding about the streets in slippers and flannel dressing gowns.

Le Mont-Dore was one of the favourite spas of the Romans. Their establishment here was much larger than the present spa. There are some slight remains of the Roman spa within the modern building. If it interests you to see what a thermal establishment is like without actually taking the treatment, this is your chance. Accompanied visits take place several times a day, apart from Sundays and official holidays, from 15th May to 30th September.

Spa towns tend to differ from other towns in that they are often situated in spots where none of the usual reasons for the existence of a town apply. Le Mont-Dore is a classic example of this, being confined to a narrow valley blocked by a mountain at one end, and so is much longer than it is wide, a form common in villages but seeming curious and unnatural in even a small town. The advent of tourism has modified this atmosphere by creating a more obvious justification for the town. Le Mont-Dore now has three times as many visitors annually for winter sports as it does for the spa.

A wide straight road leads from Le Mont-Dore the 4½km to the upper slopes of Puy de Sancy where there is a cable-car by which you can continue to the summit. Chalets, holiday villages and mountain-style hotels have been built in the vicinity of this road. The old road, narrow and tortuous, still exists and is used for the descent back to Le Mont-Dore, one-way traffic only.

In the town itself there is a funicular up to what they call the Salon du Capucin, a large, alpine meadow edged with pine and beech woods. In summer it provides the ideal place for patients and tourists to walk and get some fresh air, and in winter it is the starting point for a number of cross-country ski runs.

There are those who say that **La Bourboule**, 7km away and 200m lower down the valley, is a livelier and pleasanter place than Le Mont-Dore. For the casual visitor it is difficult to see why. Both are spa towns enclosed in the same narrow, wooded valley. Both have the same stream flowing through them, a little wider in La Bourboule but still hardly a river, though it is the Dordogne. Both are old-fashioned

spas which are trying, and modestly succeeding, to be modern winter sports resorts. They are obliged by the valley to have a similar lay-out and their architecture has much in common, with the slight variation that in La Bourboule the Dordogne is crossed by fancy bridges in shades of pastel pink and grey, looking ready for a costumed chorus to assemble and launch into something from 'The Merry Widow'. La Bourboule specialises in allergies rather than asthma so is altogether different from Le Mont-Dore for those who seek treatment for either of these conditions. For the majority of tourists there can be little to choose between them in summer. They have each about the same number of hotels and restaurants, and the same excursions can be conveniently made from either. In winter Le Mont-Dore must have a slight advantage, being higher up in a region where snowfalls below 1,000m are by no means certain every winter.

An enjoyable excursion from La Bourboule or Le Mont-Dore is to Orcival and the Manor of Cordès. Leave Le Mont-Dore by D986 in the direction of St. Nectaire but fork left after a kilometre or so on to D983 towards Clermont-Ferrand. The road runs through forest and then through a rocky valley to the Lac de Guéry, then up to the Col de Guéry at 1264m. From this point there is a spectacular view between the twin rocks of Tuilière and Sanadoire, which stand like gigantic gateposts at the top and on either side of the steep and wooded Cirque de Chausse, into the valley beyond and

The twin peaks of Roche Tuilerie and Roche Sanadoire, as seen from the Col de Guéry

Notre-Dame d'Orcival: a capital showing the punishment of the rich in Hell

away into the far distance. Do not take D80 from the Col de Guéry to Rochefort-Montagne, but continue on D983, then fork left for Orcival by D27.

Orcival is a pleasant little place nestling among hills and on the banks of the Sioulet, a short tributary of the Sioule, which you may have seen at St. Pourçain in the Bourbonnais. Even if you arrive in Orcival in early winter, as I did, it is easy to see that the village is a tourist centre from the number of hotels. Really it is more than that. It has been for centuries and still is a place of pilgrimage. It has a beautiful Romanesque church, many people would say the best in Auvergne. Such things are always a matter of personal taste and I think I prefer Notre-Dame-du-Port. One is a country church and the other in the middle of a city but in themselves they have much in common.

Notre-Dame d'Orcival is not the largest or the tallest of the Romanesque churches of Auvergne but there is none more 'right', as the antique dealers say. There was a light drift of snow over the village on the morning when I was in Orcival, no one apart from myself in the church. Perhaps the combination of circumstances, the stillness and silence which snow always seems to bring to the country, my isolation in the church, added something to its impressiveness for me. Even a momentary solitude concentrates the mind.

But the beauty of a church, like that of a boat, is a subtle business. Two boats may be the same size, have the same number of masts, similar superstructure, approximately the same lines to the hull. Yet one is beautiful and one is ordinary. Two churches may each have porch, nave, transept, choir, absidial chapels, may date from the same period, be approximately of the same proportions, and yet feel quite different. Subtleties of lighting, variations in details, in the use of the raw material, other things too complex to analyse pour into the mind and an impression is distilled. Notre-Dame-des-Miracles at Mauriac and Orcival will serve as examples from many. The church at Mauriac, fine though it is, is sombre almost to the point of gloominess; Orcival at once uplifts the spirit. The way the light falls in the interior of Orcival, rather more strongly on the choir than elsewhere, has a lot to do with it.

The church was founded by the monks of the abbey of La Chaise-Dieu (pp. 176–81) who had it built in the first half of the 12th century and with such unity that it appears to have been supervised by one man throughout. Apart from some repairs necessary after earthquake damage in the 15th century, and the early 19th-century rebuilding of the spire, damaged in the French Revolution, it is still all 12th-century, as it was built. Even the iron-work on the three sets of wooden doors, the powerful hinges decorated with human faces and birds, is that put there when the church was built. In those days apparently they had the secret of casting iron that would not rust; these hinges seem as good as ever after more than 700 years.

The exterior of the church is notable for the fact that its grace, positive as it is, comes entirely from the balance of the construction with hardly any ornamentation at all. The interior is also simple. The capitals of the slender pillars are for the most part carved with leaves, birds and demons, though one shows the traditional theme of the punishment of the miser.

On the stand behind the altar is a Virgin in Majesty, a seated Mary with the infant Jesus upright on her lap, a remote and rather severe composition, if you compare it, for instance, with the Virgin with the Bird in Riom. This statue dates from the same period as the Church (it was successfully hidden away during the religious and revolutionary troubles) and is carved in wood, painted and adorned with plaques of silver. This decoration was carefully restored in 1960. It is only 74 cm tall but gleaming in the light of the candles it has a kind of magnetism. It is a more refined work than most from this early period, also a little strange. The face of the Virgin is elongated and curiously lop-sided; the left side is that of a peasant girl, while the right shows nobility. It is worth remarking that almost all the carved Virgins in Auvergne churches, unlike those in early paintings, have quite clearly the faces of ordinary young women of the region. You still see the same faces in the streets and supermarkets. In this case the hands, for some reason redone and not very well in the 17th century, are also those of a working girl. Before leaving the church it is worth looking at the crypt which exactly reproduces the plan of the choir and is one of the finest in Auvergne. It contains a 14th-century Virgin and Child in wood as well as an altar in gilded lead by a modern sculptor, Kaeppelin.

Every year at the time of the Ascension there is an important pilgrimage to Notre-Dame d'Orcival. The Virgin is carried in torchlight procession to a place above the village where she is said to have been found nearly eight hundred years ago. It is in some ways a modern as well as a very ancient celebration, popular with young people and what used to be called 'hippies' who bring their guitars to the Midnight Mass. In recent years Notre-Dame d'Orcival has been adopted by gypsies as a patron saint and they, too, attend in numbers. The gypsies marry among themselves without the blessing of the Church but they believe strongly in baptism and bring dozens of children to the church for this ceremony.

Two kilometres north of Orcival by D27 and D216 is one of the most attractive country houses in France, the Manor of Cordès. It is really rather more than a manor though not quite a château in the grand style. It is approached by a splendid avenue of lime trees and then by tree-covered walks (the trees are hornbeams) which serve as a green background to the very attractive classic French gardens laid out in 1695 by Le Nôtre, the landscape gardener of the Palace of Versailles. Him again? you say. I agree. It is easy to get the impression that there was no one else in the business.

The house was built in the 13th century by a man called Guillaume de Chalus. In the 15th century it was extended and strengthened, being surrounded by high, defensive walls. The property passed by inheritance to the Marquis d'Allègre and the interior contains many souvenirs brought from the Château d'Allègre near La Chaise-Dieu. In the chapel there is a fine marble tomb of Yves II d'Allègre, a Marshal of France killed at the Battle of Ravenna in 1512. In the late 17th century another Marquis d'Allègre demolished the defensive walls, removed some of the battlements, put in more windows and generally made the house the charming and livable place it is today. The interior has the special interest and welcome of a historic house which has always been lived in and lovingly maintained. Each room has its own style, Louis XIII, Louis XV, Italian Renaissance, and so on. In the cellars the old guard room, or servants' quarters, still has the original well with winch and wheel.

From Cordès the D216 joins the N89 at Rochefort-Montagne for an easy return to La Bourboule. On the way the road which, for once, is not especially picturesque, passes through the village of Laqueuille. This unprepossessing village had two claims to fame both of them now forgotten.

Notre-Dame d'Orcival, one of the finest examples of the Romanesque style in Auvergne

It was the birthplace and home of Antoine Victor de Mornac who for twenty-five years robbed, murdered and terrorised the population round about. He is perhaps the most notorious of the many brigands of Auvergne and in the immediate region his name lingers on in folk memory, and not long ago was still invoked to persuade childen into good behaviour. In his day, the first half of the 19th century, he was so feared that it was the custom for people parting from each other on the road to say, 'Good-bye and God save you from Mornac'.

In 1850 at about the same time as Mornac was to be arrested for the murder of a farmer and to be condemned for the last time, another local man, Antoine Roussel, was engaged in something a good deal more homely and comfortable. He was a farmer who spent his spare time experimenting in cheese-making. He eventually produced the first of the now famous Bleu d'Auvergne, the poor man's Roquefort, from which it differs in being made entirely from cows' milk, instead of the milk of ewes. Unlike other local cheeses, St. Nectaire and Cantal, sometimes farm-made and sometimes factory-made, Bleu d'Auvergne these days is all factory-made.

Mornac, serving a life sentence, died in prison, nobody knows when. Antoine Roussel has a bust in his honour in the village, and his cheese is still sometimes called Bleu de Laqueuille.

Just beyond Laqueuille N89 turns off to the west, and D922 continues south to the junction with D996 on the left for La Bourboule. If you are leaving Puy-de-Dôme, D922 will take you south and into the département of Cantal, another part of the old Auvergne full of interest and attractions, and the subject of the next chapter.

Black Virgins

Throughout Auvergne, where the worship of the Virgin Mary is particularly strong, many of the statues of the Virgin are carved in dark walnut or cedar; with the passage of centuries these have become completely black. The origin of the black Virgins is lost in the mists of antiquity but is believed to be linked in the early days of Christianity to aspects of Byzantine worship seen by the Crusaders. Some of them are known to have been copied from icons, and the most famous, that of the cathedral of Notre-Dame-du-Puy, at Le Puy-en-Velay, was originally brought back from the Holy Land by St. Louis (Louis IX) after the seventh crusade. This original was burned during the Revolution, but another black Virgin was installed in its place in the 19th century.

Though they retained their blackness, the faces of the later Virgins changed from those of icons to those of the peasant girls of Auvergne. They are found in churches throughout this part of France. Among the best known are those at Mauriac, Besse-en-Chandesse, Murat, Notre-Dame-du-Port in Clermont, Notre-Dame-des-Neiges in Aurillac, and Marsat. Important pilgrimages still take place, especially at Le Puy on 15th August, when there is a procession through the town, and at Notre-Dame-du-Port on the Sunday after 14th May, also followed by a procession. At Besse-en-Chandesse there are two annual pilgrimages to the Virgin. On the first Sunday in July the little statuette is taken, accompanied by a large crowd, the three kilometres up to the mountain chapel of Vassivières, where she spends the summer. In September, in a ceremony known as the *dévalade*, the statuette is brought back to the church in Besse. The religious occasion is followed by a lively celebration in the town, entirely secular in style.

Overleaf: *The medieval manor of Coirdes; grounds laid out by Le Nôtre*

General Information

BESSE-EN-CHANDESSE Information: Office de Tourisme, pl Grand-Mèze (73.79.52.84).
Where to stay: Best hotel is the Mouflons, rte de Super-Besse (73.79.51.31). For something less expensive try the Levant (73.79.50.17). There are also two good hotels at Super-Besse, open only in July and August, and for winter sports.
Where to eat: The Mouflons has a one star Michelin restaurant.

LA BOURBOULE Information: Office de Tourisme, pl de l'Hôtel-de-Ville (73.81.07.99).
Where to stay: Good range of average hotels. The Parc, quai Mar-Fayolle (73.81.01.77) and the Aviation, rue de Metz (73.81.09.77) have most rooms.
Where to eat: The Auberge de Tournebride, 1.5km on D88 towards Clermont-Ferrand is pleasant. Also has eight bedrooms (73.81.01.91).

CHÂTELGUYON Information: Office de Tourisme, Parc Étienne Clementel (73.86.01.17).
Where to stay: Only 20km from Clermont and a useful alternative with several first-class hotels and many others, nearly all with restaurants. A hotel town. The Paris, 1 rue du Dr-Levadoux (73.86.00.12), near the Casino, is representative of the better than average.
Where to eat: Le Manoir Fleuri (73.86.01.27) just outside the town on D415 towards Chazeron. Le Clé des Champs a few km away at Enval (see p. 104) is another very good restaurant.

CLERMONT-FERRAND Information: Office de Tourisme: at the railway station, and also 69 bd Gergovia (73.93.30.20).
Where to stay: The city has a wide selection of hotels from the Altea-Gergovia (73.93.05.75) (see p. 98) all the way down to several which are cheap and basic. The Colbert, 19 rue Colbert (73.93.25.66) is quite large and reasonable, but has no restaurant.
Where to eat: The restaurant in the Buffet Gare Routière (Bus Station first floor) is surprisingly good. Also to be recommended the Auvergnat, the restaurant of the Hôel St. André, a little way from the centre on av de l'Union Soviétique, near the railway station (73.91.40.40). There are many others.

ISSOIRE Information: Syndicat d'Initiative, pl General de Gaulle (73.89.15.90).
Where to stay: Issoire is not really a tourist town. There are a few hotels, mostly without restaurants. I suggest the Tourette, 4km away at Parentignat (73.55.01.78).
Where to eat: Restaurant La Bergerie at Sarpoil (73.71.02.54), 11km by D996 and D999. A one-star Michelin establishment, and so not cheap, but memorable. Otherwise this is a good area to go shopping (before 12) and make up your own picnic.

LE MONT-DORE Information: Office de Tourisme, av General Leclerc (73.81.18.88), town centre.
Where to stay: There are plenty of hotels of average to modest standard with little to choose between them.
Where to eat: The restaurant of the Cascades hotel (73.65.01.36) is among the best. Le Pistounet (73.65.00.67), at Genestoux, on D996 towards Murat le Quaire, is good but small. Advisable to telephone.

ORCIVAL Information: Ask at the Mairie.
Where to stay: Several small hotels in this village. Try L'Ajasserie d'Orcival (73.65.81.54).
Where to eat: Les Bourelles used to have a simple but good restaurant. Closed in 1987 but may have reopened. Otherwise the hotel mentioned above.

RIOM Information: Office de Tourisme, 16 rue du Commerce (73.38.59.45).
Where to stay: It's a small town with three small hotels, none with a restaurant. I suggest the Mikege (73.38.07.66). La Caravelle (73.38.31.90) has more rooms and is cheaper.
Where to eat: Restaurant Les Petits Ventres, 6 rue A.-Dubourg (73.38.21.65).

ST. NECTAIRE Information: Office de Tourisme, in the Old Thermal Establishment (73.88.50.86, high season) and Mairie (73.88.50.41).
Where to stay: Savoy Hotel (73.88.50.28), or the Paix (73.88.50.20) or the Modern (73.88.50.04). Average prices.
Where to eat: The restaurant of the Modern Hotel, upper town, is well known for quality/value.

THIERS Information: Office de Tourisme, pl du Pirou (73.80.10.74).
Where to stay: Limited hotel resources in the town and the area. At ordinary level the best bet is probably the Avenue (73.80.10.05) at Pont-de-Dore 6km on road to Clermont. At Bort l-Étang, 16km to the south-west, near Lezoux, there is one of the few luxury château hotels in Auvergne, the Château de Codignat. Expensive. (73.68.43.03)
Camp site: at Bort l'Étang.
Where to eat: Chez la Mère Dépalle, also at Pont-de-Dore (73.80.10.05). This restaurant also has ten bedrooms.

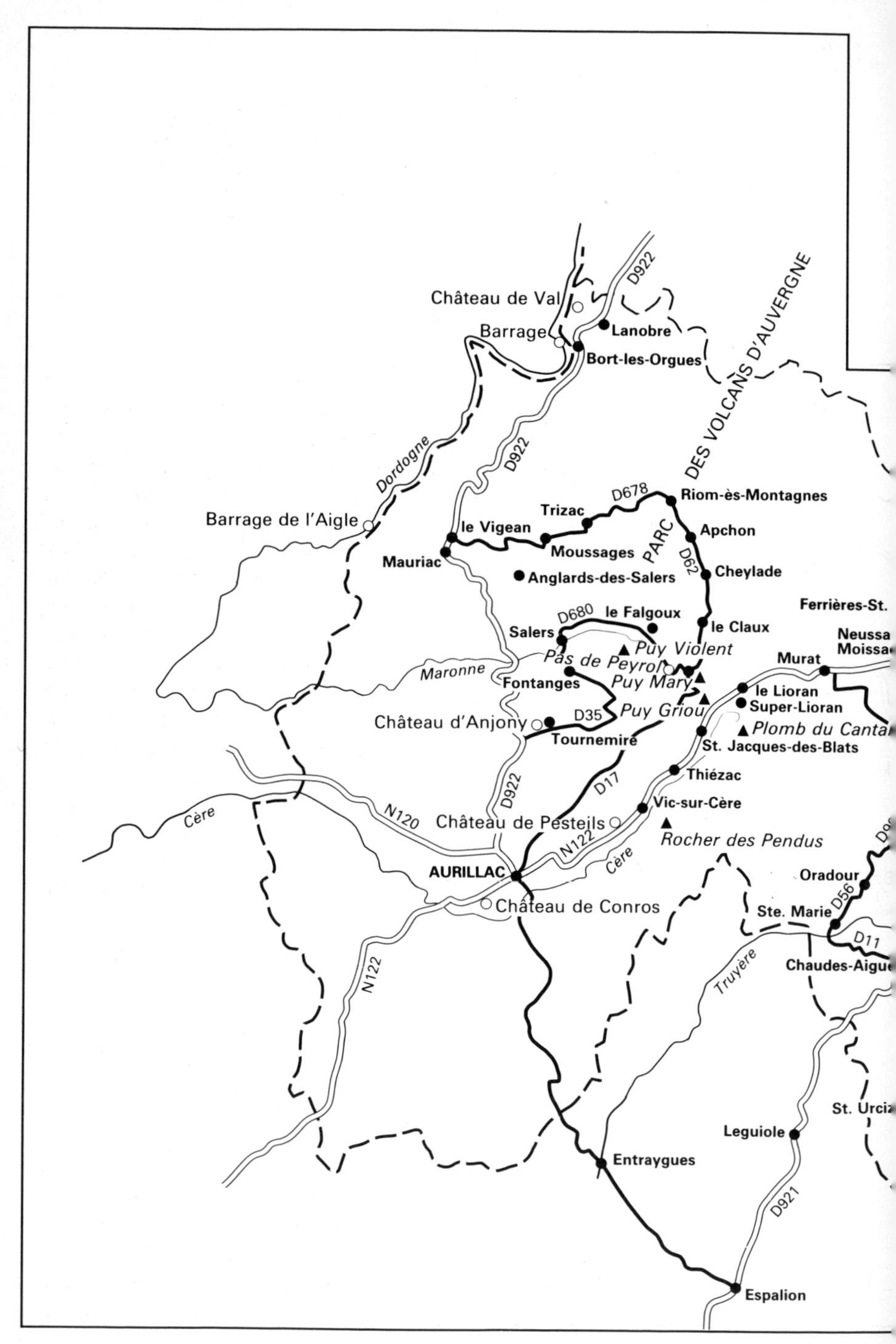
Château de Val
Barrage
Lanobre
Bort-les-Orgues
D922
PARC DES VOLCANS D'AUVERGNE
Dordogne
Barrage de l'Aigle
le Vigean
Mauriac
Trizac
D678
Riom-ès-Montagnes
Apchon
Moussages
D62
Cheylade
Anglards-des-Salers
Ferrières-St.
le Falgoux
D680
Salers
le Claux
Neussa
Moissa
Puy Violent
Pas de Peyrol
Murat
Maronne
Fontanges
Puy Mary
le Lioran
Super-Lioran
Château d'Anjony
D35
Puy Griou
Plomb du Canta
Tournemire
St. Jacques-des-Blats
Thiézac
D17
Cère
N120
Château de Pesteils
Vic-sur-Cère
Rocher des Pendus
N122
AURILLAC
Château de Conros
Oradour
D56
Ste. Marie
D11
Truyère
Chaudes-Aigu
St. Urci
Leguiole
Entraygues
D921
Espalion

7
Cantal

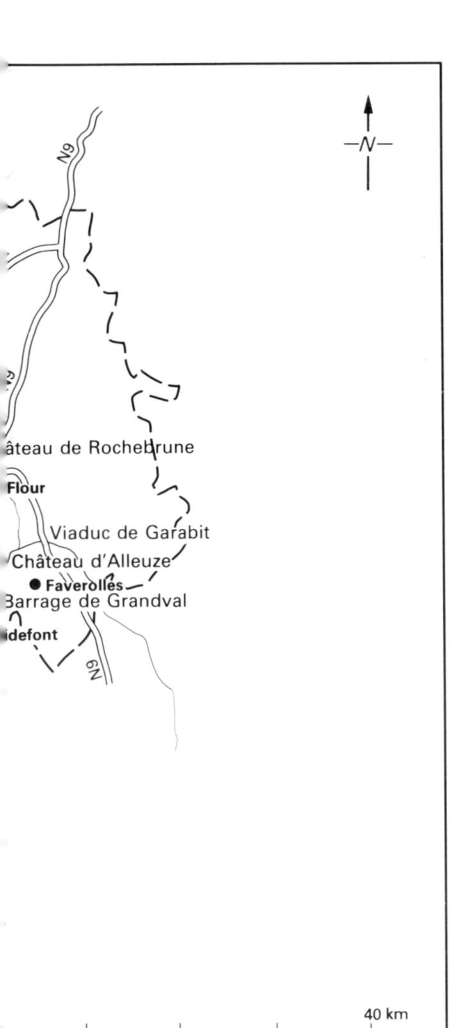

When Mount Vesuvius erupted catastrophically in AD79, blowing off the top of the mountain and burying the cities of Pompeii and Herculaneum, it was not even known that it was a volcano. There was no record of any previous eruption, no folk memory, not even a legend. A few savants said, after the event, that they had suspected that it might be, but nothing was known. It was so long before another eruption that the volcano was believed to have become extinct, but in 1631 it erupted again very seriously, and again in 1906.

Modern volcanologists, who know considerably more about the subject than their Roman equivalents did, seriously believe that every one of the volcanoes in Auvergne really is extinct. They say that the Monts du Cantal are all that remains of one enormous volcano, three times as high as Vesuvius, and more than 100km around at the base. This huge mountain was broken down by the glaciers of the Ice Ages, then by countless thousands of years of erosion by weather and running water. Among the peaks existing today that were once part of that same volcano are Puy Griou, Puy Mary, Puy Violent and Plomb du Cantal.

Broadly speaking, the peaks and uplands of Cantal occupy the centre of

The picturesque Château de Val on the lakeside at Lonabre near Bort-les-Orgues

the département and most of the practical bases for holidays or tours are situated on the lower slopes or in the valleys which surround them.

Coming from the north, the natural route into Cantal is by D922 which branches off N89 from Clermont-Ferrand. Almost as soon as you have crossed into the département there is something well worth seeing. At the village of Lanobre turn right for a short detour of about 2km to the Château de Val. This very photogenic 15th-century château, like a fairy-tale castle, once overlooked a green valley but has been given an even more beautiful setting through the courtesy of the French Electricity Authority who, by building a barrage on the Dordogne at Bort-les-Orgues, flooded the valley, leaving the Château de Val picturesquely sited on a rocky islet at the edge of a lovely lake.

The interior of the château does not quite match the glamorous promise of the exterior but there are some fine staircases and two splendid Renaissance fireplaces. It now belongs to the town of Bort-les-Orgues and serves as a setting for exhibitions every summer. There is a beach with supervised bathing next to the château, and motor boat trips can be taken on the lake, 18km long, and to the Gorges of the Dordogne. In high season the château is floodlit every night.

Wherever you are in the world and not quite sure of the way, a polite enquiry is often met with a complicated explanation including the words 'You can't miss it'. Unless it's something like the Eiffel Tower or the Taj Mahal, you can and probably will. But no one approaching Bort-les-Orgues by road could possibly miss the great concrete wall, 700,000 cubic metres of it, which forms this first barrage on the Dordogne, It's there just on your right and so much bigger and higher than you expect. Just before the town, on the right, a road leads to the barrage and crosses the top of it with lovely views of the lake. At one end there is another base for motorboat trips.

This barrage is the first step in the water staircase of the Dordogne which controls the flow of the river. There are four others almost equally important, Marèges, l'Aigle, Chastang and Sablier, which is in Limousin. Together they produce five per cent of France's electricity. Inside the hydro-electric station at the barrage of Bort-les-Orgues there is an interesting model, with sound commentary, of the whole hydro-electric system of the Massif Central.

The 'Orgues' in the name Bort-les-Orgues are huge blocks of basalt forming cliffs up to 100m high about 2km long. They were given the name *orgues* because of their alleged similarity in shape to organ pipes. It is true that they are tall and narrow, though not particularly regular in pattern. They are created by the cooling of a particular kind of lava. Similar formations exist in other places in the Massif Central but these at Bort are the most impressive, and are bound to interest geologists. They can be reached by D127, a turning off D979. A short drive brings you to Chantéry and just outside this village there are some steps on the right which lead to the foot of the Orgues.

There is nothing much of interest to the tourist in Bort-les-Orgues itself, and having seen the Château de Val, the Barrage and the Orgues, it is probably better to give the town itself a miss and carry on to **Mauriac**.

This is a quiet little town, with three quiet little hotels, which come to life only on market days. The church in the main square, Notre-Dame-Des-Miracles, is the largest Romanesque church in this part of Auvergne. It was built in the 12th century and I think it is fair to say that its size is the most striking thing about it. The interior is simple, sombre and without distinction. There is a very early font in stones of different colours, and a Black Virgin, carved in walnut wood, to whom a pilgrimage is made on the first Sunday after 9th May (see p. 123).

Mauriac lies on the eastern edge of some of the wildest and most deserted country in western Auvergne. It is a good centre for trout fishing and excursions. The road north to Neuvic crosses the Gorges of the Dordogne not far from the Barrage de l'Aigle, a lonely and beautiful spot. The road south to Pleaux and Laroquebrou snakes down into the valley of the Maronne, steep-sided, thickly forested, empty. Lovely to look at but not the place to run out of petrol.

The Barrage de l'Aigle, neither as high nor as long as the Barrage of Bort-les-Orgues, and holding back less than half as much water, 225 million cubic metres as against 470 million, produces, for reasons that only engineers can guess at, more than thirty per cent more electricity.

From Mauriac you can carry on south to the préfecture of Cantal, Aurillac, on D922. Alternatively, you can turn off left to Anglards-des-Salers and Salers, shortly after leaving Mauriac. But I suggest that those who want to explore the really splendid scenery of Cantal should choose instead D678 to Riom-ès-Montagnes, and to return from there across country to Salers, and from there to St. Cernin and Aurillac.

To follow this route turn back from Mauriac north on D922 but after a kilometre or so turn right at le Vigean on to D678. The road takes you up on to high plateaux and down into deep valleys but, apart from places where there are exceptional views, there is no particular reason to stop before reaching Riom-ès-Montagnes. The best view points are just north of Moussages, and again just after Trizac where there is a section of road with good views to the north.

Riom-ès-Montagnes unites most aspects of life in Cantal in one little town (*ès* in place names means 'of' or 'next to' — Riom of the Mountains). It has sawmills and wood industries; it has a distillery making alcohol from the gentian plant which grows profusely on

Overleaf: *The Château de Val, a fairy-tale castle reflected in the waters of the barrage lake near Bort-les-Orgues*

the Cantal uplands. It is the roots which are used, and the end product is an apéritif. It has several mechanised dairies, factories, if you prefer, making Cantal cheese and Bleu d'Auvergne. It is famous for its cattle fairs, bringing together cattle farmers and milk and cheese producers from all over the Massif Central.

It is still possible in this area to see the Cantal cheeses being made by hand in a *buron* high on the mountain slopes. To remove the last drop of whey from the freshly made cheese the farmer would roll up his trousers and kneel on top of it for an hour or more. When he got down, almost too stiff to move, a hair from his knees would sometimes be left embedded in the top of the cheese. These hairs were recognised by connoisseurs as a guarantee of authenticity. 'This', they would tell each other, 'is the real thing'. If you would like to see Cantal being made, you can probably arrange it through the local Tourist Office.

The road which runs from Riom to Puy Mary via the valley of the Cheylade and from Puy Mary on to Salers passes through the heart of the Parc Régional des Volcans. This road is one of the loveliest and most spectacular to be found anywhere. Narrow, winding, clinging to the side of the mountains, soaring between the peaks, diving into valleys with sparkling streams, then high above them with a drop so sharp that you hesitate to look down, particularly if you are the driver, it inspires in succession awe, apprehension, and boundless admiration.

Leave Riom by D3 in the direction of Murat and take the first turning on the right, the narrow D49 which dominates from a considerable height a lovely valley. With herds of red Salers cattle grazing on the green slopes, the ruined castle of **Apchon** above, the view seems to embrace in one glance the essence of Cantal. This impression is strengthened by the village of Apchon itself with its heavy stone-tiled roofs and the rugged old drinking fountain in the square. The ruins of the Château d'Apchon are a ten-minute climb from the village and the view in all directions is superb, especially to the south down the valley of the Cheylade to Puy Mary.

A 5km detour from Apchon brings you to a small chapel hidden in a clump of trees, called la Font Sainte. Every summer on 2nd July a statue of the Virgin is taken from the church in the neighbouring village of St. Hippolyte and placed in this chapel. Four times during the summer the shepherds make a pilgrimage here, the most important on the last Thursday of August, and the final one on 8th September, when the statue is carried back to the village church.

Return to D49, down into the valley, over the stream, and up into **Cheylade**. Almost every village in the Massif Central has a church with at least one interesting feature, or a few old houses, or a ruined castle, or all three. Clearly, no tourist will have the time to stop to look at all of them. There is one thing in the church at Cheylade which is rare, a vaulted ceiling panelled with hundreds of squares of oak decorated with brightly coloured designs of angels, flowers and animals.

Cheylade has a nice little hotel popular with anglers who come to fish for the plentiful local trout. About 2km beyond the village a narrow road on the right leads to a pretty waterfall, the Cascade de Sartre, only about 100m off the road. Close by is another, the

Cascade de la Roche, and a footpath leads to the adjacent Lac des Cascades, also well known for its trout. If it is the right time of day, and particularly either side of the July–August high season, you should be able to find a nice private spot for a picnic hereabouts.

Return to D262 and the village of le Claux, where there is another small hotel popular with anglers. As you leave le Claux there are marvellous views down the valley of the Cheylade with Puy Mary as a backdrop. The cliffs begin to close in on both sides of the valley and you seem to be driving into a dead end but the road attacks the flank in a series of hairpin bends and brings you up to the Pas de Peyrol. As you climb there are splendid views back down the valley of the Cheylade, of the valley of Impradine, to the Monts Dore, and to the north-west to the plateau of Cezallier.

At the **Pas de Peyrol**, at nearly 1,600m the highest pass on a motor road in the Massif Central, there is parking space, two hotels and a snack bar. On a fine day you really ought to stop here because it is one of two places in Auvergne where you can get close to the summit of one of the highest peaks by car. From Pas de Peyrol a signposted footpath leads to the summit of Puy Mary, where you are in the heart of the Massif Central with an unforgettable panorama on all sides.

The walk takes only half an hour in each direction (the ground is rough and solid shoes are advisable) and you will not be alone, but even if it is as crowded as your local park on a sunny Sunday the effect is still tremendous. Thirteen valleys radiate outwards from Puy Mary, thirteen foaming torrents tumble down these valleys. A table of orientation enables you to locate and name other peaks; the sharp peak of Puy Griou, the twin-horned summit of Puy de Peyre-Arse, and the massive, rounded Plomb du Cantal among them.

Puy Mary is named not as you might suppose for the Virgin Mary, but after an early evangelist, St. Mary or Marius, who converted most of Haute Auvergne to Christianity in the third century, as his teacher, St. Austremoine, after whom the great church of Issoire is named, converted Basse-Auvergne. According to one authority the remains of St. Mary are interred in the church Notre-Dame-des-Miracles in Mauriac but I have not been able to verify this. St. Mary's base in Auvergne was a more modest mountain, now called Montjournal, near Massiac. He chose it when he arrived from Rome because it was the chief centre of the cult of Jupiter which he intended to challenge. There are still two villages in the region which grew up around chapels which he consecrated, St. Mary le Plain and St. Mary le Gros.

From Puy Mary there is a choice between D17 through the valley of Mandailles and then the Route des Crêtes to Aurillac, another spectacular drive, and D680 via the Cirque de Falgoux to Salers. This second route has the advantage of enabling you to carry on from Salers to Aurillac and back to Plomb du Cantal, Murat and St. Flour by different roads. As you descend from Pas de Peyrol by D680 there is a short but extraordinarily steep section likely to absorb all the driver's attention and give him a rest from the inexhaustible range of views.

The road then sweeps past the cliffs of the Cirque de Falgoux and on to the Col de Néronne, then along the upper slope of the valley of the Maronne, and so to Salers.

After that magnificent but emotionally tiring drive, you are likely to arrive in Salers very much in need of a drink. What you have seen merits a moment of recollection and relaxation. Even the cool, silent types may fancy a cup of coffee.

Salers is one of the show pieces of Auvergne and deservedly so. It is attractively situated on a natural terrace above the deep valley of the Maronne, and is an unusual place in several ways. It is a walled medieval town without a castle and whose church was left outside the ramparts. Almost all its houses date from the 15th and 16th centuries and have a uniformity of style which at that time favoured towers, turrets and gables. But any suggestion of fantasy is negated by the dark, almost black, lava stone used for almost all the buildings.

Salers considers itself a peaceful, quiet place. So it is, unless you happen to be there in spring or autumn at the time of the transhumance, when the cattle and sheep are moved up to higher pastures for the summer or brought down again for winter. In that case your early morning sleep will be tintinnabulated into wakefulness as score upon score of animals, each with a bell of a different note around its neck, go ringing by, loud, fading, faint, far off but still audible.

If you do want a cow bell as a souvenir, and they can be useful for calling husbands from the end of long gardens without raising your voice, and even as dinner gongs for landladies, Salers is the place to buy one.

After Charollais, the Salers breed of cattle is perhaps the best known in France. With their rough, hairy coats and lyre-shaped horns they resemble Scottish Highland cattle who have been to the barbers for a 'short back and sides'. They are remarkable animals. They are very fertile, continuing to have calves up to an age in human terms equivalent to eighty. They give plenty of milk — about 3,000 litres a year, and as draught animals the cows are as strong as oxen, and as weather resistant as polar bears. They also have, in some areas, the unusual ability to imitate rocks. Where the volcanic rocks are red it is often difficult to tell whether you are looking across a valley at a slope strewn with rocks or with a herd of Salers cows, or a bit of both. In the latter case the ones that move are the cows.

The quality of the breed is largely due to a man whose bust has a place of honour on a column of basalt in the Grande Place, Tyssandier d'Escous. He was the son of the mayor of Salers, and it was he who persuaded the Emperor Napoleon III to subsidise a competition with prizes for the best animals of the breed. It was 1853 and 600 beasts were brought from all parts of the Massif Central — the breed had already spread far from Salers. Every year since then a similar show has been held in the canton of St. Privat, in the northern part of Corrèze.

In the old days a peasant who brought a cow to the fair to sell and had set a price on it in his mind would refuse to reduce it, and potential buyers would be so reluctant to increase offers that arguments, laced with derision on both sides, would go on for most of the morning without success. One wonders whether any

The picturesque medieval town of Salers

HOTEL

animals would ever have been sold in Auvergne, if the hour had not produced the man. In these cattle fairs he was known as the *accordaire* or bargain-maker. He would be a man well-acquainted with both parties, and choosing the right moment he would come forward. His intervention enabled these peasants, as stubborn as their mules, to save face and do business. The buyer would meet those he had bought from in the local café at midday, offer drinks all round, and settle his purchases in cash. Everyone was happy, convinced that they had fiddled everyone else, and bearing in mind the old Auvergne saying that, on the day of the fair, it is perfectly all right to cheat even your own mother.

Things happen rather differently nowadays. Instead of driving his cow to market, the farmer brings her in his Citroën truck. The dealers have arrived the night before in their big cars, formed a 'ring' and set the price, just like antique dealers, and leave the farmer little room for bargaining.

Salers is not a big village, something between 500 and 600 people. All its narrow streets lead to the Grande Place, and wherever you wander you will find something of visual interest. This is the great charm of Salers, that the whole is more impressive than any one of the parts. Two of the medieval mansions are open to the public, the Maison des Bargues, and the Maison des Templiers (in July and August only) which has an exhibition relating to local folklore and the history of Salers. The presence of a high proportion of medieval mansions in one small village (the Town Hall is not one of them, having been rebuilt in the style of the rest of the village after a fire in 1898) is a result of the unusual history of the village. During the Hundred Years War it suffered so many attacks from bands of English soldiers and gangs of brigands that the inhabitants obtained from the Duke of Auvergne the right to fortify the village, which until then had been open. Always a place apart, with poor communications, Salers became even more closed in upon itself. Then at the beginning of the 16th century Louis XII gave the village the right of self-government and in 1550 it became the seat of the magistrature for Haute-Auvergne. This introduced an era of prosperity, and it was the bourgeois families from whom the lawyers and magistrates came who were able to build these solid and impressive houses which tourists admire today.

On the edge of the village the Promenade of Barrouze offers a view over the Maronne valley and to the peaks of Cantal essentially unchanged since the Middle Ages. The church is mostly Gothic and contains a 15th-century representation of the Holy Sepulchre in painted stone with life-sized figures.

There are three hotels in Salers with a total of sixty-five rooms. The largest and newest, on the edge of the village, is the Bailliage. The Remparts has a good restaurant. The little Beffroi has only nine bedrooms but is in the centre of the village. All the hotels are quite comfortable enough to be used as a base for a few days.

Leave Salers by D35 which with several tight bends descends to the bottom of the Maronne valley, passing St. Paul de Salers on your left. Keep left to the village of Fontanges. The ruined château once belonged to the tragic Mlle de Fontanges, a mistress of Louis XIV, whose sad story I shall tell later on in this chapter. Follow on along the valley of the Aspre to St. Georges. Alternatively, for a more picturesque route, just before you reach Fontanges D135 on the left climbs steeply to the crest of the valley and follows it along the top to Le Fau, then through a pine and beech forest to the Col de St. Georges. Keep left at St. Georges on to D35 to the Col de Legal and on to Le Bruel. Here turn on to D60 for Tournemire and the Château d'Anjony. Before going on to the château, one of the most unusual in Auvergne, the village church of Tournemire is worth a look. It has a fine porch and the interior has some good frescoes, and a thorn from Christ's Crown of Thorns, brought back by Rigald de Tournemire from the Crusades in 1101.

The Château d'Anjony is built on a spur of rock commanding the valley of the Dore. Since its construction in 1439 it has been inhabited without interruption by the same family. It consists of a tall and narrow central block flanked by four round towers. Somehow it has escaped the ravages of time and was never damaged in wars or revolutions. There is only one large room on each of the three main floors. One of the towers holds the staircase serving them, and another tower contains the chapel. In the 18th century a low wing was added to provide less Spartan living accommodation but it in no way detracts from the older part.

This peaceful valley was the setting for a bizarre vendetta which lasted nearly two hundred years between the families of Anjony and Tournemire. On the one hand the Tournemire were a noble and ancient family whose fortunes had diminished steadily since the time of the Crusades. On the other hand the Anjony were *nouveaux riches*, having made their money as merchants.

The Tournemire borrowed money from the Anjony and were unable to repay it. Gradually their lands passed piece by piece into the hands of the Anjonys. Louis II d'Anjony decided to build a castle above the valley. Rigaud de Tournemire (a descendant of the Crusader) was proud and did not like the idea of someone else's castle being built on what he still thought of as his land. But Louis II d'Anjony was in a strong position because of his friendship with the Court and his support of Joan of Arc. He went ahead and built the castle.

The tension between the families rapidly grew. They would insult each other, using iron loud-hailers so that all the village could hear. There is still one to be seen at the Château d'Anjony. From insults they passed to affrays, and to mutual assassination. Over the years members of both families were slain.

Eventually they decided to bring it to an end by holding a fair fight in public. The battle between them took place in the small village square of Tournemire. On one side was a member of the Tournemire family supported by Jacques and Gabriel de St. Cernin, on the other side another Louis d'Anjony and his two sons. The fight took place in front of the local population, hoping to see blood. They were not disappointed. All the Anjony were killed. So after two hundred years the Tournemire obtained satisfaction and regained their honour.

Yes, but it is the Château d'Anjony that you have come to see, and that heap of old stone over there is all that remains of the Château de Tournemire. So? Well, like that of the Montagues and Capulets this vendetta had its Romeo and Juliet. In 1643, Michel II d'Anjony, a little boy at the time of the fight, married Gabrielle de Pesteils, heiress to the oldest branch of the Tournemire family, and so, at last, this long and bitter feud came to an end. Some of the Tournemire resorted to court actions to get their property back but they were in the wrong and they failed. The Anjony retained their castle and their descendants live in it to this day.

The Château d'Anjony contains many treasures. The walls and ceiling of the chapel are completely covered with 16th-century frescoes representing scenes from the life and Passion of Christ. The room on the first floor has an enormous chimney-piece, a splendid ceiling, superb period furniture, and a large Aubusson tapestry. In the Room of the Knights on the second floor there are more 16th-century frescoes, these depict the legend of the Nine Valiant Knights (Hector, Alexander the Great, Caesar, Joshua, Judas Maccabeus, David, Arthur, Charlemagne and Godefroi de Bouillon). There are also two life-size portraits of the first Michel d'Anjony and his wife Germaine de Foix.

The Château d'Anjony is open, in the afternoons only, from Palm Sunday to All Saints' Day. Sometimes it is the owner himself who acts as a guide for visitors.

Old houses mirrored in the river Jordanne at Aurillac

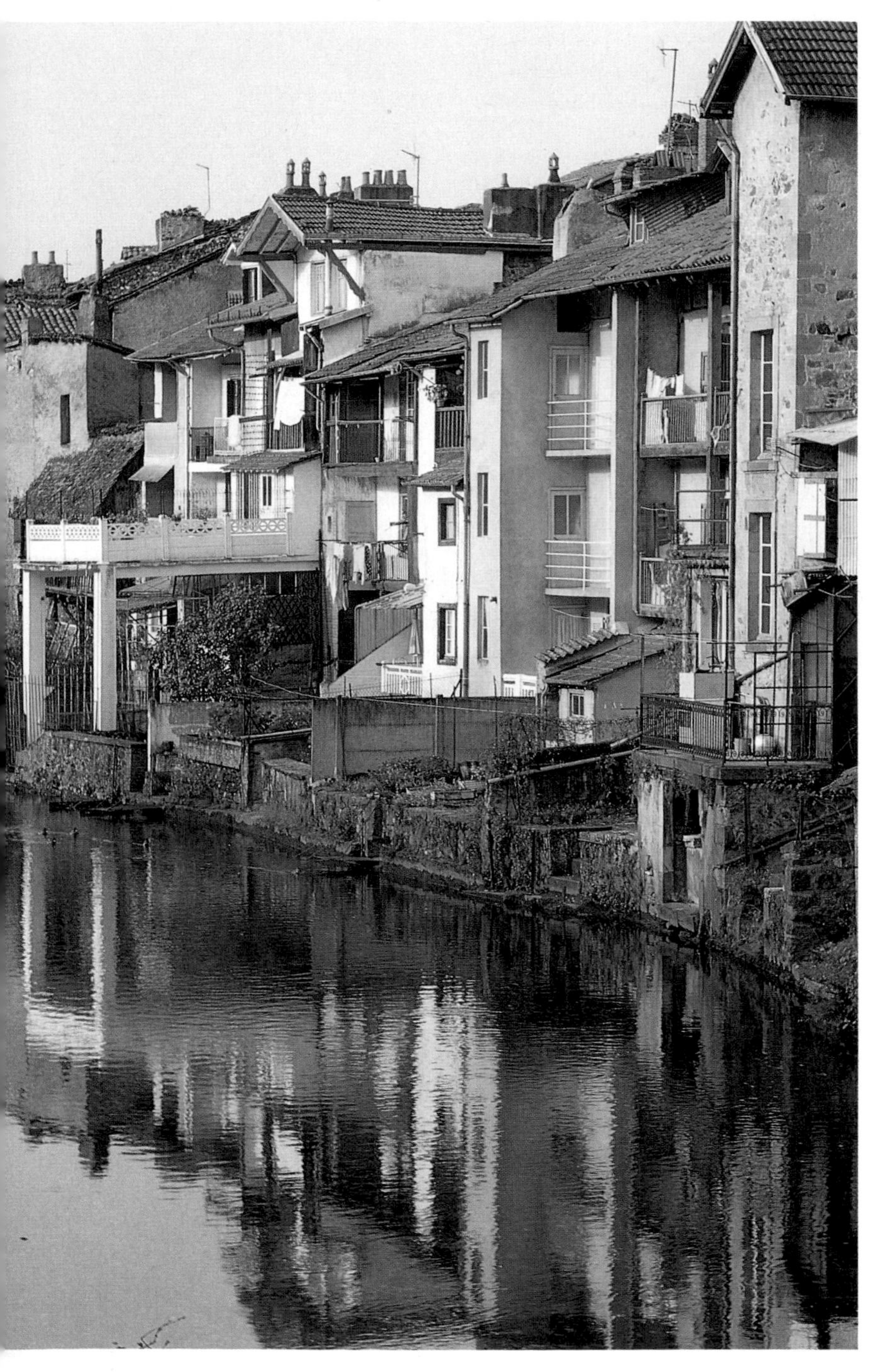

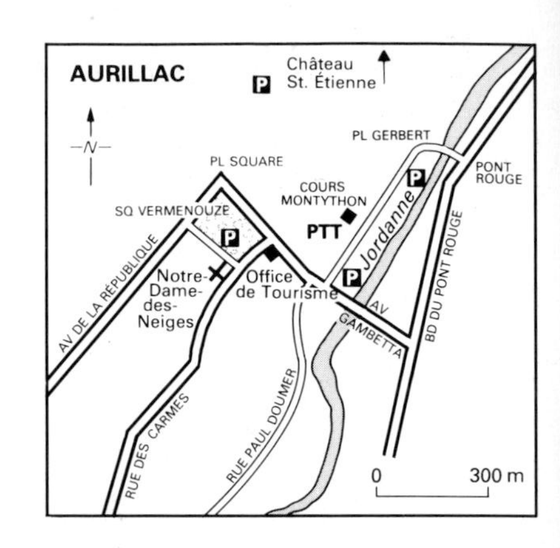

From Tournemire D166 continues to join D922, the main road from Mauriac to **Aurillac**.

In this modest town of 36,000 inhabitants, the préfecture of Cantal, you are no longer in the mountains but at their foot. After the isolated villages, the winding roads, the airy uplands, it will probably come as a relief to some visitors to be able to take their ease on a café terrace in the spacious central square, Place Vermenouze.

The old part of Aurillac is quite small, confined to a few narrow, twisting streets on the banks of the river Jordanne, and is surrounded by a modern town with smart shops, office blocks, and factories on the outskirts. I have mentioned elsewhere the pride which many towns and villages in central France take in announcing themselves as the capital of this or that, usually on a panel at the entry to the town, and often with more hope than confidence. I have not seen a notice saying so but there is no doubt that Aurillac really is the umbrella capital of France. It makes half of all the French production of standard umbrellas, market umbrellas, beach umbrellas and parasols, and garden furniture as well, and does a healthy export business. Other industries include the making of furniture, agricultural machinery and souvenir copperware. It is also an important agricultural centre, with cattle and cheese markets, and three annual agricultural fairs.

Aurillac is an excellent base for excursions and, though at first glance it may not seem so, there are things in the town itself which merit attention. The most important of them is the Maison des Volcans, installed in a wing of the Château St. Étienne. It was founded in 1972 by the local Authority in conjunction with the Faculty of Volcanology of the University of Paris South. A visit to this centre will help you to appreciate what you have seen, if you have come down from the mountains, or what you are going to see, if you are on your way to them.

It is much more than a museum. It is an active centre of research into the 'sciences of the Earth's surface and the Environment' with room for sixty students who have laboratories, workshops, library and film library at their disposal. There is a permanent exhibition relating to volcanology open to the public, with maps, photographs, wall charts, rock samples, spread through five rooms, explaining not only the volcanoes of the Massif Central but those in other parts of the world, and even on the moon and other heavenly bodies. Films are shown daily.

There is a second exhibition on the natural regions of Cantal, relating the geology and volcanic soil to the plant and animal life in different areas. It explains how the maximum benefit can be obtained from the various soils in agricultural terms, and how the volcanic stone has influenced traditional architecture.

Aurillac has two other museums of more usual type, one of Cantal in general, and a museum of fine arts. They are housed in an unlovely 19th-century building, once a barracks. But do not be put off, inside it is modernised and the collections are well arranged.

It is only five minutes' walk from Square Vermenouze to Pont Rouge from where you can explore the old town. Called the Red Bridge because it replaced a wooden structure painted that colour, it is the best spot from which to take photographs of the old houses lining the river. Adjacent to the bridge is Place Gerbert with the narrow streets of the old quarter leading off it. The statue in the square is of Gerbert who, as Sylvester II, was the first French Pope, and who died in 1003.

Gerbert was a man of extraordinary intelligence. He was just a young shepherd when the monks of the Abbey of St. Géraud, which was founded in the 9th century by the saint, and around which the town of Aurillac developed, first remarked his brightness and piety. They arranged for him to study in Spanish universities, and particularly in Córdoba, at that time the most advanced centre of European learning. He studied mathematics and medicine. He is credited with having been the first person to introduce the use of Arab numerals to the western world. He is also said to have made the first clock using weights, to have invented an astrolabe for use in navigation at sea, and to have improved the design of organs. Even as a young man his reputation was widespread. He went to Rome where he became Pope in AD999. No doubt he got the job on his merits but it is also possible that no one else wanted the responsibility since it was common knowledge that the world was going to end on the stroke of AD1000. Like a lot of other common knowledge, it turned out not to be true, and Sylvester II saw the world safely over the hurdle.

In the narrow streets around Place Gerbert there are a number of old houses with attractive façades and doorways. The most interesting are the Noailles mansion and its Renaissance courtyard at 5 rue de Noailles, the Jesuit College in rue du Collège, the François Meynard mansion in rue Vermenouze, and the Maison des Consuls in rue de la Coste.

The Jordanne was one of the rivers from which gold used to be extracted. In the 14th century a monk named Jean de la Roquetaillade of the Abbey of St. Géraud invented a better method than the sheepskin for trapping the gold. He used sloping boards covered with coarse cloth which trapped the gold in its weave. Clever enough, but he was also a prophet. Hundreds of years in advance he predicted religious strife, the loss of power by the nobility, and the fall of Royalty. He would have done better to keep it all to himself. His Bishop did not like the sound of it all and put him in prison. The Pope liked it even less and put him in the dungeons of Avignon for four years.

Aurillac is a good base for excursions and has a number of hotels. La Thomasse, in a quiet situation near the excellent sports and leisure park, is the most expensive. The Grand Hotel St. Pierre is conveniently placed between the old and new towns. The Renaissance, which has a good restaurant is on Place Vermenouze (also known as Place du Palais de Justice, or Place du Square). The best restaurants are probably la Reine Margot near the centre, and the Auberge La Baraque on the edge of town on the road to Vic-sur-Cère. The municipal camp site on the banks of the Jordanne is large and well-equipped.

Only 5km from Aurillac by N122, the road to Figeac, and D17, where it is clearly signposted at the junction, is the Château de Conros, which is open to the public on afternoons in the high season. The château, which dates from the 12th, 14th and 15th centuries, has been well restored. It has some good period furniture, and there is usually an art exhibition.

Reached from Aurillac by N122, **Vic-sur-Cère** is another pleasant little town suitable as a base for exploring this part of Cantal. The road passes through Polminhac where you will notice the Château of Pesteils on a height above the village. It is a successful blend of a 14th-century medieval keep, one of the few still standing in Auvergne, and more recent and restored living quarters turreted in Renaissance style. The buildings and the spacious terrace, with lovely views of the valley of the Cère, have been used as a setting for at least three French films. It was the home of the Gabrielle de Pesteils whose marriage to Michel d'Anjony put an end to the famous vendetta between the families. The interior is impressive, with fine furniture, 17th-century painted ceilings and 15th-century frescoes. It is open to the public in July and August.

The valley of the Cère is reckoned to be the greenest, richest and most attractive of those in Cantal. On its way to Vic, the Cère plunges down two big steps formed by glacial erosion, the Pas de Compaing and the Pas de Cère, cutting its way down through them in narrow and picturesque gorges.

Vic-sur-Cère is in two distinct parts, an old quarter on the left bank and a newer area on the right bank which developed when the long-established spa was given a boost in the 19th century. Like Salers, Vic owed its prosperity in the Middle Ages to the fact that it was a seat of the magistrature. In the old quarter there are several 16th-century houses, and a 15th-century house known as the Maison des Princes de Monaco. In medieval times Vic was the chief town of the region known as Carladès which was given by Louis XIII to the Princes of Monaco who did, from time to time, use this mansion in Vic. They lost it and the Carladès, but not their heads at the time of the Revolution.

Vic is another spa which was well known to the Romans, and has enjoyed a modest popularity for hundreds of years. In 1837, Anne of Austria, who was childless after twenty-two years of marriage to Louis XIII, whose sexual foibles have already been mentioned, and was desperate to give him an heir, made a tour of all the miraculous virgins and spas hoping that if the one would not help her, the other would. She included Vic-sur-Cère in the spas and the small chapel of Notre-Dame-de-Consolation, in the neighbouring village of Thiézac, among the holy places. Since she gave birth to a son in 1838 who came to the throne in 1843 and reigned for seventy-two years as Louis XIV, the Sun King, one might say that her tour was well worth the effort.

To the south of Vic there are three places which evoke the flavour of life in Auvergne in medieval times. Take D54 from behind the station. The road rises rapidly 300m to the Col de Curebourse (Cutpurse Pass) whose name indicates that it was a favourite spot for highwaymen. Just to the west of the pass an isolated rock is known as Rocher des Pendus (Rock of the Hanged Men). This is the place where the death sentences passed by the magistrates of Vic, some of them no doubt on cutpurses, were carried out. The Rocher des Pendus can be reached easily on foot from Cutpurse Pass. The car can be parked near the Auberge des Monts. The walk takes about twenty minutes and there are extensive views from the top and benches on which to sit and admire them.

Farther on by D54 and then D59 beyond Jou-sous-Monjou in the bottom of the valley there is a much dilapidated castle on the right, now used as a farm. It is called Cropières and it was in this noble castle that Marie-Angélique de Scorailles was born. At the age of seventeen she was introduced to the Court by one of her ambitious relatives. She at once fell into the lecherous hands of Louis XIV who, not without difficulty, as she was a simple and pious girl, made her his mistress. The golden blonde Marie-Angélique was a nice girl but what Hollywood used to call a dumb blonde. In French she was described by a contemporary as 'belle comme une ange et sotte comme un panier', freely translated 'Lovely as an angel and as thick as two planks'. In so far as he was capable of normal feelings, Louis, who was not used to being resisted, became quite attached to her and, when she gave birth to a son, created her Duchess of Fontanges. Sadly, as a result of complications during the birth, she became ill and died, only 20 years old, a few weeks later in the convent of Port-Royal. She had been 'blessée dans le service', 'mortally wounded in action', as the Marquise de Sévigné maliciously put it. It cannot be said that the King missed her for long. There was always someone ready to console the Kings of France. This time it was Madame de Maintenon.

Vic-sur-Cère has a good choice of modest hotels, all much of a muchness. There is a small, well-equipped camp site, Pommeraie, on the banks of the Cère, where reservations can be made. There is also a large municipal camp site, with a heated swimming pool.

The next village, Thiézac, situated in a particularly open and sunny part of the valley, also has a couple of small hotels and a camp site. It is a very good centre for walking in the area, as is St. Jacques-des-Blats higher up the valley. Useful maps of footpaths can be obtained from the Mairies in these villages. To the north of Thiézac on a height overlooking it, and now shaded by lime trees, is the little chapel of Notre-Dame-de-Consolation, visited for nine days of prayer by Anne of Austria. The miraculous Virgin is now kept in the church in the village.

Beyond St. Jacques-des-Blats on the way to Le Lioran the road continues to climb and passes through magnificent scenery with Puy Griou on the left and Plomb du Cantal on the right. At this point the mountain barrier between the valley of the Dordogne on one side and the valley of the Allier on the other would normally be impassable every winter, but as long ago as 1839 it was decided to drive a road tunnel through the mountain. It was dug entirely by hand and the number of workmen killed and injured in its construction was counted in hundreds. The tunnel, almost 1½km long was opened in

Courtly Love

When a man opens a door for a woman or in any other way behaves courteously towards her, she has the troubadours who lived in Auvergne and Provence a thousand years ago to thank for it.

Until the troubadours spread the new philosophy of Courtly Love throughout western Europe, women were regarded just as they are today in Japan, or Africa, or the Muslim world, useful possessions, like a horse or a hunting dog. Marriages were nothing to do with love. The idea that a woman might be seriously loved for herself was unknown to the ancient world. Great minds such as Aristotle, St. Paul, Thomas Aquinas had never heard of it. Marriages were made out of interest, to gain land, power or money, and when the alliance no longer served this purpose, the husband's object was to make another one which did.

Pierre de Vic, who came from Vic-sur-Cère, was one of the great troubadours. He was known as the Mad Monk because he preferred a Rabelaisian life of love songs and drinking choruses to religion. At the Courts of Love, a kind of medieval Eisteddfodd, held annually at Le Puy (then called Puy St. Marie), he won the Golden Spur awarded to the troubadour whose songs and general interpretation of Courtly Love, in answer to loaded questions on relationships between the sexes, were considered the best.

Pierre de Vic and his colleagues realised that women then, as always wanted to be loved and flattered. They had also noticed that many of the lords considered that sort of thing 'soppy', and spent a great deal of their time away fighting in Crusades or any other wars they could find, while their ladies languished at home wondering what to do next.

Pierre de Vic and his friends had an answer, and set it to music.

1847. A railway tunnel 30m under the road tunnel and somewhat longer was opened in 1858.

The tortuous old road via the Col de Cère (1,294m) still exists and is to be recommended in summer for its stupendous views over the whole Massif. The tunnel is, of course, quicker but the views are limited.

On the other side of the tunnel is Le Lioran, a summer and winter resort set in superb pine forests. Super-Lioran is a well-equipped and expanding ski resort, with 19 teleskis and a cable-car. It is sometimes said that 'white Lioran', the ski resort, is more beautiful than 'green Lioran', the summer resort, but that only goes to show that this is an area which has attractions in all seasons. In fact, the railway station is the only one in France which leaves travellers at the foot of a teleski in winter, and right on one of the great cross-country footpaths (Grande Randonnée 4) in summer.

The cable-car which in winter carries skiers up to within a hundred metres of the summit of Plomb du Cantal (1,855m) also works all through the summer. Walkers, pony trekkers, hang-gliding enthusiasts make this green and sublime country their province in summer. Using the cable-car makes it easy to embark upon walks across the mountain slopes and through the forests, either down again to Le Lioran (the easy choice) or, more ambitiously, along the crest which dominates the valley of the Cère, or along the Grande Randonnée 4 to Puy Mary. This latter is a day's walk to be undertaken in settled fine weather but without any real difficulty for the fit and experienced walker. In winter Super-Lioran offers 1,500 hectares of snow-fields and 50km of signposted ski-tracks.

Winter sports at Super Lioran on the slopes of Plomb du Cantal

From Le Lioran N122 to Murat follows the valley of the Alagnon and its steep pine-covered sides. On the right of the road about 2km from Le Lioran the Buron de Belles Aygues has been equipped to show some of the techniques and rural traditions of Cantal, including the complicated process of making Cantal cheese by hand.

The Alagnon is still a good trout river and was once also known for its salmon. The Administration of the Parc des Volcans recently introduced a programme of repopulating the river with young salmon. Results have been encouraging and it is hoped to make it a good salmon river once again.

Murat is amphitheatrically sited above the left bank of the Alagnon. It is an old town noticeable for the many houses roofed with *lauzes*. These are neither slates nor tiles but thick, split stones cut with one semi-circular edge so that when laid on the roof they overlap like the scales of a huge fish. They are very heavy and need strong rafters to support them, but the local saying is 'Qui bien lauze, pour cent ans pose'; in other words, if it is put on properly, you have a sound roof for a hundred years or more.

The general charm of Murat is blemished by another one of those monstrous 19th-century statues of the Virgin, overlooking the town from the Rocher de Bonnevie. It is debatable whether this colossal cast iron *faux pas*, painted white, is uglier than the one at Le Puy, painted red.

Murat is not a place which need detain the average visitor longer than is needed for a cup of coffee, or perhaps lunch at a good country restaurant, the Anglard-Messageries. It's another story for anglers. Murat is a gateway to some of the best fishing in Auvergne. The Alagnon, on which it stands, has plenty of trout, grayling and gudgeon. One of its tributaries, the Allache, which rises on the empty, almost roadless plateau of Cézallier, is also a good trout river. Nearby are the Santoire and the Rhue, two more rivers with a good reputation for mountain trout. For variety, there are a number of good trout lakes in the same area.

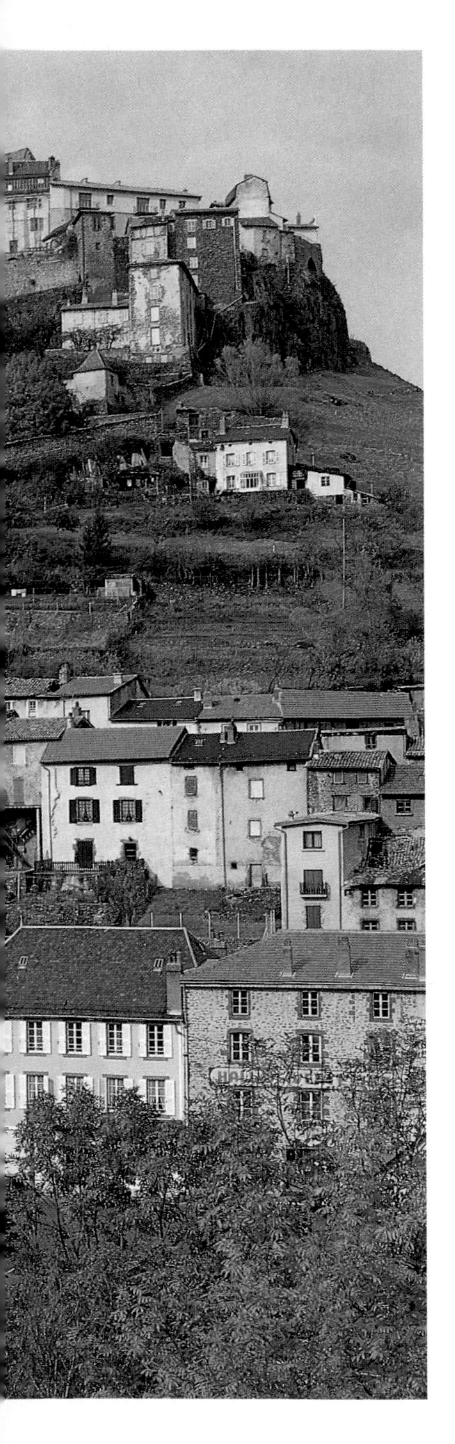

Throughout Cantal and particularly in this area there are small hotels which belong to an organisation known as the Relais St. Pierre and which specialise in catering for anglers. They will often provide a picnic basket for those who want to make an early start or be out all day. They have special facilities for storing fishing gear. They will often prepare or store fish that have been caught. In the more out of the way villages the hotelier can often supply the necessary fishing card. Among such hotels are the Hôtel de la Santoire, at La Carrière de Ségur-les-Villas, actually on the banks of the Santoire; the Hôtel du Midi at Pont du Vernet, within fifty metres of the Alagnon, and the Hôtel l'Oustalou at Ferrières-Ste. Marie, also very close to the river. Full information on the Relais St. Pierre can be obtained from the Fédération des A.P.P. du Cantal, 14 Allée du Vialence, 15000 Aurillac.

The direct road from Murat to St. Flour is D926 but it makes a nicer, if slightly longer, drive to follow N122 along the valley of the Alagnon as far as Neussargues-Moissac and there take D679.

St. Flour is dramatically situated on a cliff at the edge of a plateau but this is not evident from the direction of Murat, as you are already on the plateau as you approach St. Flour. The approach from the north or better still from the east shows the town to great advantage. There is a lower town at the foot of the cliff and the older, upper town on the plateau. These days St.

St. Flour: lower town, in the foreground, and the old town with its stern cathedral, on the plateau

Flour is very much a crossroads town whose hotels always seem to have coachloads of tourists disembarking or about to embark.

Largely due to its easily defended position St. Flour has a less colourful history than some other towns of the Massif Central. It was never captured by anyone, though the brave and resourceful Captain Merle, the Huguenot soldier, came near to succeeding on the night of 9th August 1578. Some of his men succeeded in scaling the ramparts but made too much noise. Unfortunately, the consul, Brisson, was a light sleeper. He heard them and sounded the alarm bell, rousing the townspeople who managed to repulse the attack.

St. Flour has a good selection of hotels. The Europe, in the upper town, has a dining room with a panoramic view over the valley of the Lander, as well as first-class food.

It is a town of more interest as a centre for exploring in all directions than as a destination in itself. Nevertheless, as always in the towns of Auvergne, there are several things worth looking at. If you are not going to stay there, it is a place to spend an hour or two wandering around while you digest a good lunch. The cathedral is in severe Gothic style, the exterior having a formidable, almost fortress-like look about it. The interior is spacious and dignified. On the left of the ambulatory a life-size Christ in dark wood dates from the 15th century, perhaps earlier. It is known as 'le bon Dieu noir' and is the only black Christ in France.

The old town in front of the Cathedral is not extensive, a lot of it now forms a pedestrian shopping area where you can buy all kinds of souvenirs of Auvergne, including the cow bells and *bouffadous* already mentioned, and sheepskins of good quality.

On the other side of the town there is a spacious square known as Allées Pompidou, with a statue of the former French President who was an Auvergnat and deputy for St. Flour, though not from the town itself. He was born in the small village of Montboudif, near Condat, between the plateaux of Cézallier and the Monts Dore. The house where he was born is open to the public.

St. Flour is the easiest place to find out what is meant by the word *orgues* in place names such as Bort-les-Orgues, already mentioned. If you did not see them there, you will be able to see them here. The right-hand side of the road down from the upper town to the lower town consists in places of a black cliff in the form of these basalt pillars.

It is possible to stay several days in St. Flour, taking a worthwhile excursion in a different direction each day. One of the best is to the Viaduct of Garabit on the river Truyère, the chief tributary of the Lot, which it joins in Entraygues. In a region of wonderful rivers the Truyère is in several ways the most remarkable. It has kilometre after kilometre of gorges, countless tributaries, many lakes and fiord-like inlets, and waterfalls. If it were not for the fact that much of it is quite inaccessible by road, it would surely be as well known as the Tarn.

The large number of tributaries and the almost complete absence of roads and villages in its valley made it a natural choice for hydro-electric development. It was sufficient to build five barrages to create an enormous reserve of water.

Some idea of the grandiose beauty of the Truyère and its lakes and inlets can be obtained at Garabit about 12km south of St. Flour by N9. There are two hotels with viewpoints over the lake, the Beau Site and the Panoramic, and both have parking space and good restaurants.

The remarkable viaduct of Garabit carrying the Paris-Béziers railway line over the gorge was one of the great engineering feats of the late 19th Century. It was built in 1882–1884 by Gustav Eiffel and it was the lessons he learned here that enabled him to build the 300-m Eiffel Tower of the Universal Exhibition in Paris in 1889. The viaduct is 564m long and when it was built it carried the railway 123m above the surface of the river. With the building of the Barrage de Grandval in 1959 the water level has risen to within about 40m of the platform. The lake that you see at this point was created by the building of this barrage and is 27km long.

Because of the difficulty of access by road to most of the river, the easiest and best way to see something of its beauty is by boat and this can be done from here. The Garabit Hotel, down at the lakeside, which belongs to the group of fishing hotels, the Relais St. Pierre, is beside a beach and boat moorings and can arrange motor boat trips on the lake. They operate from 1st May to 1st October. On Sundays and Wednesdays in July and August there is also a restaurant boat on which lunch can be taken during the trip. This is also sometimes available on other days by arrangement. One of the most enjoyable journeys is down the lake to the very romantically sited ruins of the Château d'Alleuze; this trip takes about two hours.

The Château d'Alleuze can also be reached by road from Pont de Garabit. It is a place to be seen and photographed — it would have been dear to 19th-century English water colour artists had they known about it — but it is a complete ruin and of little interest to visit. Take D13 to Faverolles, then to Auriac de Faverolles for the views. Then carry on to the Belvédère de Mallet, another spot for the photographer. Here, the viewpoint is a five-minute walk from a parking place which is just beyond a sharp left-hand bend, turning away from the lake. (If you are going to venture off the main roads in Cantal, the Michelin map No. 76 is really essential.) Then at the village of Fridefont turn right on to D40 to the Barrage de Grandval, cross the top of the barrage, and in Grandval at the junction with D48 turn right for the Château d'Alleuze. This is a good area for finding a picnic spot on a fine day. D116 via Villedieu will take you back to St. Flour.

Another good drive south of St. Flour is to Chaudes-Aigues and Laguiole by D921.

Chaudes-Aigues, cosily sited along the deep valley of the Remontalou and surrounded by lovely mountains, is an unusual little town. In English its name means 'Hot Waters', and it has seven hot springs. One of them, the Source du Par, supplies the public fountain (near Place du Marché) with water not far off boiling point at 82°C. The housewives of Chaudes-Aigues traditionally

Overleaf: *One of the greatest iron bridges of the 19th century, Eiffel's Viaduct of Garabit, over the Truyère*

use this fountain to warm their soups, cook eggs, and wash the calf's head, pig's feet, vegetables, or whatever they may be preparing for lunch. In rustic France the only important meal of the day is at lunch time; the farmers take only a light snack in the evenings and go to bed early. For hundreds of years this natural hot water supply has been piped into the houses of Chaudes-Aigues for heating, which is virtually free. It also heats the school and the public swimming pool. It is the only town in Europe to benefit in this way from its own hot water supply. A similar system exists in Iceland.

Though, once again, it was known as a spa to the Romans, Chaudes-Aigues fell into disuse because of its isolation and poor road communications. It was not until the construction of a new Thermal Establishment in 1964 that it became a spa again. Its waters are not only hot (from 52–82°C) but contain bicarbonates, soda, and are mildly radio-active. They are thought effective in the treatment of rheumatism, sciatica and allied conditions.

If you feel that all this can be left to others and that your own joints are in fairly good working order, you might like to tackle the 17km of narrow, winding but spectacular road which is one of the few that will take you to and actually across the Gorges de la Truyère. This is D11 west from Chaudes-Aigues to Pont de Tréboul. After about 7km it is worth taking the trouble to detour by the right fork up to the hamlet of Espinasse where there are superb views of the Gorges, then back again the short distance to D11 and on to Pont de Tréboul.

This is a modern suspension bridge built to replace the 14th-century stone bridge built by English troops during the Hundred Years War which was drowned, along with the village of Tréboul, when the Barrage de Sarrans was built in the 1930s, transforming this section of the Truyère into a lake 35km long.

If you turn right, having crossed the bridge, on to D56 towards Ste. Marie there are more magnificent views, and this particularly rustic little village contains a sophisticated surprise. Its simple church contains two stained-glass windows designed by Jean Cocteau. I have not been able to find out why or how this happened, but Ste. Marie is only about fifty contorted kms from the Château de Pesteils, near Vic-sur-Cère, which Cocteau used as a setting in making his film *Le Retour Éternel.*

From Ste. Marie you can carry on by D56 to Oradour, a pretty road, to the junction with D990. Near this junction there is a 15th-century castle with a 13th-century keep, the Château de Rochebrune. It is open to visitors (except on Tuesdays) and holds exhibitions of contemporary painting during the summer season. At the junction turn right and 3km farther on right again on to D48 for Neuvéglise. This little town has two small hotels with goodish restaurants, and a 4-star camp site. It is little more than a kilometre from D921 for St. Flour.

Instead of taking this closer look at the river Truyère and its lakes and gorges, you could continue south from Chaudes-Aigues on D921 to Laguiole. If you are beginning to think about eating it might turn out to be a good idea, because Laguiole has what is

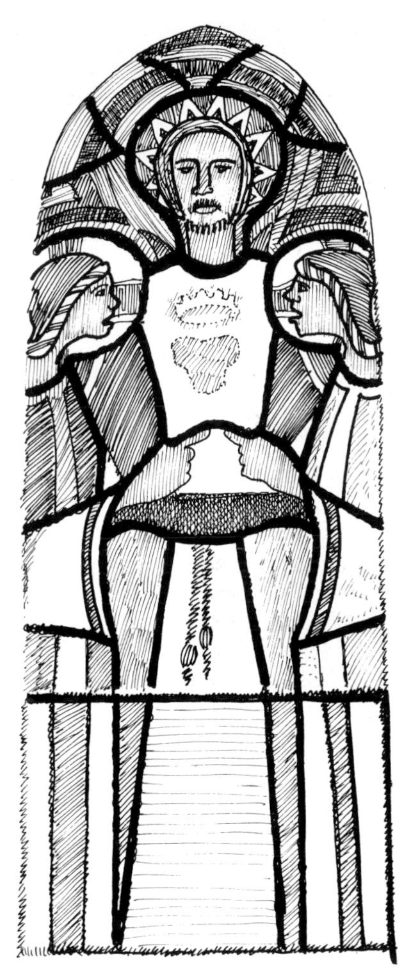

Stained-glass windows by Jean Cocteau in the village church of Ste. Marie, near Pont de Tréboul

probably the best restaurant in the Massif Central.

Monsieur Bras at 'Lou Mazouc' is one of the rising stars of French cuisine, and his reputation is already widespread in southern France. With two Michelin stars the restaurant is not cheap but at one hundred francs for the cheapest menu, it is not expensive either at this standard. The Lou Mazouc also has a few reasonably priced bedrooms. *Mazouc* is the word used in this area instead of *buron* to describe the stone shelters high on the pastures where in summer the cows were milked and the handmade cheese produced. It is not a large restaurant so, in season, it is a good idea to arrive on the dot of 12 noon or, better still, telephone a reservation.

Laguiole (which is pronounced La-ee-yoll) is one of those towns which concentrate the life of its region. It is the chief cattle market of Aubrac, a vast cattle-producing upland which, although it does not look like it, is also of volcanic formation. It is a dome similar to those near Clermont-Ferrand but much flattened due to the liquidity of the lava produced by its volcanoes. The pastures are at an average altitude of more than a thousand metres. On this high plateau the snow comes early and stays late and it is possible to graze the cattle there for only twenty weeks a year. Traditionally they leave their stables in the valleys on 24th May and are brought down again on 13th October. When they leave in the spring it is a festive occasion, the cows often having a bunch of flowers between their horns or a flag attached to their bell collar.

There are few roads across this empty plateau (the last wolf was killed here only ten years ago) but it is interesting to note that the Romans, who liked straight lines because they had not invented a pivoting axle, put their road from Lyon to Rodez straight across the crest of the Aubrac.

The 13th-century Château d'Alleuze, among the most picturesque ruins in Auvergne

Laguiole is just in Aveyron close to the borders with Cantal and Lozère. So from here you can continue south to the charming town of Espalion, on the Lot, and then along the Lot valley to Entraygues and from there to Aurillac. Or you can turn east to St. Urcize, which has one of the better Romanesque churches, and then by way of Nasbinals and Marvejols to Mende and the Cévennes.

But if you wish to see Le Puy, and it would be a mistake to be in this part of the world without visiting it, because it is a town unlike any other, it would be better to return directly to St. Flour. The road from St. Flour to Le Puy is the natural route from Cantal into Velay and offers the most attractive approach to this fascinating town.

The Barrage of Grandval on the Truyère creates and holds back a lake 27km long

General Information

AURILLAC Information: Office de Tourisme, pl du Square (71.48.46.58).
Where to stay: Good selection of rather better than average hotels, of which La Thomasse can be recommended for its quiet situation near the Sports complex (71.48.26.47). No restaurant. More modestly priced, the Renaissance (71.48.09.80).
Where to eat: La Reine Margot, 19 rue G.-de-Veyre (71.48.26.46) is a very good reasonably priced restaurant. Another good one, slightly cheaper, is La Cremaillère at Les Quatre Chemins, 3.5km on the Tulle Road (71.48.10.70). Or La Baraque, on the edge of town on the Vic-sur-Cère road.

CHAUDES-AIGUES Information: Office de Tourisme, 1 av Georges Pompidou (71.23.52.75).
Where to stay: The Beauséjour (71.23.52.37) is the largest of the three modest hotels. (When there is not much to choose between hotels I recommend the largest on the grounds that you will have a better chance of finding a room.)
A few kms away at Neuvéglise there is a first-class camp site.
Where to eat: Aux Bouillons d'Or (71.23.51.42) is more a restaurant than a hotel but it does have some rooms.

LAGUIOLE Information: Ask at the Mairie.
Where to stay: Grand Hôtel Auguy, av de la Pépinière (65.44.31.11).
There are several camp sites in the area, and here, as in many other parts of the Massif Central, there are many places nearby where individual camping is permitted.
Where to eat: The restaurant Lou Mazouc is probably the best in the whole of the Massif Central, as far as standards of cuisine are concerned. Two Michelin stars. Advisable to reserve in advance in summer season (65.44.32.24).
Not too far away, the restaurant of the Hôtel Remise at St. Urcize is simple but well known for its regional dishes.

LE LIORAN Information: There is a seasonal tourist office (71.49.50.08), or ask at the Mairie.
Where to stay: There are three hotels at Super-Lioran, open for winter sports, and in summer for July/August and a week or two either side. Best is probably Grand Hôtel Anglard et du Cerf (71.49.50.26).
Where to eat: The restaurant of Anglard et du Cerf is very well known and reasonably priced, and down at Le Lioran itself the restaurant of the Auberge du Tunnel (71.49.50.02) also has a good reputation.
Leisure: In summer a very good walking centre. In winter, a lively winter sports resort.

MAURIAC Information: Office de Tourisme, pl Georges Pompidou (71.68.01.85).
Where to stay: Try the Écu de France, 6 av de Ch.-Périé (71.68.00.75).
Where to eat: For a change, in one of the other two hotels.
Leisure: There is good fishing in the area.

ST. FLOUR Information: Office de Tourisme, 2 Pl d'Armes (71.60.14.41) (near Hôtel-de-Ville).
Where to stay: A list of all accommodation in the town and neighbourhood is available from the Tourist Office, and includes camp sites. Several hotels of good average standard, of which the Nouvel Hôtel-Bonne Table has the largest number of rooms (71.60.05.86).
Where to eat: The Grand Hôtel des Voyageurs (71.60.34.44) in the upper town near the Cathedral has a restaurant strong on Auvergnat dishes and wines. The Hôtel Europe (71.60.03.64) also has a good value restaurant.

SALERS Information: Syndicat d'Initiative, Grande Place (71.40.70.68) and Mairie (71.40.72.33).
Where to stay: Hôtel Bailliage (71.40.71.95), and see p. 138.
Where to eat: The restaurant of the little Hôtel Remparts (71.40.70.33) is generally reckoned to be the best.

VIC-SUR-CÈRE Information: Office de Tourisme, av Mercier (71.47.50.68).
Where to stay: Several average hotels. Try the Beauséjour (71.47.50.27) or the Bel Horizon (71.47.50.06).
Six kms away by D54 the Auberge des Monts at the Col de Curebourse is in a pleasant position.
Where to eat: In town, the restaurant of the Bel Horizon is perhaps best value. That at the Auberge des Monts (71.47.51.71) is very good, and strong on Auvergnat dishes.

Overleaf: *Simple but impressive, the Chevet of the fine Romanesque church at St. Urcize near Laguiole*

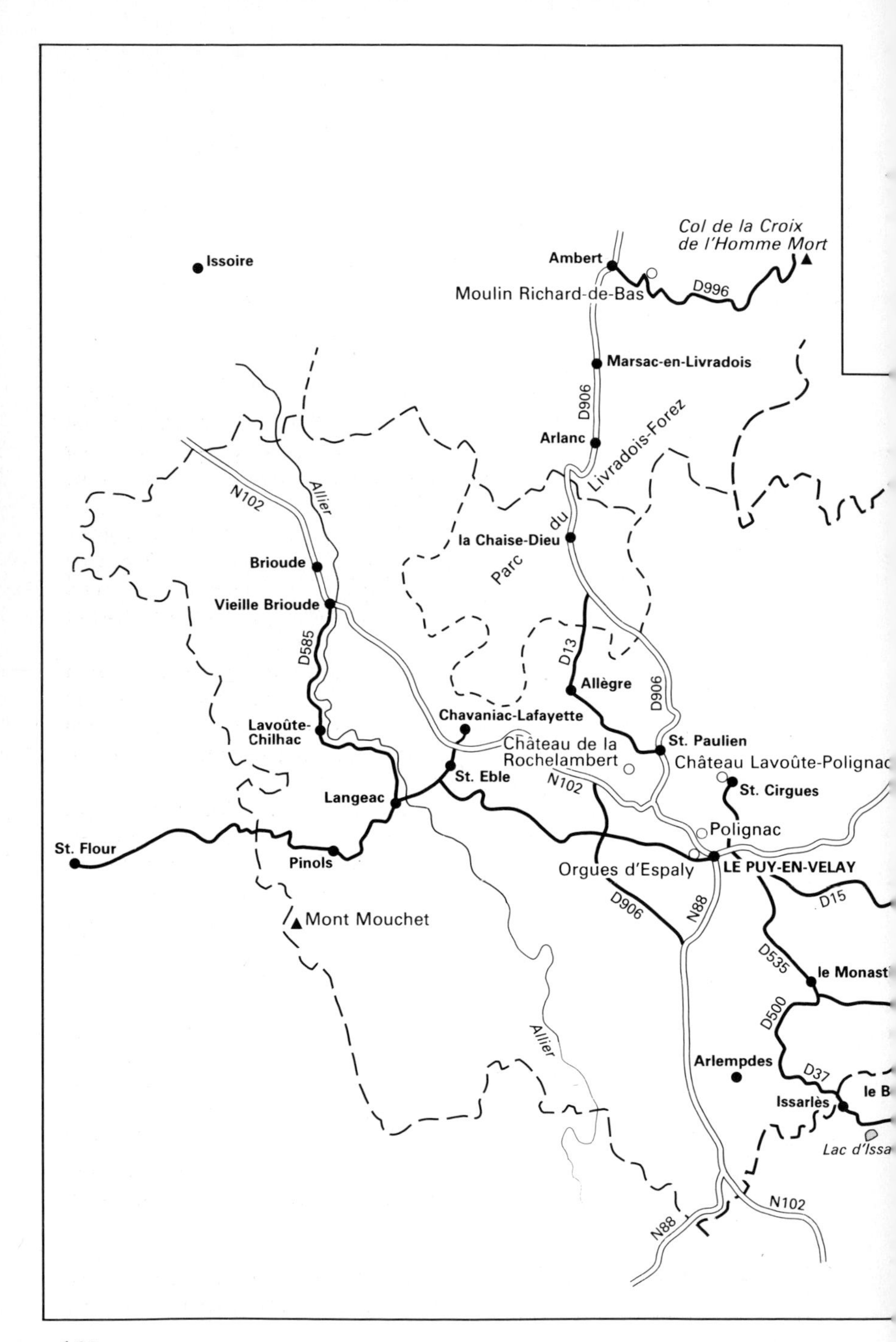
Col de la Croix
de l'Homme Mort
Issoire
Ambert
Moulin Richard-de-Bas
D996
Marsac-en-Livradois
D906
Arlanc
Parc du Livradois-Forez
N102
Allier
la Chaise-Dieu
Brioude
Vieille Brioude
D585
D13
Allègre
D906
Lavoûte-
Chilhac
Chavaniac-Lafayette
Château de la
Rochelambert
St. Paulien
Château Lavoûte-Polignac
St. Eble
N102
St. Cirgues
Langeac
Polignac
St. Flour
Pinols
LE PUY-EN-VELAY
Orgues d'Espaly
D15
D906
N88
Mont Mouchet
D535
le Monast
D500
Allier
Arlempdes
D37
le B
Issarlès
Lac d'Issa
N102
N88

8
Haute-Loire: Le Puy, Velay

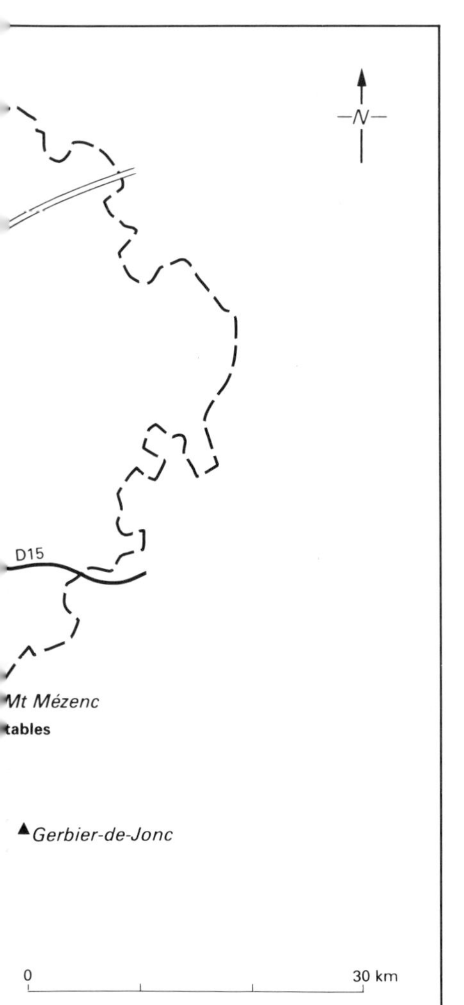

In the scenic symphony of the Massif Central the region called Velay, which forms a large part of the département of Haute-Loire, is a spacious, slow movement with lively passages. It is a lonely countryside which has seen a colourful history, rich in romantically ruined castles, fallen reputations and forgotten heroes, and masterpieces of religious architecture.

As a whole the region is rather short of hotel accommodation and in summer it is probably wiser to secure a base and make excursions than to attempt a place-to-place tour which might prove impossible to follow as planned. In winter many of the hotels are closed, the weather can be inclement and, unless you are a keen cross-country skier, for whom there are several centres, it is better to stay away.

The town of Brioude, tucked away in the north-west corner of the département, has several good small hotels and a reasonable camp site nicely placed beside the Allier. Issoire to the north, la Chaise-Dieu to the east, Le Puy to the south-east, the Gorges of the Allier to the south, St. Flour and the volcanoes of Cantal to the south-west, are all within easy driving distance.

Brioude has a fine romanesque church, St. Julien de Brioude, the largest in Auvergne. It is named after the martyr, St. Julien, a Roman soldier beheaded for his Christian faith. This basilica has some odd things about it, including a 19th-century roof of shiny tiles, but is is full of interest, and has a beautiful apse with five radiating chapels. Six different kinds of stone in varying shades of red, rose, brown and grey were used in the construction of the church, and give its interior a warm and welcoming light. The stones of the nave were cleaned some years ago and the work not only brought up the freshness of the original colours but also exposed some curious frescoes in which red and green devils are seen torturing the damned.

The carved capitals are almost a reference work of the themes common in Auvergne churches: men carrying sheep or donkeys, a miser being chastised, a roped monkey, scenes from hell, fabulous beasts, faces peering through leaves, and so on. There are also some fine statues, including a Virgin in childbed, a 14th-century carving in coloured wood, and an unusual leprous Christ carved in wood at about the same time and which came from the leper hospital at La Bajasse, near Brioude.

Some years ago during restoration work, a floor paved in neat patterns with pebbles from the bed of the Allier was uncovered, and beneath that pieces of Gallo-Roman mosaics suggesting that here, as in so many other places in Auvergne, a pagan temple preceded a Christian church.

In the past the Allier was famous as a salmon river, and Brioude was an important centre for salmon fishing. Today, although salmon are still found in the Allier, it would be a lucky man who caught one. For each salmon landed here hundreds are caught in Scotland. However, for trout and other fish, Brioude is an excellent centre. Three kilometres to the south-east a small barrage has created a lake well-equipped for watersports, near where the Allier leaves a series of gorges.

Leaving Brioude by N102 in the direction of Langeac and Le Puy turn off at Vieille Brioude on to D585 which links a number of pretty villages perched above the gorge. The most picturesque is St. Ilpize on a spur of rock on the opposite side of the river from Villeneuve-d'Allier to which it is linked by a frail-looking suspension bridge.

At Lavoûte-Chilhac, a 15th-century hump-backed bridge joins the two banks. The village has the impressive ruins of a Benedictine abbey, and a Gothic church with a large 12th-century Christ in wood, 15th-century choir stalls, and a lovely carved wooden door from the original 11th-century church. In the adjacent village of St. Cirgues the small church has some interesting late 15th-century frescoes around the choir.

From Lavoûte-Chilhac continue on D585 down the valley of the Allier to Langeac, then cross the river on to D590 and after 4km fork to the left on to D114 a road which, with fine views on the right, takes you through the village of St. Eble to the junction with N102. Cross this route nationale on to D613 to the village of Chavaniac-Lafayette.

The village, once simply Chavaniac, was renamed in honour of the Marquis

Le Puy-en-Velay, the chapel of St. Michel d'Aiguilhe on its lava rock in the foreground

de Lafayette, the French general who was a champion of American Independence and who fought against the British with the Revolutionary army. Marie Joseph Paul Yves Roch Gilbert du Motier was born in the castle here in 1757. The château was originally built in 1701 and was restored in 1781. In 1916 it was sold by Gaston de Sahune Lafayette, a great-grandson of a cousin of the Marquis, to the Lafayette Memorial Association. The pleasant château with its strange coolie-hatted towers is maintained in perfect condition by the American association. The well laid out grounds and gardens with their neatly clipped hedges and topiary work are worth a visit in themselves. But the museum, and the commentary, show that the Americans think a lot more of Lafayette than do the French, who considered him a brave soldier but a vain and foolish man. He was certainly brave, and he was certainly vain; he loved to be seen, splendidly uniformed, charging about on his pure white horse. And it is natural that the cynical French should consider him foolish, since he was always on the wrong side, fighting for lost causes, against what he saw as tyranny. He was against what he thought was the tyranny of the British in America, against Louis XVI and Marie-Antoinette and the tyranny of the Court, and after the Revolution he was against the tyranny of the people. In middle age he opposed Napoleon, and then Charles X, and during the reign of Louis-Philippe he died as he had lived, in opposition. Foolish? Perhaps. In the end he earned the best of all distinctions. He was well-remembered, and honoured, by his friends.

From Chavaniac return to N102 and conveniently back to Brioude.

There are very few places in France to which the Michelin Red Guide awards three stars just for the site alone. **Le Puy** is one of them. Despite its familiarity in photographs, the first sight of this town is enough to persuade the visitor that it is a place unlike any other.

I particularly like the approach from the west by D590 from St. Flour by way of Pinols and Langeac, but it can be equally well done by N102 from Brioude. For the last few kilometres towards Le Puy these two roads follow more or less the same course within a few kilometres of each other, and from both there are splendid views.

D590 from St. Flour passes first through the Monts de Margeride and forests of huge pine trees. Just before the village of Pinols a small road, D41, turns off to the right to Mont Mouchet, headquarters of the Resistance movement in the area during the Second World War, and where there is now a Resistance museum and national monument.

Beyond Langeac, in the valley of the Allier, the road climbs up to the plateau again and offers panoramic views of the Loire and the slopes of the Velay mountains rising on the other side. Those who believe there are no majestic views without dramatic peaks will find this vast prospect of multi-coloured fields and forest a revelation.

It is impossible to come upon le Puy itself by surprise, since the authorities, in the interest of both road safety and tourism, have provided parking at intervals on all the roads that lead down to Le Puy, so that visitors can stop to admire the view and take photographs.

Today the town is a commercial crossroads and carries heavy traffic and

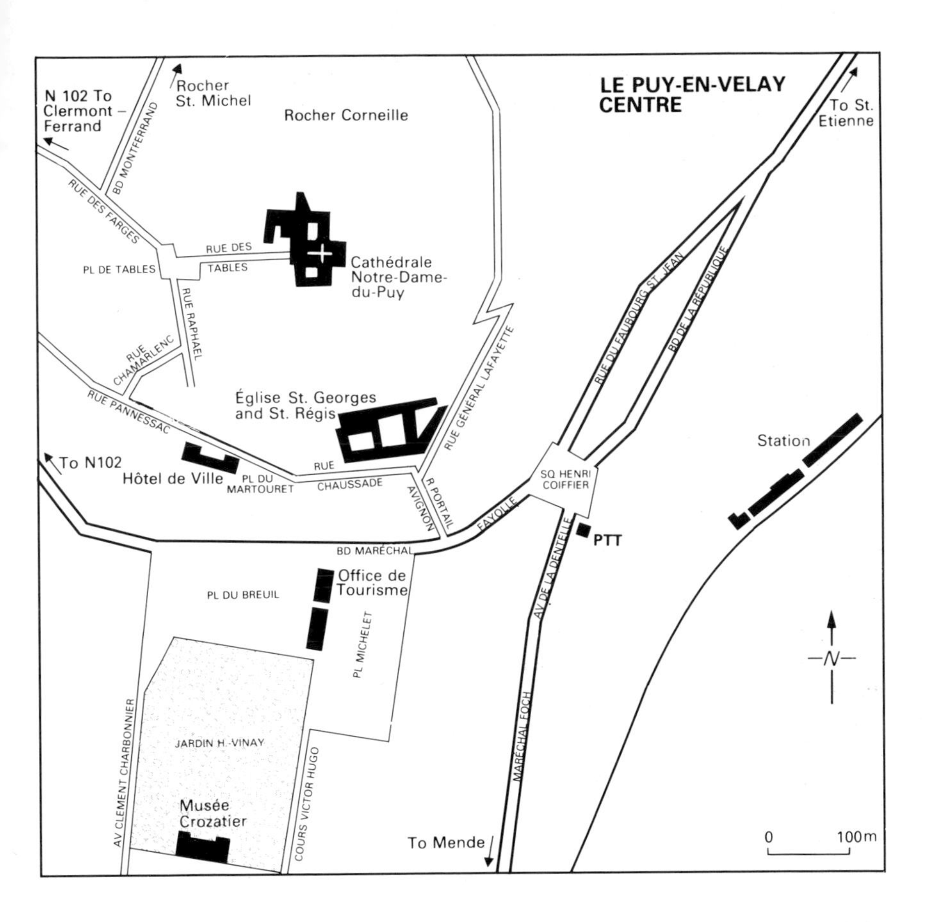

yet remains impressive, individual. It is not difficult to understand the spell-binding fascination it held for the pilgrims of the Middle Ages, when, without all the dross of modern urbanism, it was so much more concentrated.

The town is situated in a great bowl with a slightly domed floor, and high rims surrounding it on all sides, except where the river Loire has cut its way through in the south and north. Le Puy is actually on the Borne, a small tributary, and about 3km from the Loire itself. In the centre of the bowl volcanic activity has left outcrops and giant pillars of basalt. The town has developed around these strange rocks which rise up to 122m above the lower streets.

The most individual is the Rocher St. Michel, easily recognised by its isolation, its narrow sugar loaf shape, and the small chapel which crowns the peak, its minaret-like spire making the rock seem even more pointed.

Two hundred and sixty-eight steps lead up to the chapel, but the lung-testing climb is worth it both for the view and the chapel itself. It was a

Façade of Notre-Dame-du-Puy, a style showing strong Oriental influence

bishop of Le Puy named Gotescalk who, after making one of the first pilgrimages to St. James of Compostella, had the original chapel of St. Michel d'Aiguilhe (aiguille = needle, from the shape of the rock) built in the year 962. Most of the present building dates from the 11th century, and is irregular in shape following the contours of the rock, which in places forms part of the floor and has been worn smooth over hundreds of years by the feet of the faithful. The rounded arch above the entrance, with its trefoil decoration and coloured mosaics, suggests Oriental influence. Inside, the centre of the building consists of the earlier 10th-century chapel. Modern stained-glass windows, the work of Jacques le Chevalier, were put in place in 1955. They diffuse a lively, coloured light throughout the simple interior. A number of precious objects found beneath the altar in 1955 are exhibited behind a grille in the wall.

From a distance the Cathédrale Notre-Dame-du-Puy, on its basalt rock above the town, is impressive and adds considerably to the ensemble. The best way to approach it is by the ancient rue des Tables which joins the foot of the grand staircase leading to the cathedral entrance. Amateurs of religious architecture should not miss this cathedral which must be one of the most unusual in Europe. It is bound to arouse an opinion of some kind in every visitor.

The climb up rue des Tables affords time to assess the west façade of the cathedral as you approach it. This façade has been variously described as 'curious', 'interesting', 'remarkable'. These are kinder judgements than those that came to my mind. I find the 31 Romanesque arches and the multicoloured chequerboard patterns of the five-storey façade confused and rather ugly. The geometric arrangement of coloured stones, found again in the cloister, the palm and leaf themes used in the sculpture of some capitals and friezes, and the multiform arches with trefoil decoration, are all ultimately derived from the work of the builders of the Omayyad rulers of Moorish Spain.

None of this is surprising in the historical context of the period. Throughout the 11th and 12th centuries movement and cultural exchange between southern France and Moorish Spain was continual. Also, Adhemard de Monteil, Bishop of Le Puy, was the spiritual leader and Papal Legate for the first crusade in 1095. Many influential men from the region

Le Puy: lace-making by hand is a traditional craft in the region

took part in this crusade and brought back their impressions.

The interior of the church is austere but the grace and height of the spacious nave and its unusual six-domed roof make it impressive. In contrast with the general simplicity of the interior, the main altar is an ornate affair of veined white and dark rose marble with a good deal of bronze decoration applied, and large gilt panels and stars framing the black Virgin, crowned and in a pose calling to mind a coronation scene. This is not the original black Virgin of Le Puy, said to have been offered to the cathedral by St. Louis (Louis IX) on his return from the seventh Crusade and which was burned during the French Revolution. The present one is a 19th-century work installed with great ceremony in 1856.

Details of pillars and capitals, Notre-Dame-du-Puy

To the left of the altar the north transept has some good frescoes — the martyrdom of St. Catherine on the wheel, the two Marys at the tomb of Jesus, and a remarkable St. Michael, dating from the 11th century, more than 5m high and said to be the largest painting in France. A time switch on the pillar between the smaller frescoes enables them to be illuminated.

In the Chapelle des Reliques (Reliquary Chapel) there is a large mural painting, in the style of the late 15th century, representing four of the liberal arts (Grammar, Logic, Rhetoric and Music). It was discovered in 1850 under old whitewash by Prosper Mérimée (the well known 19th-century writer) who, as Inspector of Historical Monuments, was responsible for restoration work being carried out at the time.

At the back of the church on the right, the Cathedral treasure is displayed in the Sacristy. The best pieces are a 15th-century Pietà, painted on wood, a head of Christ in copper chased with gold, and a 600-page Bible on white and purple vellum, illuminated and written in gold and silver, which was made by the monks of St. Fleury-sur-Loire at the end of the 8th century.

After the overall sobriety of the interior of the Cathedral, the fine cloister is a lively contrast. Its coloured stonework alternating between red, white and black recalls a similar use of stone in the arches of the mosque (now cathedral) of Córdoba. The rhythm of the graceful curves of the vaulting, the refinement of the wrought iron grilles, the sculpture on the friezes and cornice alive with symbols of good and evil, together make it one of the most attractive cloisters in France. Though much restoration was done in the 19th century, it dates essentially from the 12th.

Le Puy was already a bishopric by the 5th century AD and it was a Roman architect, Scutarus, who built the first Christian church on the site now occupied by the Cathedral. At the end of the 11th century a new church was built, but the growing religious importance of Le Puy and the steady increase in the number of pilgrims who halted there on the way to St. James of Compostella soon created a need for a larger church.

It does not seem to have occurred to the religious authorities that they might put a new cathedral somewhere else in Le Puy. They wanted to keep it where it was because that particular rock had been a place of worship from time immemorial. The Druids had a temple there. Indeed, the Pierre des Fièvres (the Fever Stone) outside the west façade entrance is believed to be a Druid ceremonial stone. It was supposed to have the miraculous power to cure the sick or paralysed, if they slept upon it. It seems likely that here, as in so many other places in Auvergne, the Druid cult was followed in Roman times by the worship of the god Mercury, and then came the Christian Church.

If it was force of habit that kept the Cathedral in a traditional place of worship, it was another essentially human characteristic that made it physically possible to do so, stubbornness. The rock platform was not big enough for the architects to enlarge the nave as they wished to do. All right, they said, in effect, if the rock is not big enough we will make it bigger, and then we will enlarge the cathedral. So they constructed two great pillars to carry the platform for the extension of the nave, a 12th-century *tour de force*, which they repeated fifty years later to enable them to build farther over space. Their work lasted until the 19th century when the whole edifice was in danger of falling down and had to be considerably reinforced and reconstructed.

Above the Cathedral the Rocher Corneille rises in a basalt pillar, the highest in the town, which is surmounted by a statue of Notre Dame de France. The climb up to the foot of the statue may be found tiring by some but on a good day worth it for the extensive view of the town and the old quarters just below. The statue itself, erected by subscription in 1860, is more than 15m high, weighs 112 tonnes, and was cast from 213 cannons taken at the Battle of Sebastopol. It is in every way a clumsy work and is painted a nasty shade of red, presumably a protection against rust. All in all it must rank as one of the ugliest religious monuments in the world. The locals like it, but most visitors are blind to its merits. Anyone fortunate enough to have seen, for example, the magnificent Christ the Redeemer in Rio de Janeiro, the foot bathed in clouds and the statue seeming to float above them, will know what an opportunity has been lost here.

In order to see something of the old town, walk down rue Raphael from Place des Tables (bottom of rue des Tables) and turn off into rue de Charmalenc and from there into rue

Overleaf: *The impregnable fortress of Polignac with a history going back 2000 years to the oracles of Apollo*

Pannessac, where there are a number of 17th- and 18th-century houses.

On the other side of the town the Musée Crozatier in the Jardin Vinay, behind the Préfecture, has a superb collection of the lace for which Le Puy was famous. The making of lace by hand has been a craft practised by the women of this region for hundreds of years. It was first mentioned in a text in 1408. In the 19th century there were seven hundred women engaged in teaching the art to young girls, but the lace makers became fewer as machine-made lace flooded the market. Not to be beaten Le Puy, too, switched to mechanical production and in the 1930s had about a hundred workshops producing machine-made lace, but, as the fashion for lace itself declined they began to close down and there are now only a few left.

On the other hand, due to the recent efforts of one woman, Michèle Fouriscot, the making of lace by hand is enjoying a revival. As a result of her enthusiasm the subject is now taught in schools and in 1976 a National Conservatoire for making lace by hand was founded. Lace makers can be seen at work at the Centre d'Initiation à la Dentelle du Puy (2 rue du Guesclin), where there is also an exhibition of lace of the 17th century onwards. In summer there are often lace makers at work in rue des Tables, conveniently placed for tourists to take their photographs on their way up to the Cathedral.

Apart from lace the Musée Crozatier has a surprisingly strong collection of other kinds. On the first floor in the Salle Cortiale there is a collection of furniture and *objets d'art* from the Middle Ages. It includes a marble group showing Alinorda, sister of Pope Clement VI, and her five chidren, which came from the Pope's tomb at la Chaise-Dieu. They must have been part of the group of 44 family mourners which originally formed part of the tomb, and which some guide books suggest were all destroyed by the Protestants in 1562. On the second floor there are several rooms of paintings from the 15th century onwards. There are attributions to Rubens, de Heem and Salomon Ruysdael. In another room on this floor there are Aubusson tapestries of the 17th century and a collection of Limoges enamels. The ground floor has mineralogy of the region, early architecture, Christianity in Le Puy from its origins to the end of the Middle Ages, local history from the Renaissance to the Revolution, and a room with working models of early machines.

On the outskirts of the town, in the district of Espaly-St. Marcel, there are two more volcanic outcrops and a strange geological formation of fluted rock in a cliff above the Borne, known as the Orgues d'Espaly (reached via N102). There are fine views from this site.

In Espaly, the rock to the west has the ruins of an old castle once used by the Bishops of Le Puy. It was built in 1270 and destroyed during the religious wars. The rock to the east is surmounted by a 15m concrete statue of St. Joseph, holding the child Jesus with one arm, gesturing to heaven with the other, and looking down, one is tempted to say, with disgust, at the Basilica of St. Joseph, another concrete construction, the façade of which looks more like a hastily run up Hollywood set for a musical version of Ivanhoe than a church. It is an extraordinary caricature of a medieval castle.

The antidote lies about 3km from the centre of Le Puy at Polignac, where a flat-topped basalt rock is crowned by the ruined fortress of the Polignac family. In the Middle Ages they were the masters of this region, due to the impregnability of their castle magnificently sited on this steep-sided rock.

Not much remains to see of the castle apart from the Keep, and that was rebuilt at the end of the 19th century. Among the fallen stones a mask of Apollo is pointed out. Tradition has it that the Polignacs were originally priests of Apollo, with a temple and a famous oracle on the rock. Those consulting the oracle left their offerings in a room at the foot of the rock and whispered aloud their problems. They then climbed slowly up the rock to the mask of Apollo which at once thundered out its reply, no doubt with the aid of a loud-hailer concealed behind the stone. What the astonished pilgrim did not know was that the room where he whispered his problem was connected to a well shaft, said to be 80m deep, which acted as a sound box so that every word could be heard by. the priests above who had their reply ready by the time he had struggled up there. Well, it makes a good story.

What is sure is that the chief interest of the site today is its historical associations. If any family can be described as illustrious, it is a fair term for the Polignacs who were already viscounts when Héracle de Polignac died in 1098, at the age of 23, before the walls of Antioch, fighting in the first Crusade. Like many of the warlords of the Massif Central the Polignacs were guilty of excesses and brigandage during the Middle Ages, but they held their power and became more respectable as time went by. In 1713 it was Melchior de Polignac, a dignitary of the Church, a man of letters and skilful diplomat, who negotiated the Treaty of Utrecht. In the same year he became a Cardinal, and was made a member of the French Academy.

The fortunes of the family reached their height towards the end of the same century. Yolande de Polastron, wife of Jules de Polignac, was a very close friend of Marie-Antoinette. This friendship brought her great sums of money, priceless jewellery, and a Dukedom for her husband. Their son, Auguste Jules, became a friend of the Comte d'Artois, brother of Louis XVIII.

The Polignacs were leaders in the extravagant behaviour of the Court and did much to excite the jealousy and hatred of the people. They were well aware of it, and when the Revolution came were among the first to emigrate. They went to Russia where Catherine the Great, because of their royal connection, gave them an estate in the Ukraine. They did not return after the Revolution but their son, created a prince by the Pope, became Prime Minister when his friend, the Comte d'Artois, came to the throne as Charles X. Both this King and his Prime Minister were extreme reactionaries and are remembered today for two things. It was under their administration that Algeria became French, and it was the edicts issued by Polignac on 25th July 1830, restricting the liberty of the Press, dissolving the Chambers and altering the electoral laws, which immediately provoked the 1830 Revolution (27th–28th July). After three days of fighting in Paris (it was an entirely Parisian revolution, over before the rest of the country heard of it), the King was driven from the throne.

There is another Polignac castle at Lavoûte-sur-Loire, also with an interesting story and evidence that when the mighty fall they are often able to save something from the wreck. The château of Lavoûte-Polignac is about 18km north of Le Puy by D103. It stands proudly above a bend of the Loire on the edge of a rocky cliff, a site made for a fortress, and there has been one here since the 13th century.

What you see today is a classic 17th-century château with a rectangular façade flanked by two round towers, but most of it is a very good reconstruction. The château had been in and out of the hands of the Polignacs and when they bought it back for the last time in 1888 all that was left was a two-storey building and the lower part of the towers. The restoration was done with complete accuracy inside and out, to the extent of bringing great fireplaces of the right period from yet another Polignac castle. It was in the salon here in 1592 that agreement was reached between the Catholic League and the Protestants, bringing peace in the religious wars. The château contains some superb period furniture, and portraits of the family, including Cardinal Polignac, who was born there, and of the Duchess Yolande and her husband, the friends of Marie-Antoinette, and of the Jules de Polignac whose stupidity brought about the fall of the government and his king and ended the greatness of his family. Today the average Frenchman associates the name Polignac with a Cognac brandy, a rather good one.

The road which runs past the ruined fortress of Polignac carries on to La Chaise-Dieu which, like Le Puy, is both a religious centre and a place unlike any other. On the way the drive takes you through some of the loneliest and wildest country in France.

A few kilometres from Polignac is the village of St. Paulien which has a moderately interesting Romanesque church. From St. Paulien a short detour (2.5km) leads to the Château de la Rochelambert. This pleasantly situated 16th-century castle is interesting for its association with Aurore Dupin, Baroness Dudevant, known to novel readers as George Sand, who used it as a setting in her novel *Jean de la Roche*. One of her fellow pupils in the English convent in Paris had been the future Marquise de la Rochelambert, with whom she remained friendly, and she had stayed in the castle. It remains today just as it was at the time of her visit and among the remarkable art collection are some of George Sand's own drawings.

From St. Paulien D13 climbs steadily to the large village of Allègre, overlooked by the ruins of a 14th-century castle, strange gate-like ruins, where the wall between two towers has fallen leaving the battlements in place. In clear weather the climb from the village to the ruins is rewarded with extensive views across to the Velay mountains and the Mézenc plateau. There is an orientation table on the spot.

From Allègre D13 passes through the empty, forested heights of the Regional Nature Park of Livradois-Forez, a region depopulated, now almost deserted, because of the near impossibility of making a living there. It is a country of memories and legends where the few people left scratch a

The splendid early Gothic abbey church at La Chaise-Dieu

Château of La Rochelambert, used by George Sand as a setting for one of her novels

living from the forest clearings, or from the forest itself. Small sawmills produce wood for construction or telegraph poles. Even the lichen off the trees, which is used as a fixative in the perfume industry, is sold.

The park was established in 1982 and its Administrative Committee was formed in 1984, although it is not yet fully operational. The objectives in setting up this Regional Park are more than simply the preservation of a wild and beautiful area — more than half of it is thick forest. Some of them are defined as follows: to stop the population drain — by the development of cultural tourism (by this they mean activity holidays, walking, riding, cycling, skiing, fishing, etc.); by improving the income and standard of living of those engaged in agriculture (it hovers around subsistence level at present); by organising and reinforcing the financial resources of local agriculture; by harmonising the sometimes competitive relationhip between farming and forestry; by encouraging young people to take up farming; to increase forestry production and the manufacture of wood products within the area. To facilitate this development the park has been divided into six regions each with its own 'town' at the centre. In fact there are only two real towns within the limits of the park, Thiers and Ambert, and they are small.

It all sounds sensible and ambitious but where will the money come from? The region does not have the same impetus from existing tourism as the Parc des Volcans, or the Cévennes which is a subsidised National Park, and the attitude of the French authorities is similar to that of the World Bank to the Third World — but of course we are willing to invest — if we can see a profit. It will be a slow business.

The road keeps on up through the trees and it is almost a shock, when one is beginning to think in terms of primeval forest, to come upon the isolated village of La Chaise-Dieu, and the great church which looms over the little red-roofed community.

This lonely sanctuary had its origins in the 11th century when Robert de Turlande, a canon of the church of St. Julien de Brioude, decided to do penance through a life of extreme simplicity. After searching the depths of the forest for four days, he chose this clearing on the cold ridge between the valley of the Allier and that of the Loire. He set up a monastery there. At the time of his death more than three hundred monks had joined him, attached to the Benedictine order, and a small village had grown up around his house of God, Casa Dei — the origin of the name Chaise-Dieu.

Nothing remains of the church he had built in 1043. It was replaced in the 14th century by the wish of Pope Clement VI. In his young days this Pope, whose name was Pierre Roger and who came from Limousin, had been a monk at Chaise-Dieu, and wished to be buried near St. Robert. In commanding the reconstruction of the abbey church of St. Robert, the Pope was ordering a magnificent funeral monument for himself. Work on the new church began in 1344. It was built by Hugues Morel, architect of the Palace of the Popes at Avignon. He built in the simplest Gothic style with a minimum of elaborate technique and decoration. He was aided by Pierre de Cébazat who had been responsible for completing the cathedral at Clermont-Ferrand.

The early Gothic abbey church of St. Robert, at La Chaise-Dieu

The combination of the Pope's generosity — he spared no expense for his own resting place — and Morel's great talent and sure taste has produced a church remarkable for its blend of strength and refinement. Perhaps because he was sensitive to the contrast between the sun of Provence and the rough winter climate of La Chaise-Dieu, Morel built to last in great weather-resistant blocks of granite. His work still stands today looking much as it did in the 14th century.

The church is approached uphill by a small square which has a very rustic 17th-century fountain. The west façade gives at once an impression of grave solidity. The statue on the central pier of the porch is of St. Robert. Inside, the feeling of simplicity, grace and strength is even more marked. Perhaps because of its isolation, the church is one of the few religious monuments of France which has kept almost all its original furnishing and decoration.

Pope Clement VI died in 1352 and was buried here while the church was still being built. His tomb still occupies its place in the centre of the choir but was badly damaged in the Huguenot attack on the church in 1562. The 44 marble figures of family mourners grouped around the tomb when it was installed were nearly all destroyed then. What remains is the recumbent white marble statue of the Pope, a masterpiece of Gothic sculpture, on its black marble base. The tomb is framed by two tiers of beautifully carved 14th-century choir stalls, 144 of them. Above the stalls around the Choir is a very fine set of tapestries, made in Brussels and Arras, and presented to the church by the abbot, Jacques de Senectaire, in 1518. They are arranged in groups of three, each with a scene from the New Testament in the centre, with one from the Old Testament on either side.

In the aisle of the left (north side) of the Choir there is the famous mural painting of the Danse Macabre. This 15th-century work, 26m long and 2m high, has been restored. It is divided into three panels, the one on the right representing the rich and powerful of the world, the one in the middle the bourgeoisie, and the one on the left the artisans and workmen. Each character is being led by his skeleton into the Dance of Death. This theme, illustrating the impartiality of Death, was often used by the Church in the Middle Ages to remind the faithful of their Christian duty and to be prepared always to appear before God.

This tempera painting, its severity relieved here and there by warm tints, contrasts the grace of the living with the contorted ugliness of the skeletons, and is one of the best surviving works of its kind. The contemplation of this particular work by the musician, Honegger, is said to have inspired his well known Danse Macabre.

17th-century fountain in the village square, La Chaise-Dieu

In the same aisle there are two 14th-century tombs. It is not known for certain who is buried there, but the tradition is that one is the tomb of an Archbishop of Rouen, uncle of Pope Clement VI, and the other of Edith, widow of Edward the Confessor, who, after her husband's death, came to finish her days at La Chaise-Dieu. As Edward had been dead for nearly three hundred years when this church was rebuilt, one must assume that Edith was first interred in the 11th-century church.

The choir is closed off by a triple arched rood screen added in the 15th century, in the Flamboyant Gothic style. Above it there is a fine figure of Christ, dating from 1603, and in the side arches there are 14th-century wooden statues of the Virgin and of St. John. The fine organ surround was installed in 1683 and restored ten years ago.

Nothing much remains of the original monastery apart from two galleries of the 14th-century cloister and a few buildings used as a hospice. In one of the rooms just inside the hospice, the Salle de l'Écho, two people standing in opposite corners with their backs to each other can carry on a whispered conversation with ease. This arrangement is said to have been used in several places in the Middle Ages to enable lepers to be confessed.

The building of the Abbey Church of St. Robert was completed by the nephew of Pope Clement VI, who had also become Pope. The total cost was two million gold francs, a very large sum for the time.

La Chaise-Dieu is the setting for an annual festival of French music which takes place at the end of August, beginning September.

D906 winds slowly down through a deeply forested part of the Livradois-Forez Nature Park to the small town of Arlanc. Like Le Puy this was once a famous lace-making centre and is, also, in a modest way, reviving the art. A small museum in the town centre has an exhibition of antique lace, and professional lace makers explain the various stages of the craft and their work is offered for sale.

From Arlanc, 16km of wide straight road lead to the peaceful town of Ambert. About halfway, in Marsac-en-Livradois, there is an unusual museum. When in the 14th century the Church abandoned the imposition of public penance, societies of voluntary penitents were formed whose members took it upon themselves to absolve the sins of others. This they did by practising piety and charity and by carrying out disagreeable tasks such as the care of the sick and the burial of the dead during epidemics.

In Auvergne there were two of these societies, the Black and the White Penitents, and in this museum in Marsac there is an exhibition which represents many aspects of the Company of White Penitents. Every year, on the Thursday before Good Friday, the Penitents walked in procession through their villages, and the museum includes a model of such a procession. The custom has died out except in the village of Saugues, also in Haute-Loire, where it continues to take place as it has done annually for more than four hundred years.

Ambert, set in its fertile valley, surrounded by wooded hills, and watered by the Dore, a good fishing river, is a place that seems apart from the world, a quiet, unhurried town. Something in the air here must stimulate the intellect since Ambert has produced far more than a normal proportion of scholars and writers for such a small town. One of them was Henri Pourrat, a writer once well known throughout France, and still revered in Auvergne. His parents kept a genteel haberdashery in the town and Pourrat was meant to be a civil servant but was taken ill with consumption. His doctor advised him to spend plenty of time in the open air and to eat raw eggs. Pourrat took his fate philosophically — in those days people almost invariably died from tuberculosis — there were two other brothers to carry on the family — but followed his doctor's orders. He walked lazily in the countryside, taking with him a pocketful of raw eggs, and chatted with the peasants. One day he heard a folk tale, a story which exists in varied forms in many European countries, sometimes called The Story of the White Eyes, often the Tale of the Severed Hand. It concerns a young girl, who through unusual circumstances is left alone in the family farmhouse. She forgets to close one of the seven doors of the house, and at night a man emerges from hiding and attacks her. She fights back and in the struggle two of his fingers are cut off. He flees, swearing vengeance. The girl says nothing to her parents on their return. A year or so passes and, as was the custom, the parents arrange her marriage. At the wedding feast the girl recognises her husband as the man who attacked her.

It's Enough to Drive You Mad

Remarkable powers have been attributed to some of the mineral springs in Auvergne. There is one at Jarrix, near Ambert, which is known as La Fontaine des Timbrés, the translation of which is The Fountain of the Loonies. Those who drink its waters are said to feel that they are going mad. If they have been told in advance that this is likely to happen and they still drink the water, one wonders whether, in fact, much change takes place. It is in any case not too desperate a situation because there are other springs which restore sanity to those who have lost it.

Others are said to be able to turn you to stone, if you stay in the water long enough, though it seems likely that only those among the more serious cases who had drunk long and deep at the Fountain of the Loonies would try it. There is certainly a petrifying spring at St. Nectaire where souvenirs consisting of petrified mice, leaves, flowers and fruits were sold. The water of the spring was directed over shallow steps where the objects to be 'petrified' were placed. In a few days they acquired an attractive coating of white crystals.

Weaving all kinds of other tales around it, Pourrat wrote the first volume of his great saga of Auvergne life, *Gaspard des Montagnes*. He sent it to the newspaper *Le Figaro* which had just announced a literary prize competition. The jury of already famous French writers, including Colette, awarded him the prize unanimously.

It was 1921. Pourrat carried on writing. He worked sitting in a wheelbarrow in a neighbour's garden facing the mountains, swallowing his raw eggs and leaving a small mountain of shells at his left hand every day. He wrote three more volumes of *Gaspard* and seventy other works. His brothers died, one in an accident, and one of a chill. Henri Pourrat married, brought up a family, ate raw eggs by the thousand, and died in 1959, aged seventy two. So much for eggs and the dangers of cholesterol.

Ambert was once famous for paper making. Today this has been replaced by a number of small industries, furniture, prefabricated wooden houses, spare parts of cars, and the manufacture of clothing. But of the former three hundred paper mills, one remains, a tourist attraction unique in France.

The Moulin Richard-de-Bas is a few kilometres out of town in the Lagat valley, off the Montbrison road. It was founded in the 14th century, the exact date is not known, but it continued in normal commercial production until 1938. It was revived a few years later by the Association de la Feuille Blanche, a group of amateurs of beautiful books and old crafts.

You can watch the manufacture of high quality paper in all its stages and by the same methods that have been used here for hundreds of years. There is also a museum of paper making and a bookshop which sells superbly bound books and special editions printed on the hand-made paper from this mill. More than 100,000 people visit the Moulin Richard-de-Bas every year.

About 25km from the mill on the road to Montbrison there is a pass called the Col de la Croix de l'Homme Mort. It recalls the assassination in 1795 of a 20-year-old paper maker, Thomas Richard, son of the family who owned the mill, who was stabbed to death by one of his workmen.

Le Puy is an excellent base for many other excursions, but hotel rooms should be booked well in advance in summer. The centre of the town can be crowded and noisy and for those who like peace and quiet at night the Moulin de Barette, 8km out on N88, the St. Étienne road, is a possible alternative. It has some rooms in the old mill, more in spacious and comfortable motel accommodation in the grounds, and a good restaurant.

Going south from le Puy there is a good tour taking in Le Monastier-sur-Gazeille, Arlempdes, Issarlès, Mont Mézenc, and Gerbier-de-Jonc, the source of the Loire.

To reach Le Monastier leave Le Puy by the road to Valence and directly after crossing the Loire turn right on to D535, and a little farther on, after passing under a bridge, take the right fork for Le Monastier. This is still D535 and it is about a 20km climb up to Le Monastier situated at about 915m, and above the right bank of the Gazeille.

It was at Le Monastier that Robert Louis Stevenson spent 'a month of fine days' before setting out on his travels through the Cévennes with his temperamental donkey, Modestine. Apparently he did not think highly of the inhabitants of Le Monastier. 'It is,' he wrote 'notable for the making of lace, for drunkenness, freedom of language, and unparalleled political dissension ... Except for business purposes or to give each other the lie in a tavern brawl, they have laid aside even the civility of speech.'

Nevertheless he admitted that everyone was anxious to be kind and helpful to him as a stranger and ... 'this was not just from the natural hospitality of mountain people, nor even from the surprise with which I was regarded as a man living of his own free will in Le Monastier when he might just as well have lived anywhere else in this big world. It arose a good deal from my projected excursion southward through the Cévennes. A traveller of my sort was a thing hitherto unheard of in that district, I was looked upon not with contempt, like a man who should project a journey to the moon, but with respectful interest like one setting forth for the inclement Pole ...'

Perhaps Stevenson was being a little hard on Le Monastier which, in summer, is an attractive place with some nice old houses. There is also an impressive church, clearly a close relation of the cathedral at Le Puy. It has a similar, if simpler, polychrome façade with white and red stones arranged in geometric patterns. In the high season only, 5th July to 15th August, the church treasure is exhibited to the public in the sacristy. It includes some valuable pieces, among them a reliquary bust of the 11th century carved in wood and decorated with silver and precious stones. There is a similar one, of St. Foy, in the abbey of Conques.

At the exit from the village to the south the road forks. Take the right-hand side and follow D500 in search of Arlempdes, a difficult place to come at from any direction, being served only by pretty but winding and poky roads. Perhaps the simplest way is to keep on D500 as far as the hamlet of Les Arcis where there is a right turn, D54, down into the valley by way of Vielprat and so to Arlempdes. This village is a curious, fey sort of place, very old, fortified, with a gate built in the year 1066. The boulder-strewn torrent which rushes through the valley is none other than the Loire. Above the village a fractured basalt rock bears the ruins of a feudal castle built by the Monlaur family in the 13th century, a fortress which played its part in the bloody struggles of the Middle Ages. It must still have been in use in the 16th century since the stones carry a coat of arms of Diane de Poitiers, a lady who seems to have been an intrepid traveller throughout France — well protected, of course, as she was what the French so charmingly call the *douce amie* of Henry II.

The village stands at a point where the Loire enters a wild gorge. In the summer dry season it is often possible to walk the few kilometres through the gorge in the bed of the river to the village of Goudet, which Stevenson reached for lunch on his first day's walk (by a completely different route) from Le Monastier. 'It stands,' he wrote 'in the green end of a valley with Château Beaufort opposite on a rocky steep and the stream as clear as crystal lying in a deep pool between them. Above and below you may hear it wimpling over the stones, an amiable stripling of a river which it seems absurd to call the Loire. On all sides Goudet is shut in by mountains; rocky footpaths practical at best for donkeys join it to the outer world of France, and the men and women drink and swear in their green corner, or look up at the snow-clad peaks in winter on the threshold of their homes in an isolation you would think like that of Homer's Cyclops . . .'

Back in Arlempdes there is a pleasant little inn, the Manoir, where a good meal can be had at a reasonable price.

From Arlempdes take the road back up to Les Arcis, turn left on D500 back towards Le Monastier then, after the descent to the Loire and immediately after crossing it, turn right on D37 to the village of Issarlès and continue on to the Lac d'Issarlès. A small summer resort has grown up around this beautiful crater lake renowned for the purity and the lovely colour of its water. In the 1950s it was the cause of one of the first ecological arguments in France. The French Electricity Authority planned to build an underground hydro-electric power station, for which the Lac d'Issarlès would serve as a reservoir. This involved diverting part of the Loire into the lake, and it was feared that the lake would become turbid, lose its famous colour and cease to be a tourist attraction. The Electricity Authority therefore agreed to filter all the new water entering the lake.

The power station and eighteen kilometres of tunnels were built and, under the lake, an inlet for the water into the system; the whole scheme cost £12 million and took 2,000 workmen five years to complete. The lake remains as beautiful as ever and, constantly refilled by the Loire, produces 300 million kWh every year.

To continue to the source of the Loire at Gerbier-de-Jonc carry on from Lac d'Issarlès by D16 to the village of Le Béage, about 8km. Take the right fork in the village and then a sharp right on to D122 to Ste. Eulalie. If you happen to be there on or about 15th July, the annual Flower Fair will be in progress. Medicinal plants, herbs and lovely flowers, notably violets, from the mountain slopes are sold. On the volcanic soil they grow in profusion and in spring the ground is a purple carpet of violets with large, perfumed flowers. Together with the strongly scented herbs (one of the delights of Auvergne cookery is the rich and penetrating flavour of the local herbs) they are set to dry, and by July are ready to sell. Most are bought for use in the pharmaceutical and perfumery trades.

Serious walkers may like to know that from Ste. Eulalie the GR 7 passes over the Suc de Seponnet (Suc is a word used in this part of the Cévennes to describe a volcanic peak) to Mont Mézenc, crossing uninhabited country with limitless views.

At a junction just beyond Ste. Eulalie D122 goes off to the right. Keep straight on, the road is now D116 for about 4km to Gerbier-de-Jonc where the Loire rises in the pastures of the lower slopes. You are already more than 915m up and this awkwardly shaped volcanic cone is only a few hundred metres above the surrounding country. One talks of the source of the Loire and for a hundred years or so there was one farmhouse (it is shown with the peak on an old 50 franc French stamp) with water spurting beside its walls whose owners made a living showing it to visitors as the source of the Loire. It is still there, but as more and more tourists came, some of the quicker-minded local people realised that there were several streams on Gerbier-de-Jonc, and now there are several inns and cafés, each with its own trickle of water and the 'true' source of the Loire. Who knows? And does it matter? When I went to find the source of the river Lot, which, about 200m wide, flows past my house, I arrived in the correct place not far from the village of Le Bleymard only to be told, 'Well, it often is hereabouts, but we have had a couple of dry seasons and you will find it about three kilometres farther down the valley,' and so I did.

It is a short and easy climb to the top of Gerbier-de-Jonc, and from it range after range of volcanic mountains can be seen.

The Loire starts off happily southwards towards the Mediterranean, only about 160km away, but comes up against the solid rock of the Suc de Bauzon and turns west and then north and takes 965km to reach the Atlantic.

From Gerbier-de-Jonc take D378 to the village of Les Estables, and then D361 to Le Monastier will put you back on the road to Le Puy.

Les Estables, which at more than 1,370m claims to be the highest village in the Massif Central, is a classic example of what tourism can do for a poor and struggling village. Until a few years ago it was a place where shepherds and foresters earned a miserable living, often cut off by snow in winter. Then tourism gave it a chance and Les Estables has taken it and effected a modest revolution in its circumstances. Its three small inns have been modernised. A holiday village of cosy south-facing chalets has been built. Smart shops have been opened, as have simple installations for cross-country skiing. Footpaths and ski-tracks have been signposted. In summer it is a fishing and walking centre.

All this is due to its proximity to the highest mountain in the Cévennes, Mont Mézenc. At close to 1,830m this mountain, shaped like the big-top of a

Murder at the Inn

On the road from Le Puy to Aubenas, the N102, there is a lonely inn called the Auberge de Peyrebeille, set in a wild landscape of moors, forests and deep gorges.

In the early 19th century, travellers arriving at nightfall on foot or on horseback often felt that it would be dangerous to continue on this isolated road, and opted to stay the night. For those with fat purses it was a serious mistake. Over the years, 53 clients were knocked out, robbed, had their throats cut, and were chopped into small pieces, boiled and fed to the pigs.

The chief actors in this gruesome business were the innkeeper, Pierre Martin, his wife, Marie, their two daughters, their nephew, and Jean Rochette, a servant. At their trial in Privas, the innkeeper and his wife, and the servant, were condemned to the guillotine. The daughters had married and gone away and were never brought to trial.

The execution took place on 2nd October 1833, in the farmyard of the inn. Thirty thousand people are said to have gathered to see the spectacle. Temporary bars and market stalls were set up. Marie Martin was first upon the scaffold and is said to have spat upon the Cross that was offered her. Pierre Martin died professing repentance. The servant cried out, 'Cursed master, what have you made me do?'

When it was over, there was music, and the crowd enjoyed a good country dance, the famous *bourrée* of Auvergne.

The inn has been rebuilt and today sells postcards and souvenirs of its grim past. There are rooms to let, but not many people stay there.

circus, with rock outcrops at each end, dominates a region of volcanic mountains which, being far from the main centres of the Massif Central, and a little apart from the main body of the Cévennes, are much less well known, almost forgotten, both by tourists and the authorities, than those of Puy-de-Dôme and Cantal. Between the granite plateau of Margeride and the limestone heights of the Vivarais to the east there are about a hundred volcanoes of various types. Those between Mt. Mézenc and Gerbier-de-Jonc are often of the Peléen type, worth mentioning because they have two special characteristics. They erupt with a lava which is too thick to flow freely and which solidifies without forming a crater. This often gives them a bizarre shape. The stook-like Gerbier-de-Jonc, bent over at the top is an example. Secondly, their rock is phonolithic — when it is struck it resounds and it is this quality which in some places makes you feel that the earth is hollow beneath your feet.

Mt. Mézenc is an approachable mountain best seen from the south and the east. The roads which encircle the base are narrow but perfectly drivable. From Les Estables it is possible to drive within twenty minutes' walk of the summit. These mountains have their own grandeur but are, perhaps, less scenically attractive than the main body of the Cévennes, described in the next chapter.

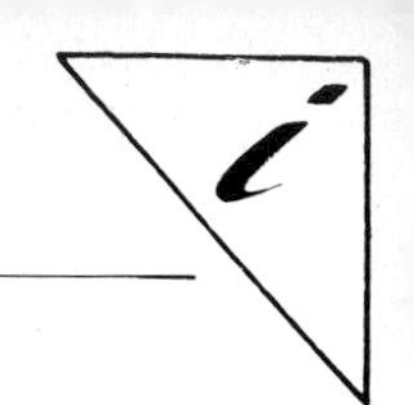

General Information

AMBERT Information: Syndicat d'Initiative, pl de l'Hôtel-de-Ville (73.82.01.55) and in high season, pl G.-Courtial (73.82.14.15).
Where to stay: Another small town with small hotels, of which Le Livradois is the best known (73.82.10.01).
Where to eat: The restaurant of the Livradois is unanimously regarded as the best in this part of Auvergne. Not expensive and well above average.

BRIOUDE Information: Syndicat d'Initiative, 3 bd Dr-Devins (71.50.05.35).
Where to stay: The Poste et Champanne (71.50.14.10) is reasonably priced and has a good value restaurant. It also has an annexe. I have never stayed in a satisfactory hotel annexe and I believe it is a good rule to avoid them if you possibly can. No doubt there are exceptions, somewhere.
Where to eat: If not at the above hotel, at the Restaurant Julien (71.50.00.03), an unpretentious and rustic atmosphere, high standards of cooking, and very good service.

LA CHAISE-DIEU Information:: Syndicat d'Initiative, pl de la Mairie (71.00.01.16).
Where to stay: Surprisingly, with less than 1,000 inhabitants, La Chaise-Dieu has four small hotels. Au Tremblant (71.00.01.85) is the largest.
Where to eat: Either at the Tremblant, which is good value, or at one of the other hotels, of which the Moderne at Sembadel Gare (71.00.90.15), 6km by D906, is the cheapest.

MOUDEYRES This is a small, pretty village on D36 from Le Puy to Les Estables and Mont Mézenc. I mention it only because of the Auberge Pré Bossu, a charming cottage inn with a one-star Michelin restaurant, and ten very comfortable bedrooms, and one suite. High up in forested mountains, peace and fresh air. Not cheap, but reasonable for what it is (71.05.10.70).

LE PUY-EN-VELAY Information: Office de Tourisme, pl du Breuil (71.09.38.41); and in July and August only at 23 rue des Tables near the Cathedral, (71.09.27.42).
Where to stay: In Le Puy itself the hotels, though half empty most of the year, are heavily booked in season, and it is advisable to book well ahead. The Hôtel Chris'tel is in a quiet situation and of a high standard (71.02.24.44). The Régina, also good, is close to the main circular boulevard (71.09.14.71).

The Moulin de Barette, at Pont de Sumène, 8km by N88, is a hotel with the addition of a well-furnished motel (cottages), and also a camp site (71.03.00.88).
Where to eat: Au Petit Vatel, 9 pl Michelet; or le Bateau Ivre, 5 rue Portail-d'Avignon (71.09.67.20).
The restaurant of the Hotel Chris'tel is also good.

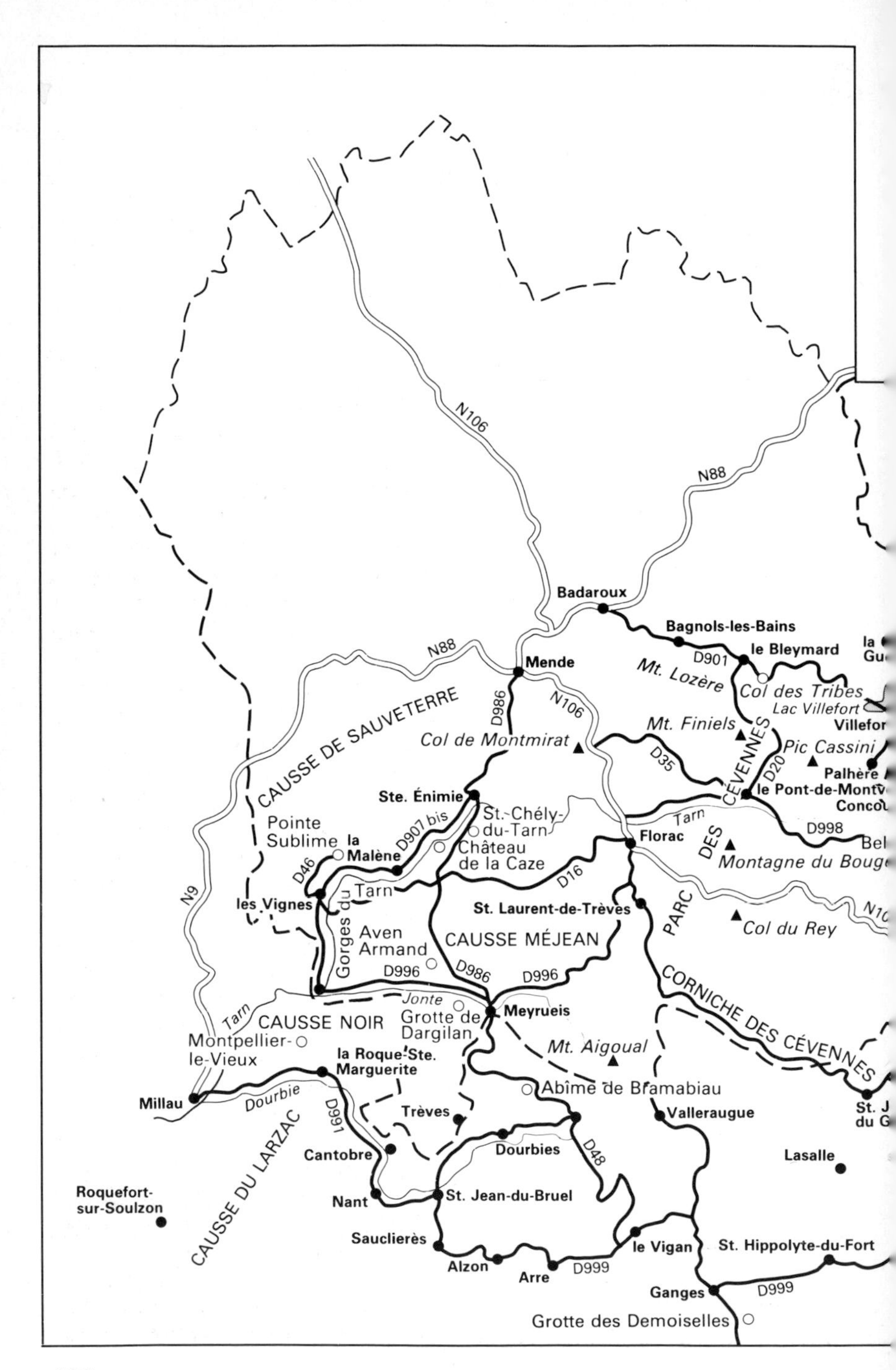
N106
N88
Badaroux
Bagnols-les-Bains
le Bleymard
D901
Mt. Lozère
Col des Tribes
Lac Villefort
N88
Mende
D986
N106
CAUSSE DE SAUVETERRE
Col de Montmirat
Mt. Finiels
CÉVENNES
Pic Cassini
D20
Palhère
D35
Ste. Énimie
St.-Chély-du-Tarn
Pointe Sublime
la Malène
D907 bis
Château de la Caze
Tarn
D998
Florac
DES
D46
Tarn
D16
les Vignes
N9
Gorges du
St. Laurent-de-Trèves
PARC
Col du Rey
Aven Armand
CAUSSE MÉJEAN
D996
D986
D996
CORNICHE DES CÉVENNES
Jonte
Meyrueis
Tarn
CAUSSE NOIR
Grotte de Dargilan
Montpellier-le-Vieux
Mt. Aigoual
la Roque-Ste. Marguerite
Abîme de Bramabiau
Millau
Dourbie
D991
Trèves
Valleraugue
CAUSSE DU LARZAC
Cantobre
Dourbies
D48
Lasalle
Roquefort-sur-Soulzon
Nant
St. Jean-du-Bruel
Sauclierès
le Vigan
St. Hippolyte-du-Fort
Alzon
Arre
D999
Ganges
D999
Grotte des Demoiselles

9

Lozère, Cévennes, Gorges Du Tarn

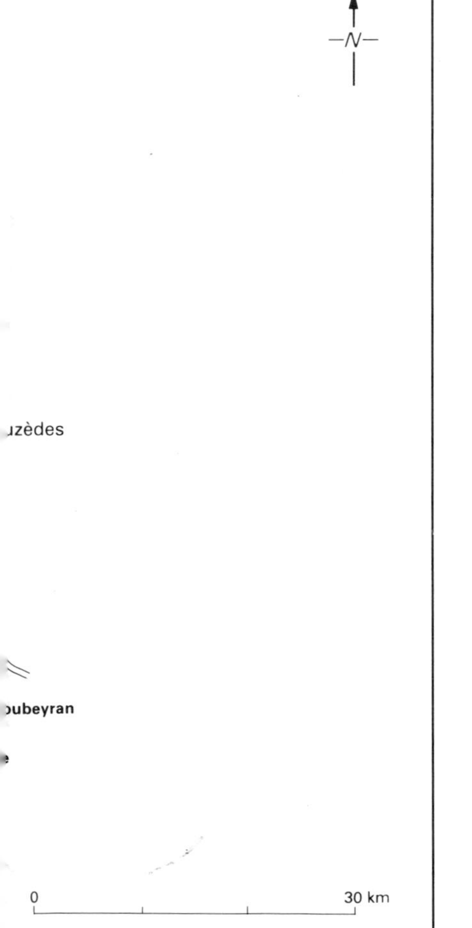

After the magnificent scenery of Auvergne travellers moving on south to the Cévennes mountains may well be wondering whether what they are about to see can possibly match what they have seen, whether there will be anything new or different. The region known as Cévennes is, if anything, wilder and more remote than even Auvergne, and is in many ways different. There are two simple reasons for this. First, these mountains are granite and schist, belonging to the age when Europe first rose from the sea six hundred million years ago. Unlike the volcanic rock and the even more porous limestone plateaux of Auvergne, they are impervious to water, and the soil is different. Secondly, they are farther south, the sun is warmer, and their southern slopes facing the Mediterranean grow plants, like lemons and bananas, never seen in Auvergne. But different soil also means different plants, so everywhere the countryside has a new aspect.

Like Puy-de-Dôme and Cantal the département of Lozère takes its name from a mountain but of an altogether different kind. Mont Lozère is a huge granite upland more than 35km long and reaching 1,699m at the peak of Finiels, the highest point in the Massif Central which is not of volcanic origin.

Apart from one or two places on its lower slopes, this once thickly forested mountain is now bare of trees and is sometimes called 'the Bald Mountain'. It is crossed by only one road from north to south, the D20 from Le Bleymard to Le Pont-de-Montvert, but is ringed by roads which run from Mende to Villefort, then to Génolhac, and from there to Le Pont-de-Montvert and on to Florac, where the N106 leads north to Mende.

Mende, the préfecture of the most sparsely populated département in all France, was once encircled by walls. Its 12th-century ramparts have long since been replaced by a wide boulevard enclosing the old streets of the town centre.

Like St. Flour and Aurillac this little country town is more a base for excursions in all directions than a tourist destination in itself. Having said that, it is fair to add that the Gothic cathedral which dominates the town is worth a visit. It was originally built in the 14th century on a site on which there had been several previous churches. The crypt is reckoned to date from the 3rd century, when Christian missionaries first came to this region.

On Christmas night in the year 1579 the Huguenot soldier, Captain Merle, attacked and captured the town. He blew up the existing spires of the cathedral and some of its walls. It was restored about fifty years later. Inside the main door, on the left, there is a souvenir of Captain Merle's attack, a 2.5m long iron clapper of what was believed to be the largest bell in Christendom. It weighed 20 tonnes and was smashed by Merle's troops. Some fine Aubusson tapestries dating from 1708 hang beneath the stained-glass windows of the choir. The cathedral also contains one of the many black Virgins of the Massif Central, this one carved in Lebanon cedar wood.

Mende once had a thriving wool industry and was particularly well known for its serge cloth, but this activity ceased about a hundred years ago and Mende became a sleepy, and far from prosperous town. In recent years it has revived and there is now a modern business and industrial area around the old town.

It is an ideal place from which to begin a tour of the Mont Lozère region and the rest of the Cévennes. Leave the town by N88 signposed Langogne which crosses the Lot and follows its winding course, From Badaroux the road climbs up to the Col de la Tourette. Not far beyond here take the right-hand fork, D901, which crosses the Lot again and follows the southern bank to **Bagnols-les-Bains**. This village, pleasantly situated on the Lot, little more than a rippling stream here, seems ordinary at first sight. But as you walk around it, an indefinable attraction makes itself felt. Like some English villages there is nothing special about it, it's just likeable. In fact, this unassuming little place is a very ancient spa and — yes, you have got it in one — its four medicinal springs were first discovered and used by the Romans. Today Bagnols treats heart conditions linked to rheumatism. But with its sheltering hills, its chuckling river and its fresh mountain air, it is the kind of place that must surely be good for any indisposition, and a certain cure for city stress.

From Bagnols the road winds and climbs to the village of Le Bleymard where the D20 leads up and over Mont

The Beast of Gévaudan

Was it a wolf? Or an escaped performing bear turned man-eater? A werewolf? A homicidal maniac? In the Gévaudan region in the southern Massif Central in the three years from 3rd July 1764 scores of people were attacked by some kind of monster. Nearly all the victims, many of whom were killed and eaten, were young girls or small children.

The monster was seen eighteen times by witnesses who were not attacked, or escaped. Several of them said it stood on its hind feet and seemed to make 'human' gestures. There were many who believed the monster to be a man disguised in an animal skin.

On 19th June 1767 a wolf hunter named Jean Chastel shot the largest wolf ever seen in the region. But was it the monster? There were those who were suspicious of the Chastel family. The father was known to practise sorcery, and the younger son, Antoine, lived wild in the woods with a pack of dogs and half-tamed wolves. Was he the mad sadist?

Was it coincidence that Chastel killed the monster just after a short spell in prison imposed for his rough treatment of one of Louis XV's hunting masters sent to investigate the monster? Or had the prison experience persuaded the Chastels that enough was enough? Either way, there were no more attacks.

A hundred years later Robert Louis Stevenson found the story still fresh in local minds, though he seems not to have taken it seriously. He was wrong. The exact truth will never be known but there is no doubt at all that there really was a beast of Gévaudan.

Lozère, with spectacular views on both sides. On the way up to the Col de Finiels you pass on the left the Chalet du Mont Lozère. In summer this is a hostel for pony-trekkers, and for walkers using the national footpath, Grande Randonnée 7, which crosses Mont Lozère from north to south. The complex includes a hotel which, in winter, becomes a ski centre, particularly for cross-country skiing.

A signposted footpath leads from the chalet to the peak of Finiels. On a clear day the walk, which takes about three hours there and back, offers splendid views to the plateau of Margeride in the north, and far to the south-east.

From Col de Finiels, its highest point, D20 descends to **Le Pont-de-Montvert**. This village has its place in history as the scene of the murder, on 24th July 1702, of the Catholic Inspector of Missions to the Cévennes, the Abbé de Chayla, by a group of Protestants. This was the first action in the bloody revolt of the Camisards (see p. 25). Today, Le Pont-de-Montvert is a popular centre for walkers. A large modern building includes a hostel for them, as well as a permanent exhibition of the natural history and way of life on Mont Lozère.

An alternative to taking D20 at Le Bleymard is to continue on D901 to Villefort, then D66 and D362 to

Florac: the young Tarn and the towering cliffs of the Rocher de Rochefort

Génolhac, and D998 to Le Pont-de-Montvert. This is a longer but very beautiful route which climbs first to the Col des Tribes, a watershed between the Lot flowing west to the Atlantic, and the rivers that flow east to the Ardèche, the Rhône and the Mediterranean. The road follows the wooded valley of the Allier and then crosses the attractive crescent-shaped lake of Villefort.

This spacious lake was formed when the gorge of the Allier was dammed by a hydro-electric barrage. It is now equipped for watersports of all kinds and has made Villefort a popular holiday centre. With its plane trees, its boule players and cafés, **Villefort** seems already to have the scent of the south about it, although it is at the foot of Mont Lozère. There are two small hotels and several camp sites, and good excursions in the area.

Only 8 km away is the unusual village of **La Garde-Guérin**, first established in the 10th century on the old Roman road from Languedoc to Auvergne, then the only road in the region. It needs only a glance around and very little imagination to understand the risks of travelling this road a thousand years ago. It was infested with highwaymen and it was the Bishops of Mende who decided to establish a strong point on the plateau in its wildest part. The village was protected by a castle and consisted mostly of fortified houses inhabited by a group of knights who protected travellers on their way and were permitted to charge a toll for doing so. A few of their houses, with mullioned windows, still remain. Today, Le Garde-Guérin has a few artisans and stock farmers, and a small but comfortable inn. The keep of the old castle still stands and offers panoramic views as far as Mont Ventoux beyond the Rhône.

Nearby is the Belvédère du Chassezac. A few minutes' walk from the parking place is a point where the cliffs fall sheer to the fierce torrent of Chassezac far below. It seems impossible that rubber boats could make the passage through this wild and chaotic river, one of the most difficult in France, but it has been done a few times by specially trained teams.

There is hardly a road in all this area which is not a spectacular drive and from Villefort to Génolhac there is a choice of two routes. D906 continues southwards crossing and recrossing the railway and passing the attractive village of Concoulès. A longer route by D66 and D362 first heads west up the valley of Palhère towards Pic Cassini. Near the Chalet de Chantegrive it turns south-east and a little farther on passes a small road on the right signposted to Mas de-la-Barque. Both these places have teleskis and simple installations for cross-country skiing used by people staying in Villefort in winter. Mas de-la-Barque is also used by pony-trekkers in summer.

The road climbs to the Plateau de la Croix de l'Ermite and then descends slightly to the Belvédère des Bouzèdes. From this point, more than 1,300m up, there is a good view to the south-east and of Génolhac 800m below. The road then winds down through pine, beech and chestnut forest to this pretty village whose red-tiled roofs, flowers and fig trees seem to belong more to Provence than the Massif Central.

To continue the circuit of Mont Lozère take D998 from Génolhac to Florac via Le Pont-de-Monvert. This is yet another beautiful route lying between the slopes of Mont Lozère to the north and those of the Montagne du Bougès to the south.

It would be an exaggeration to describe **Florac** as beautiful, yet with its orchards and flower gardens in the valley of the Tarnon, and protected by the great cliffs of the Rocher de Rochefort, it is a very welcoming little town with something of a Shangri-La atmosphere about it.

If peace seems to be its keynote now, the past history of Florac, like that of so many towns in the Massif Central, was violent. Ancient capital of one of the seven *baronnies* of Gevaudun, it was repeatedly sacked and fought over by warlords. Its castle was destroyed, rebuilt, destroyed again. When times at last became more peaceful, the patched-up building served as a prison, then a salt warehouse, then a hospital, and eventually fell into disuse. But its history was not over With the recent growth of tourism it was realised that Florac was a natural centre for trips in all directions; to the Gorges du Tarn, the Causse Méjean, Mont Lozère and the Cévennes. So, when the National Park of the Cévennes was set up in 1970, Florac was made its headquarters. The Administrative offices were installed in the castle and the building was given a new lease of life. It has been intelligently restored and with its long façade flanked by small towers, and its fine entrance, it now makes an impressive building. The former kitchen, recognisable by the huge fireplace, has become a salon for meetings and receptions. The ground floor also includes an Information Centre devoted to the National Park. The first floor is an exhibition hall where displays relating to the wild life in the Park are arranged.

A short but agreeable walk from the centre of the town is the Source du Pêcher, a spring which bursts from the foot of the Rochefort cliff and crosses the old town before tumbling into the Tarnon. These and other streams in the neighbourhood make Florac a popular centre for trout fishing.

The National Park of the Cévennes is a paradise for walkers and amateur explorers of all kinds whether they choose to travel on foot, on horseback, by bicycle, in canoes, or, like Robert Louis Stevenson, with a donkey. This last is a method chosen by some families, as the donkey can easily carry tired children as well as camping equipment. Two of the great national footpaths of France, the GR 7 (Vosges-Pyrenees) and the GR 5 (Alps-Atlantic Coast) cross on the massif of Mont Aigoual. There are signposted footpaths for walks of from 8 to 20km in all areas of the Park, and during the summer months guided walks with commentary are regularly arranged. Full information on all leisure activities can be obtained from the office in the castle at Florac, or from any of the fourteen Information Centres in the park, six of them open all year round.

About a quarter of the 320,000 hectares of the Park is forested. The central zone, 84,000 hectares, is strictly controlled to preserve its wild life and within it hunting, camping and caravanning are forbidden. The peripheral zone includes villages, hotels, camp sites and *gîtes*.

Lovers of the great open spaces can enjoy another part of Mont Lozère by taking the road north from Florac towards Mende, turning off on to D35 at Col de Montmirat. This narrow road, almost everywhere more than 1,200m up, offers kilometres of utter solitude with no sign of life apart from an occasional flock of sheep or herd of goats, and only a couple of tiny hamlets before the short sharp descent into Le Pont-de-Montvert.

An even more spectacular and somewhat easier drive is the road from Florac to St. Jean-du-Gard, the Corniche des Cévennes. Like many other good things in the Massif Central and Auvergne this lovely road owes its origin to the region's violent past. It was constructed at the beginning of the 18th century to enable Louis XIV's

Above: *Spiked boots and a barrel with internal spikes both used for dehusking chestnuts.*
Below: *A hand-made fireside bench with holes for the farmer's cats*

troops to penetrate into the Cévennes to put down the revolt of the Protestant Camisards.

Leave Florac by D907 which follows the valley of the Tarnon. After about 5km keep to the left at a slightly misleading road junction and take D983 to St. Laurent-de-Trèves. This village is well known to students of natural history because, on the plateau above it, traces of dinosaurs which lived there 190 million years ago have been found. Beyond it the road climbs to the Col du Rey where the Corniche des Cévennes begins. When I took this road it was early afternoon and it was a superb drive but it is reckoned to be at its best towards evening, when the slanting light of the sun picks out the crests and emphasises the depth of the valleys.

St. Jean-du-Gard is situated on the left bank of the Gardon, a small river that looks innocent enough in summer, but is subject to sudden and violent floods, known as *gardonnades,* after heavy rainstorms in the mountains. When I say heavy I am not joking. The total of the annual rainfall of London or Paris has been known to fall on the slopes of Mont Aigoual within two days. Volumes of water such as this combined with the impermeability of the granite soil produce a rise in the level of some rivers of as much as five metres within a few hours and the raging torrent carries all before it including, sometimes, the bridges. In 1958 half the old bridge at St. Jean-du-Gard was carried away. It has since been rebuilt.

In the past this town lived on silk and chestnuts. An interesting museum has been set up in a former coaching inn, explaining the importance of the chestnut, which they called 'the bread tree', and the mulberry, called the 'tree of gold' because of the prosperity it brought to the life of the region through the silk industry. This museum, the Musée des Vallées Cévenoles, also covers many other aspects of the crafts and traditions of the Cévennes, and is a good deal more interesting than many small museums.

There is plenty to visit in the area of St. Jean-du-Gard. One really worthwhile trip is by a very pretty route along D50 through Mialet to Le Mas-Soubeyran and the Musée du Désert. This is another very interesting small museum, and is established in the house of Roland, the leader of the Camisard revolt (see p. 25). His bedroom is furnished just as it was in his time and altogether this museum gives a complete evocation of this bitter revolt and of the daily lives of those who conducted it.

Not far from Roland's house is the Grotte de Trabuc. Once inhabited by prehistoric men, then used by the Romans, then by brigands, it was also a home and a hiding place for groups of Camisards. It is also an impressive cave with its fair share of stalactites and stalagmites. In one place there are a large number of small stalagmites called 'the hundred thousand soldiers' because, if your imagination is sufficiently elastic, they resemble an army of infantry. I do not know what you have to drink first.

A few kilometres farther on D50 brings you to Générargues where a right turn leads towards Anduze. On the way you come to the Bambouseraie de Prafrance, a really unusual botanical garden well worth seeing. Its 34 hectares contain a 10-hectare bamboo forest with more than twenty varieties, from those you can eat to those you can build houses with, as well as many other trees and plants brought from the Far East. The garden was formed more than a hundred years ago by Eugène Mazel who travelled to Japan and China to study the mulberry trees on which the silk worms and so the whole silk industry depended. That the garden has thrived so well is strong evidence of the warm micro-climate of this region.

This interesting garden is on the outskirts of the pretty town of Anduze, another Protestant stronghold. It was the headquarters of one of the most important Huguenot nobles, the Duc de Rohan, who fortified it so well that when Louis XIII and Cardinal Richelieu sent a military expedition against it, the troops preferred to leave it alone and attacked the nearby town of Alès instead. After the peace of Alès in 1629 the Duc de Rohan was obliged to negotiate and, though he obtained concessions, the fortifications of Anduze had to be destroyed. Only the Tour d'Horloge which dates from 1320 was left standing.

The old railway line which ran between Anduze and St. Jean-du-Gard via Mialet was closed down in 1960, but has since been reopened as a tourist attraction. Railway enthusiasts will like the old steam engine which belches out huge clouds of black

A view from the lovely Corniche des Cévennes, the route from Florac to St. Jean du Gard

smoke as it puffs its way slowly across viaducts and through tunnels following the river valley. The railway operates from May to September.

The silk industry of the Cévennes which had fallen on hard times has been revived in recent years. At St. Hippolyte-du-Fort, about 18km from Anduze by D982, or by more scenic but much narrower roads from St. Jean-du-Gard through the village of Lasalle, there is a museum of the Cévennes silk industry. It covers the techniques of making silk from ancient times to the present day and reveals some curious facts about the industry. The eggs of the silkworm moths were incubated in small sachets which the local women wore between their breasts; and the silkworms required a tonne of mulberry leaves for every 25 grammes of eggs, in other words they ate forty thousand times their own weight before they went into cocoon; and each cocoon produces up to one kilometre of silk thread. The problem was that before it could be unwound the start had to be found. This was done by agitating the cocoons in boiling water. The museum has a shop, open from May to October, which sells items made of silk. Lengths of Cévennes silk are once again supplied to the fashion houses of Lyons and Paris.

St. Hippolyte-du-Fort lies at the southern limit of the Cévennes proper on D999, a road that farther west comes close to the massif of Mont Aigoual. Those who are enthusiasts for caves and grottoes may like to make the short detour from this road, at Ganges, to the Grottes des Demoiselles, one of the most impressive of the many caves in this area.

You may have noticed that I have some difficulty in being enthusiastic about caves. There is no doubt, however, that the Grotte des Demoiselles ranks pretty high in the underground league. Caves are often measured by comparison with cathedrals; in this case with Notre Dame de Paris which would find plenty of room, if for some reason it should be decided to move it, in the 100m long, 60m wide and 50m high main space of the Grotte des Demoiselles. This particular cave was discovered in 1770 and described ten years later. It was not properly explored until the end of the 19th century, when the great French alpinist and speleologist, Édouard-Alfred Martel, repeatedly risked his life in subterranean expeditions in the then totally unknown underworlds of the Cévennes and Auvergne, including this grotto. Its name is said to have been given to it by local peasants who held in awe this great cavern beneath their sheep pastures, and in their mind peopled it with fairies, the 'demoiselles'.

Apart from being a convenient base from which to visit the Grottes des Demoiselles, Ganges is a small industrial town with another claim to fame. It is a 'capital', this time of silk stockings. They were made here for the court of Louis XIV, and it was a father to son industry until silk stockings were replaced by nylon. A few small factories managed to survive by converting to the new yarn and today Ganges has a reputation for producing the highest quality nylon stockings.

There is hardly a vestige left of the Château of Ganges which was the scene of a truly horrible crime in the mid-seventeenth century. It was the home of the Marquis de Ganges whose wife, Diane de Roussan, was called 'La Belle Provençale', and was one of the loveliest women at the court of Louis XIV. The Marquis was a villain and his brothers, the Abbé of Ganges and the Chevalier de Ganges, were a good deal worse. They made repeated advances to their beautiful sister-in-law and were steadfastly refused.

They planned a terrible revenge. First they pointed out to the Marquis that if his wife were to die, he would enjoy her enormous fortune. It seems that he found nothing wrong with this idea, because one morning in 1667, before the Marquise was up, the Abbé and the Chevalier burst into her bedroom. One of them held a glass of poison, and the other a pistol in one hand and a sword in the other.

'Madame,' said the Abbé, 'in a few moments you must die. Choose now whether it shall be by this pistol, this sword, or by this poison.'

The Marquise pleaded with them without success. She chose the poison, begging them to fetch a priest as soon as she had drunk it. They watched and then went on the errand. As soon as they had left, she dressed rapidly, took the sheets from her bed, knotted them, let herself down from her window, and fled into the town. The two murderous brothers soon tracked her down in the house where she had taken refuge, attacked her and left her for dead with seven sword wounds. But she was strong as well as resourceful. It was not the sword cuts that killed her but the poison, after nineteen days.

The murderers were condemned to be broken alive on the wheel and the Marquis was banished.

Mont Aigoual is a moody mountain, sometimes sinister, sometimes glorious. At 1,600m it is not as high as Mont Lozère but it is more conventional in shape, steep-sided and thickly forested. It is subject to storms awe-inspiring in their ferocity. When the French Alpine Club built a refuge near the summit, they thought it wise to use anchor chains embedded in the rock to make sure that the roof could not be blown off. They say that on a clear morning after rain it is possible to see Mont Blanc, more than 300km to the north, and Mont Canigou in the Pyrenees, 240km away in the south-west. But it would be a lucky person who arrives there by chance on such a morning, because Mont Aigoual has a magnetic attraction for clouds; it is a weather breeder.

The French National Meteorological Office has an observatory there, which they were careful to build in blocks of granite fit for a Crusader castle. It is the steep southern slopes of the mountain and the valleys of the Hérault and Gardon rivers which draw up the huge cumulus clouds that break in diluvian rainstorms. This peak, exposed to all winds, gets about 2m of rain a year. As it falls in such great volumes at once, there are more dry days than wet. In summer it is often burned by a fierce southern sun, and in winter lies under a cap of snow as much as 3m deep.

There are now nearly 15,000 hectares of beech and pine forests on its slopes, yet only a hundred years ago it was denuded of trees. Here and in other parts of the Cévennes the thick forests were ruined by neglect, by glassmakers who cut the trees down to make the charcoal they needed, and the passage over the years of countless flocks of sheep who ate every new shoot. It is due to a re-afforestation policy started in 1875, not yet complete, that Mont Aigoual is now so richly wooded.

Four important roads, six of the long distance footpaths, and the great drovers' road from the Languedoc, once a Roman road and now in many places a cross-country ski-track, all meet near the summit.

From Ganges D999 carries on towards Mont Aigoual by way of Pont-d'Hérault where there is a turning to the north, D986, which arrives on Mont Aigoual via Valleraugue. Alternatively, by following D999 to Le Vigan and then D48 the heights of the mountain are reached near Lespérou. This must be an impressive drive in any weather. Several places are shown on the map as belvederes and no doubt they offer wonderful views. I cannot say of what exactly because on the afternoon that I drove over Mont Aigoual by this route the mountain was in one of its most sinister moods. The

Causse Méjean above the Gorges du Tarn near Les Vignes

rain bucketed down and even without the sheets of water a doomsday gloom made it almost impossible to see anything except on the frequent occasions when the lightning sizzled beside us. The thunderclaps would have made Hercules jump. In such weather it hardly seemed worth carrying on to the highest point so I turned off at Lespérou down towards Meyrueis on D986.

After a few kilometres the road comes to the parking for the Abîme de Bramabiau. This extraordinary abyss has been created, and is still being extended, by the Bonheur, a stream which is only a tributary of the Trèvezel, which is itself a tributary of the Dourbie, in turn only a tributary of the Tarn. But this little river is an object lesson in the power of water to erode limestone, and its consequences. Tumbling down from the upper slopes of Mont Aigoual it disappears in a crack in the small limestone plateau of Camprieu to reappear, much reinforced, as a waterfall 700m farther on at the foot of a cliff. Visits which follow the underground course of the river have to be suspended from time to time, because the Bonheur is subject to violent floods which damage the installations and make it unsafe.

But it's always possible to get close to the waterfall and to explore the grottoes. There are guided visits from April to the end of September, and at particular times in October and early November. The whole tour takes about an hour and a half, including the descent on foot and the climb back by the woodland path.

From Bramabiau the road winds down 300m to Meyrueis. After the wild slopes of Mont Aigoual, **Meyrueis**, tucked down in a valley where the streams of Bétuzon and Brèze meet the Jonte, has a cosy atmosphere, though it is still more than 600m above sea level. It is a very good centre for exploring the mountains, the plateaux and the gorges in the region. Here you are north of the granite mountains and on the edge of an area of great limestone plateaux. Meyrueis stands near the entrance to the 20km of the very picturesque Gorges de la Jonte, and also offers easy access to three of the most famous grottoes in France — the Abîme de Bramabiau, the Grotte de Dargilan and Aven Armand.

The Grotte de Dargilan was

A peaceful stretch as the Tarn begins to emerge from the Gorges near Le Rozier

discovered in 1880 by a shepherd following a fox he saw enter a crack in the rock. He enlarged the crack and going forward found himself in a huge cave. He thought he had come upon the entry to Hell and fled. It was not until eight years later that it was explored by Martel and six companions.

Like the shepherd the visitor enters at once into a huge room where stalagmites (those that are built up from the ground) are still being formed. In one place the water has eaten away a deep hole in the rock which leads down, by a staircase, to a further series of caves. There are more than twenty in the system, six of them open to the public. Some are wide, some narrow, one has a small lake, and all have interesting formations in the rock. The visit lasts an hour and those who are not fit will find the climb back up the three hundred steps somewhat tiring.

The underground river Bonheur in the abyss of Bramabiau, near Meyrueis

The Aven Armand, 11km northwest of Meyrueis on D986, is considered to be one of the underground wonders of the world. I have tended to use the word cave or grotto for the sake of convenience, but for those who are not knowledgeable about holes in the ground, this is perhaps the place to explain why these three similar natural phenomena are called three different things — *abîme, grotte* and *aven*. An *abîme* is a chasm, a *grotte* is a cave, and an *aven* is what in English is called a pot-hole (such as gaping Gill in Yorkshire). All three of them are due to the porosity and solubility of limestone rocks in water.

A pothole occurs where water breaks through the surface of a limestone plateau and gradually eats away a huge hole (Aven Armand is 210m deep, twice the depth of Gaping Gill.) Over thousands of years the constant erosion of water pouring down this hole creates a system of linked caves. Every drop of water that falls from the roof or down the walls of these caves leaves behind a tiny proportion of the mineral salts it contains and stalactites begin to form from the roof downwards. The drops that hit the floor build with infinite slowness the pillars of crystals that rise from the floor, stalagmites.

Aven Armand is exceptional in two things. First, its great size. At the bottom of its main shaft there is a cave, yet another that would easily take Notre Dame de Paris. Secondly, for the beauty of its forest of stone, a collection of more than 400 stalagmites, including the tallest in the world at more than 30m, which really do resemble petrified trees, especially pines and cypresses, and here you need little imagination to accept this.

The beauty of the spectacle is enhanced by clever lighting which in places makes the rock seem translucent. Access to the forest of stone is made easy by a little electric train which runs 200m through the rock, taking the visitor down about 50m at the same time, to a balcony which even handicapped people can reach in safety, and from which the greater part of this striking curiosity can be seen. When he came out after his first exploration Martel, who had already seen many things of this kind, said 'I thought I was waking from a dream'.

The tour takes about one hour. Aven Armand is open for accompanied visits from the end of March to the beginning of November and in the June to August period it does not close at lunch time. It opens at nine in the morning and it is strongly recommended that you arrive there as early as possible to avoid the considerable crowds that build up later in the day. (This advice applies to all other important sites mentioned in this book and, indeed, to all others anywhere in the world. A few people can share their wonder, enhance the interest, too many destroy it altogether.) Aven Armand is well furnished above ground with parking space, children's playgrounds, picnic areas, and a bar and souvenir shop.

The landscape of this part of the Massif Central is characterised by the large limestone plateaux already mentioned briefly. They are called in French *les Causses*. Four of them, de Larzac, de Sauveterre, Méjean and Noir, are known as 'Les Grands Causses'. These flat uplands add greatly to the variety of the scenery, not only because their erosion by water has created the spectacular caves, potholes and majestic gorges of the Massif Central, but also because their openness and size is in direct contrast to the mountains, just as their elevation and exposure is opposed to the warmth and sheltered fertility of the valleys that separate them.

They provide yet another spectacle found only in this part of the Massif Central. In certain places the limestone contains a proportion of magnesium which makes it more resistant to erosion than in other areas. This resistant limestone has broken down more slowly, leaving on the surface huge rocks which, from a distance, look like ruined castles or even villages, to such a degree that they have been given names of towns, Nîmes-le-Vieux, Montpellier-le-Vieux.

Meyrueis: the Clock Tower, a remnant of the old fortifications

In other places where there were large deposits of soft and hard rock side by side, erosion has worn down the softer rock, leaving exposed cliffs of the harder rock in vast natural amphitheatres. Perhaps the most impressive is the Cirque de Navacelles in the valley of the Vis, separating the relatively small Causse de Blandas in the north, from the thousand square kilometres of the Causse de Larzac in the south.

The road which leads from Meyrueis to Aven Armand, D986, carries on across the Causse Méjean to Ste. Énimie at the eastern end of the main part of the Gorges du Tarn. The Causse Méjean is the most elevated the Causses, almost everywhere well over 1,000m, and consequently has a harsh climate, very cold in winter, blistering sun in summer, and a wide difference in all seasons between day and night temperatures. To the east of this road, which runs almost due north and south, the plateau is stony with frequent outcrops of rock, and has a population of less than two per square kilometre, tough farmers who look after flocks of more than 19,000 sheep. To the west of the road the Causse Méjean has more trees and some crops are grown in saucer-shaped depressions where fertile soil has collected over the years. In this part of the Causse Méjean, as on the Causse de Sauveterre, the plateau is broken here and there by wooded ravines as much as 100m deep.

Le Pont de Capelan, an ancient bridge at Meyrueis

In summer, the Causse Méjean is a botanist's paradise. Rock plants nurtured carefully in English gardens grow wild in every nook and cranny. I noticed several that I used to have in my garden in Sussex. In places vast tracts of scarlet poppies form lakes of colour under the great arc of blue sky.

About two-thirds of the way across one meets the D16 which crosses the Causse from west to east, from les Vignes in the Gorges du Tarn to Florac, into which it makes a vertiginous and difficult descent. From this cross roads, the road from Meyrueis which has been picturesque all the way becomes even more dramatic, as it comes close to the Gorges du Tarn. As you begin the descent towards Ste. Énimie there are many places where the depth and the great cliffs of the gorge can be seen, often with white clouds sailing through far below you.

When I first saw the Gorges du Tarn, I was a student. Three of us had spent a few days in Paris during the summer break, then decided on impulse that we would go down to the Mediterranean. We hired a small French car, a Dauphine, and drove doggedly southwards on secondary roads. At one point, I think it was at Sévérac-le-Château, we saw a signpost to the Gorges du Tarn and, again on impulse,

Looking into the Gorges du Tarn from the Roc des Hourtous, off the D16 crossing Causse Méjean

took the road. None of us knew what to expect or had even heard of the gorge. When after about 20km we got our first sight of it and started on the precipitous descent to les Vignes (the road has since been much improved), we were astonished beyond belief. It was a very different thing to visit a natural wonder that you have read a lot about and seen pictures of from coming upon something magnificent unexpectedly.

I have since visited and flown through the Grand Canyon of Colorado and sensational though it was I think I was less surprised, because I knew roughly what to expect, than I was by the Gorges du Tarn. It is not in the same class as the Grand Canyon, it is nothing like so long, so wide or so deep, but its dimensions — 80km long and up to 600m deep — are sufficient to make it very impressive and in places awe-inspiring.

The Tarn rises 1,524m up on Mont Lozère and pours down its young valley as a torrent receiving a number of tributaries. When it reaches the Causse it follows faults in the rock and has cut its way down forming the canyon that now separates the Causse Méjean from the Causse de Sauveterre. In the 80km of the gorge from Florac to le Rozier there are no more open tributaries, but the river is swollen by forty subterranean streams all of which, with three exceptions, enter the river as waterfalls direct from the rock face.

Ste. Énimie is an ancient and attractive village which, in summer, has some of the worst aspects of modern tourism pasted on it, like pancake

Ste. Énimie

Once upon a time there was a beautiful princess called Énimie. She lived in the 7th century AD and she was the sister of Dagobert, the King of the Franks. She was so lovely that all the lords of the Court wished to marry her. Énimie refused them all, saying that she meant to devote her life to the Church.

But King Dagobert obliged her to accept one of his barons. No sooner had the wedding been arranged than Énimie fell ill with leprosy. The royal doctors failed to cure her, and her suitor found that he had urgent business in other parts.

In a vision Énimie saw an angel who told her to travel south to the Gévaudan region where she would find a fountain that would restore her beauty. After a long and difficult search she found the fountain of Burle. She bathed in its water and all traces of her illness disappeared.

She set off for home, but the disease returned. She went back to the fountain and the miracle was repeated. But each time she tried to leave the leprosy broke out again. Understanding that God wished her to stay there, Énimie founded a convent, where she died in AD 628, after a life devoted to charity.

The fountain of Burle and the remains of the convent can still be seen. The story of Ste. Énimie is told in modern ceramic tiles in the 12th-century church of the village which bears her name.

make-up mistakenly applied by an old but once beautiful actress.

The Gorges du Tarn have been a star tourist attraction for nearly a hundred years. Even before the First World War, when there were very few private cars, tourists came in considerable numbers by rail. As the family car became commonplace over the years, the tourism steadily increased because, unlike some other spectacular gorges, those of the Verdon and the Ardèche, for example, this one is followed through the bottom from end to end by road. The D907bis has enabled countless thousands to enjoy one of the great natural spectacles of Europe, and to travel this road on a sunny day out of season, able to stop as and where you want, is a really memorable experience. It has to be said, however, that it is not quite the same thing in the July/August high season, when more than three thousand cars a day follow each other in caterpillar processions along the road.

The traffic jam is not always confined to the road. The river, for most of the year fast-flowing, becomes a lot tamer in summer. The result is that in many parts of it there are flotillas of canoes and rafts, not a few of the canoes clearly in the hands of youngsters who have no idea how to manage them. They make a nice splash of colour, most of them are red, and give scale to photographs. At the same time the hysterical shouts of those who have lost control of their boat echo from the rock walls of the canyon and do little to add to the grandeur of the scene. On the other hand, how they do enjoy themselves!

If at the height of this crowded summer season you begin to feel that you are, almost literally, in a tourist trap, not even this sensation can destroy the scenic marvels of this road through the gorge.

Following the D907bis in the direction Ste. Énimie-Le Rozier, the first important site is at St. Chély-du-Tarn where the river has carved out a great natural amphitheatre with cliffs more than 300m high. It faces diagonally a similar cirque on the other side of the river, the Cirque de Pougnadoires. Every night from the beginning of June to the end of September the gorge at St. Chély is floodlit from 8pm to 11pm and there is a Son et Lumière show. It is a purely personal view but I do not find natural wonders suitable subjects for this sort of spectacle. They turn something real into something artificial, like the coloured searchlights they play on the spray of Niagara Falls at night, without improving it in any way. The great sweep of this defile between the Cirque de St. Chély and the Cirque de Pougnadoires is best seen by taking one of the boat trips that run regularly in summer from St. Chély du-Tarn.

A few kilometres farther on, after the Cirque de Pougnadoires, the 15th-century Château de la Caze is sited between the road and the river in a pleasant frame of trees and imposing rocks. This château still has a slightly medieval look, with turrets and high walls, but is now a small luxury hotel (14 bedrooms) in the Relais et Châteaux hotels group, and has a 1-star restaurant.

At La Màlene, the next village, there is another pleasant hotel based on a 15th-century fortified manor house, the Manoir de Montesquiou. La Malène is a very old crossing point between the Causse de Sauveterre and the Causse Méjean, and at the times of the transhumance great flocks of sheep still cross here.

Beyond La Malène the river enters the most striking part of the gorge, les Détroits (The Narrows), and immediately beyond this section there is another natural amphitheatre, the Cirques des Baumes, where the rock of the cliff face is many-coloured, mainly red, but with white, black, blue, grey and yellow, as well as the occasional green of shrubs and trees. The walls of the canyon fall sheer to the river, and above them a second cliff, set back a little, soars to more than 500m above the river.

It is well worth taking a boat trip from La Malène through this part of the gorge to appreciate its full beauty. It should be done, if possible, in the morning, when the light is most effective. The system for boat trips is that you drive your car beyond the departure point and park near the disembarkation point. Passengers are then taken back by bus to the departure point and come down river by boat to rejoin their cars.

The next village, Les Vignes, is situated at another ancient crossing point between the Causse de Sauveterre and the Causse Méjean, at a spot where the gorge opens up into a sunny valley. Before going on from here it is worth taking the trouble to drive up out of the gorge to see the lovely views of it from the top. From Les Vignes D995 climbs up in tight hairpins to the Causse de Sauveterre. Take D46 to the right and continue to St. Georges-de-Lévéjac. Here, take the road to the right to the *Point Sublime* which gives a marvellous view of a long section of the Gorge.

After les Vignes the canyon closes in again but remains wider than in the early part of this route, so that the cliffs have more vegetation. In places it is almost luxuriant.

Just inside the Gorge before it ends at the village of Le Rozier where the Tarn is joined by the Jonte, flowing out of its own splendid gorge, is the surprising Grand Hôtel de la Muse et du Rozier. Surprising because of its unusual architecture, a sort of Le Corbusier version of a medieval castle. It is striking and, I think, successful. It is a comfortable and expensive hotel (35 rooms and 3 flats) built in a pleasant garden right beside the river, and the road.

It is one thing to drive along this road at the bottom of the canyon but the full beauty of this natural marvel cannot be appreciated without tackling at least some of it from above and on foot.

For those who are keen and experienced there are some really good walks starting from Le Rozier, up on to the Corniches du Causse Méjean.

A good all-day walk starts from behind the church in Le Rozier and follows the national footpath GR 6A up to the deserted hamlet of Capluc, then to the Col de Francbouteille, then to the Col de Cassagnes. The footpath is well-marked and well-maintained. At the Col de Cassagnes turn right without going into the village itself and after about one hour's walk the Belvédère de Vertige is reached more than 400m above the Jonte flowing through its canyon. From here the path descends steeply by the Pas du Loup and leads to a huge isolated rock called the Vase de Chine and, soon after, a similar rock called the Vase de Sèvres, with fine views down to Le Rozier and across to the cliffs of the Causse Noir. Then, by way of the Ravine of Echoes and the Brèche Magnifique the path leads back to Capluc and Le Rozier. This lovely walk takes about seven hours and,

An eroded rock called 'the Sèvres vase' above the Gorges du Tarn

although there is one spring of drinking water on the way, it is advisable to take your own supply of water and, of course, your provisions. You won't find a supermarket up there.

Those who are sound in wind and limb but somewhat less ambitious can enjoy a taste of wild grandeur by following the same route but for about an hour only, to the top of a crest which gives panoramic views both of the Tarn and the Jonte. At Capluc, only about half an hour out of Le Rozier on this route, there is a path to the Rocher de Capluc — a short walk, but to get to the summit of the rock necessitates climbing metal ladders and steps cut in the face of the rock. From the top there are superb views of the junction of the Tarn and the Jonte and of perched villages on the Causse de Sauveterre. The climb should not be attempted by anyone subject to giddiness.

Another good walk can be started from the isolated village of Cassagnes which (I understand, I have not tried it myself) can be reached by car via Le Truel on D996, the Corniche de la Jonte, which runs from Meyrueis to le Rozier. I mention this walk on the recommendation of a friend who says it takes only three hours there and back, but should be tackled by tourists who are fit, alert, agile and have a good head for heights. It concludes, that is the walk there does, with the ascent of the Rocher de Cinglegros, which is achieved with the help of nine metal ladders, six ledges with handrails, stone steps cut into the rock, and iron crampons fixed in the rock face. I admit that I have never tried it and am never likely to, as I suffer from an unusual fear of heights. But I have no difficulty in believing those who assert that the view of the Tarn gorges from the top of the Rocher de Cinglegros is incomparable.

From Cassagnes the rock is reached via the Col de Cassagnes, where you take the path to the right. After about twenty minutes there are some rocks which give an impressive view down into a deep ravine. After another twenty minutes the Sartane spring is found on the right, if it is not dry, as it sometimes is in summer. Shortly afterwards the footpath forks, keep to the left to the Pas des Trois Fondus and the Rocher de Cinglegros. The path leads down and soon comes to a natural terrace with a fine view of the Cinglegros gap. The path on the left of the terrace leads steeply down by Le Pas des Trois Fondus to the bottom of the ravine that isolates the rock, and there the climb begins.

As the footpaths are so well-marked and maintained, those who intend to venture only a short way can probably manage without maps, but serious walkers are well advised to obtain the ramblers' maps showing the national footpaths (Grandes Randonnées). These are most easily found in the paper shops in the towns of the region concerned, but there never seem to be enough to go around so they may have to be hunted for. (See box on p. 45.)

As an alternative to Meyrueis or Florac, the lively little town of Millau is an excellent base for excursions in the Cévennes and the southern Massif Central, particularly to the Gorges du Tarn, the Causses, the Gorges de la Jonte, and also by D991 into the valley of the Dourbie.

Though not on quite the same scale as the Gorges du Tarn, the Dourbie is, all the same, extremely beautiful and dramatic, and in some ways more varied, having a number of interesting sites, as well as two gorges quite unlike each other, three if you count the side gorge of the Trévezel.

The whole of this route from Millau to L'Espérou on Mont Aigoual along the valley of the Dourbie is exceptionally picturesque. From the first village, La Roque-Ste.-Marguerite, a narrow road leads up to the Causse Noir and the Chaos de Montpellier-le-Vieux (which can also be reached from Millau by D110). A little farther on there is a prettily sited mill on the right of the road, and not far beyond this point a good view of the perched village of St. Véran, where the tower that can be seen is all that remains of the château which was the home of the Marquis de Montcalm, who died on 13th September 1759, on the Heights of Abraham, Quebec, fighting General Wolfe. At the junction of the Dourbie and the Trévezel is the extraordinary village of Cantobre with its ancient houses perched on the extreme edge of a promontory jutting out into space from the Causse.

The road continues to Nant, at the end of the first gorge of the Dourbie, and on to St. Jean-du-Bruel. Between these two towns the road, now the D999, runs through a wide and fertile valley, an oasis of vines, orchards and market gardens. This sunlit bowl was first cultivated by the Benedictine monks of the monastery of Nant, who began by draining the marshy land as long ago as the 7th century. (What would the social history of Europe have been without the monks of the Middle Ages and their vineyards and farms, their patient teaching of the peasant farmers, their libraries, and their continual movement from place to place exchanging ideas?)

From St. Jean-du-Bruel D341 climbs to the Col de la Pierre Plantée at over 800m, where there is a fine view over the lower valley of the Dourbie. A road on the left, D47, leads via Trèves to the narrow and chaotic Gorges du Trévezel, at one point no more than 30m wide. Carrying on from the Col de la Pierre Plantée D341 becomes a corniche dominating the Dourbie from about 300m. From Dourbies to the next village, Laupies, the road is very narrow with tight bends and difficult crossing places, and should be driven with great care.

From L'Espérou, Millau can be regained by taking D48 down the slopes of Mont Aigoual to Le Vigan, where D999 runs west by Bez, Arre and Alzon to Sauclières. At this point it turns north to St. Jean-du-Bruel and

Cantobre, a village perched on the cliffs above the valley of the Dourbie

Nant, and the canyon of the Dourbie in the reverse sense.

In Roman times **Millau**, which had plenty of water, plenty of clay and plenty of wood for furnaces, was the site of one of the most important potteries of the day. A kilometre to the south of Millau, on an archaeological site called Graufesenque, excavations have revealed the foundations of a village of potters which had a main street, a canal, houses for slaves, and great furnaces capable of baking thirty thousand items at the same time. It has been calculated that at least four hundred potters worked there, and it is known that their products were exported all over Europe, to the Middle East, and even as far as India.

The museum in Millau, installed in an 18th-century mansion, has a very good collection of pottery and objects from this site.

In more recent times Millau has been famous for its leather. The innumerable sheep on the Causses supplied not only milk for the famous Roquefort cheese, and wool but, inevitably, sheepskin. For hundreds of years Millau was the most important glove-making centre in France, producing hundreds of thousands of pairs per year, including those ordered by the rich and fashionable, which were sewn finger by finger.

One of the consequences of the Second World War was that society became less formal. One of the minor aspects of this informality has been that people do not wear gloves nearly as much as they used to. The glove industry in Millau was badly affected and the town's economy was in decline for a number of years. But fashions change. Gloves may be old hat, to coin a phrase, but leather jackets, leather skirts, leather trousers have become universally popular. Millau is all smiles and activity again, supplying good leather to the top end of the fashion market, and making many fine items in the town. They can be seen in the smart shops in Place des Mandarous, and Place de la Tine.

It is an easy drive of about 25km from Millau to Roquefort-sur-Soulzon, without any doubt at all France's capital of cheese, if not the world's.

The manufacture of this cheese is now such a big industry — seven million cheeses are produced every year — that not even the great flocks of sheep on the Causses can provide enough milk to meet the demand. About 30 per cent of it has to be imported from Corsica and the Pyrenees. Though the cheese is now made in large modern dairies, it becomes Roquefort only because all of it is matured in the seven levels of caves which were created thousands of years ago, when part of the mountain of Cambalou fractured and slid away from the main part. These caves are the home of a form of penicillin, accurately called *Penicillum glaucum roquefortii*, which is dispersed by the currents of air throughout the galleries, and which thrives in the steady temperature of 7–9°C. The three months' ageing of the cheese can only take place successfully in this one environment and that is why a Roquefort can only come from Roquefort. Not even the Japanese can imitate it.

Conducted tours of the caves take about three-quarters of an hour. In summer, as it can be 30°C outside and 9°C inside, it is a good idea to wear a sweater.

Millau is well equipped to receive tourists. There are a number of good hotels, two of them of a high standard. One, the International, is large, and one, La Musardière, is small. There is an excellent municipal camp site on the banks of the Tarn, and others near by.

La Musardière has only 12 bedrooms, but it has a 1-star restaurant with a well deserved reputation for excellence. In an absent-minded moment you might fancy yourself in the dining room of a Georgian hotel somewhere in the English countryside, say Hereford, or Taunton. But not while actually tasting the food. That comes from another world. One can buy Roquefort in any supermarket in France, but at La Musardière they serve a Roquefort as far removed from the supermarket brands as Château Margaux is from *vin ordinaire*. Even in the best restaurants there can be a tendency towards a slight weakening of standards as you approach cheese and 'desserts'. Not so at La Musardière where gastronomic marvels are performed right through to the coffee.

I have finished this tour of Lozère and the Cévennes at Millau but, of course, it could equally well be started there. But then one would be tempted to start with the Gorges du Tarn which is fine if that is all there is time to see.

The fantastic rocks of the Chaos of Montpellier le Vieux, above the Dourbie, near Millau

But the pleasure of travelling through beautiful country has something in common with the pleasure of the theatre. There should be a certain amount of suspense and a natural order of things which produces the best effect — not many plays would survive having their third act put first — and for those who are spending time on touring this region, the Gorges du Tarn are perhaps better left for the final curtain.

General Information

BAGNOLS-LES-BAINS Information: Office de Tourisme, Esplanade Mont Cotton (66.47.64.79).
Where to stay: Three hotels in this village, all the same size, all with quiet gardens. The Pont (66.47.60.03) has a swimming pool, and the Commerce (66.47.60.07) does not have private bathrooms.
Where to eat: The restaurant of the Hôtel Commerce is simple, but has an excellent reputation.

FLORAC Information: Office de Tourisme, av J.-Monestier (66.45.01.14).
Where to stay: Grand Hôtel du Parc. A pleasant, comfortable, roomy hotel, but not that grand (66.45.03.05).
Le Rochefort, a new hotel on the edge of town, will appeal to some for its modernity. One of those that could be anywhere in the tourist world (66.45.02.57).
Where to eat: The restaurant of the Grand Hôtel du Parc is very good.
Leisure: Gorges du Tarn. Walking, riding, serious cycling.

GORGES DU TARN Information: Ask at the Mairie, St. Énimie (66.48.50.09), or, at western end, the Office de Tourisme, av Alfred Merle, Millau.
Where to stay: Hotels in the Gorges tend to be above average in comfort and expense; Château de la Caze, at la Caze (68.47.51.01) and Manoir de Montesquiou, at La Malène (68.47.51.12). These are both in very old, historic buildings. Grand Hôtel du Rozier et la Muse (65.60.60.01) is a modern hotel near Le Rozier. Apart from these there is the Hôtel Gévaudan at Les Vignes, halfway through the Gorges. This is a good average hotel, much cheaper than those above (66.46.81.55).
Where to eat: The three expensive hotels have good, expensive restaurants. Château de la Caze has a Michelin star and is very expensive.
Leisure: Boating, canoeing and rafting on the Tarn. Superb walks for serious walkers.

MENDE Information: Syndicat d'Initiative, 16 bd Soubeyran (66.65.02.69).
Where to stay: Several good average hotels on the circular boulevard, so ask for a quiet room. The largest with a restaurant is the Pont Roupt (66.65.01.43). Slightly more up-market and a little farther out is the Lion d'Or (66.49.16.46).
Where to eat: The best restaurant, locally accented cooking, is that of the Lion d'Or. Cheaper, but good value, is that of the Hôtel France (66.65.00.04).

MEYRUEIS Information: Office de Tourisme, Tour de l'Horloge (66.45.60.33, high season) or the Mairie (66.45.62.64).
Where to stay: The Renaissance is a comfortable hotel in a 16th-century mansion (66.45.60.19). The Grand Hôtel Europe et Mont Aigoual (66.45.60.05) does not offer the same atmosphere but is very reasonably priced.
Where to eat: The Grand Hôtel has one kitchen but two dining rooms, rustic for the Europe part, modern for the Mont Aigoual. Good country cooking. The same family have been in charge here for nearly a hundred years.

The Renaissance is slightly more up-market, pewter plates and so on, but very good.
Leisure: Good centre for gorges and grottoes.

MILLAU Information: Office de Tourisme, av Alfred Merle.
Where to stay: Two first-class hotels. One, the International, very large for the provinces (110 bedrooms) (65.60.20.66) and the other, La Musardière, very small (12 rooms) (65.60.20.63). Apart from these there is a number of average hotels of which the largest with its own restaurant is the Moderne (65.60.59.23).
Where to eat: Both the first-class hotels have first-class restaurants with a Michelin star. Another good restaurant at the Château de Cresseils, 2km on the road to St. Affrique. Also has 30 rooms (65.60.16.59).

ST. JEAN-DU-GARD Information: Ask at the Mairie.
Where to say: Hostellerie Château de Cabrières (66.85.13.26), 1km by D153. Pleasant grounds and swimming pool. Not too expensive. Or at Hôtel L'Oronge (66.85.30.34).
Where to eat: Restaurant Corniche des Cévennes (66.85.30.38). Good regional cooking.

VILLEFORT Information: Office de Tourisme, rue Église (66.46.80.26).
Where to stay: Try the Balme (66.46.80.14), or the Mont Lozère (66.61.10.72) in Génolhac, the next village.

At La Garde-Guérin, 8km from Villefort by D906, the Auberge Regordanz is simple, comfortable and in an exceptional position (66.46.82.88).

There are a number of average camp sites both at Villefort and Génolhac.
Where to eat: The restaurant of the Balme Hotel is the best.
Leisure: Bathing and boating on the Villefort lake. A good centre for walking.

Useful Addresses

Maison de l'Auvergne, 194 bis, rue de Rivoli, 75001, Paris (42.61.82.38). (Also answers enquiries for départements of Lozère and Haute-Loire.)
Comité Régional du Tourisme
45 av Julien, B.P. 395, 63011, Clermont-Ferrand (73.93.04.03).
Maison des Gîtes de France
35 rue Godot-de-Maury, 75009, Paris (47.42.25.43). (for cottages)
La Chaîne Camping Massif Central
31 rue Eugène Gilbert, 6300 Clermont-Ferrand. (for camp sites, etc.)
N.B. Several British tour operators offer cottage and camping holidays in Auvergne, some of them of very good standard.
Parc Régional des Volcans
Centre d'Information du Parc des Volcans, 28 rue St. Esprit, 63000 Clermont-Ferrand.
Parc Régional Livradois-Forez, St. Gervais sous Meymont, 63880 Olliergues.
Parc National des Cévennes, Château de Florac, B.P. 15, 48400, Florac.

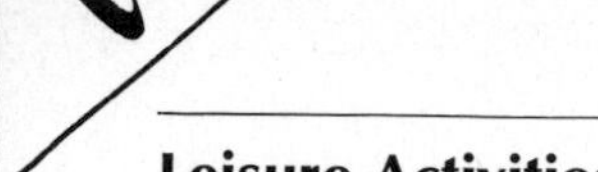

Leisure Activities

WALKING Comité National des Sentiers de Grandes Randonnées 92 rue de Clignancourt, 75883 Paris.

Association Chamina, 5 rue Pierre-le-Vénérable, 6300 Clermont-Ferrand (73.92.82.60).

RIDING There are many riding and pony-trekking establishments in Auvergne, over twenty in the département of Lozère alone.

Association Nationale pour le Tourisme Équestre
12 rue du Parc Royale, 75003, Paris.

Comité Départmental de Tourisme, B.P. 4, Place Urbain V, 48002 Mende.

FISHING A group of small hotels caters specially for anglers (fishing cards, live bait, picnic baskets, free cooking of your own catch, storage of fish, etc.).

Hotels Relais St. Pierre
Association Nationale de Promotion du Tourisme de Pêche, 5 rue Pierre Vernier, 25290 Ornans.

Maison du Tourisme, 22 rue Guy de Veyre, B.P. 8, 15018, Aurillac (or any other of the département tourist offices). There is superb fishing in all départements of Auvergne and throughout the Massif Central.

CANOEING AND KAYAKS Ligue Auvergne de Canoe-Kayak
M. Yves Lecaud (President), 32 rue Charles Péguy, 63800 Cournon.

CYCLING Cycle tours are arranged throughout the Massif Central, and bicycles can be hired at numerous places in each département. Any Tourist Office or SI will give full information.

Association Chamina, 5 rue Pierre-le-Vénérable, 63000 Clermont-Ferrand (73.92.82.60).

If you want to use your own bicycle the above association organises tours based on SNCF railway stations on the Paris–Marseille line which crosses the region.

Facilities exist for a very wide range of more specialised activities open to tourists, including pot-holing, hang-gliding, sailing, ULM flying, etc. Any main tourist office will answer queries or send addresses of the appropriate societies.

N.B. Addresses are correct at the time of writing but people do move.

Index

Songs of the Auvergne p62